Memoir of
Andrew J. Byrne
(1830–1911)

ORIGINAL WRITING

Text of original memoir (325 pages, 70 paintings and 5 poems) by
Andrew J. Byrne (1830-1911) edited by Nicola Morris.

ISBN: 978-1-906018-39-9

A CIP catalogue for this book is available from the
National Library.

Printed by Biddles Ltd., King's Lynn, Norfolk.
Published by Original Writing Ltd., Dublin, 2008.

Buy online at www.originalwriting.ie/bookshop

To my grandfather, Andrew J. Byrne,
(1830–1911)

AND

THE MILLIONS OF IRISH MEN AND WOMEN WHO,
LIKE HIM, DEPARTED THE SHORES OF IRELAND
TO FAR FOREIGN LANDS WITH HIGH HOPES AND
HEAVY HEARTS BUT, UNLIKE HIM,
NEVER TO RETURN HOME.

Contents

Introduction

'Who is he?' 'That's my father, your grandfather, Andrew Byrne' mother replied.

I was looking at an old-oval framed photo, the man in a military uniform, looking very distinguished, moustached, rich head of hair, a good-looking 36 year old.

'Now read all about him' said mother, handing me a ledger book. I opened it and gazed with fascination and excitement at all the colourful paintings of ships, steamboats, prairies, towns, soldiers in battle scenes, military uniforms, cathedrals, beautiful handwriting flowed on and on, concluding in five poems pertinent to his experiences. He travelled North, South, East and West of the central United States, by foot slogging, stagecoach, steamboat, rail, sail, ship and finally steamships, crossing the Atlantic Ocean eight times. He accumulated ten years of broken military service in Uncle Sam's army. Wounded twice, imprisoned twice, married twice, twice an enlisted private, (Uncle Sam's army & John Bull's militia), also a member of the Fenian Brotherhood and worked in the building trade as a bricklayer in Ireland, England and the USA.

In 1849 he fulfilled a dream to see the New World. He departed on the barque *Confidence* from Custom House Quay, Dublin for New Orleans. Shortly prior to his departure he married his girlfriend, Maryan Cassidy.

> *'What might have been had I not wed*
> *Is far beyond my knowledge.'*
>
> AJ Byrne poem, 'Musings"

These lines sum up his frame of mind at the time of his departure. In 1873 life gave him a second chance to find happiness when he married Honora Connors from Clonmult, Co. Cork, in Albany (his first wife, Maryan Cassidy, died in New York in 1865). In 1875 he returned to Dublin and raised a second family of two sons and four daughters. Only 45 years of age, he returned to his work in the building trade. In his retiring years he enthusiastically compiled this memoir over a span of eleven years, completing it in 1909.

The gestation period for this memoir to see light of day in book format has taken a hundred years. His date of birth precedes mine by a hundred years. In reading the memoir he comes across as a self-educated man of humility and honesty. His strong adventurous spirit is displayed in his social, political and military commitments in the USA and Ireland. He participated in events greater than himself and risked his life in doing so, as did hundreds of thousands like him.

Seamus B. Condon Col. (R)
Dublin, 2008

Editor's Note

TWENTY YEARS AFTER HE RETURNED to Ireland for the last time Andrew J. Byrne started writing his memoirs. Over the course of about ten years he produced three hundred and twenty five handwritten pages that detail his life from his earliest childhood memories to his eighth and final transatlantic journey, returning to Ireland with his second wife and young children. This original memoir included a preface and extended appendix of comments on Irish history and politics as well as several poems penned by Byrne himself. He completed his memoir in 1909.

The original manuscript is illustrated with decorations at the top of each page and contains watercolour paintings illustrating Byrne's experiences. The paintings include images of emigration ships, battlefields, buildings in Ireland and America, military dress, flags and landscapes. Byrne painted each illustration himself, although some are copied from images published in newspapers of the time. We have selected paintings that best illustrate the key events in the memoir and experiences of Andrew J. Byrne.

Andrew J. Byrne, as he tells us himself in the opening chapter of his memoir, received very little formal education. He attended small local schools and seems to have been very engaged with learning. What is so interesting about his memoir is that, despite his limited early education, he has written an articulate and engaging account of his life and times. Byrne is clearly well read and, although some spelling conventions appear beyond him, the text is entirely accessible and should not pose difficulty for the modern reader. We have made every effort to retain original spelling and punctuation. In most cases it is easy to distinguish his intention with certain misspelt words. In those cases where unusual spellings interrupt the flow of the narrative, the correct spelling has been provided in parenthesis. For example, instead of 'few' Byrne uses 'fue' and for 'their' Byrne uses 'there'. These idiosyncrasies do not interfere with the reading of the text. However, for the word 'eye' Byrne uses 'iey', this spelling is rather more disruptive and the correct spelling has been inserted in parenthesis. There are many examples of this throughout the text. These 'errors' in their own way provide an insight into the character of Andrew J. Byrne. His intelligence seeps through the text, but just lacks the finesse that would have been provided by a more formal education. It is also notable that as one progresses through the memoir the quality of Byrne's writing improves. It would seem that over time the process of recalling and writing down his memories helped him to formalise his style as he became more comfortable with spelling conventions and structure.

One issue with the text of his memoir is the term 'nigger'. Byrne uses this term after his arrival in New Orleans. In all cases where it appears in the text it is not in a derogatory context and we have retained the word. The term offers an insight into the use of the word in the mid 19th century in the Southern states of America. Although its very presence in the text may cause offence, none is intended, neither by Byrne nor the publisher, and the word is maintained in order to protect the integrity of the memoir and the experience of Byrne in the new world.

In order to make the memoir more accessible we have removed a numbre of passages and sections and this has been denoted in the text. These pertain to Byrne's account of events that he did not experience directly and also to events considered irrelevant to the progress of his own personal story. They have been removed in order to focus on Byrne's own experiences and create a more fluid narrative.

The collection of material left by Andrew J. Byrne also includes a Civil War regimental pipe, original 19th century photographs of Byrne in Army uniform, his pension application papers and two large scrapbooks filled with notes and newspaper cuttings and also two framed Commissioning Certificates signed by Horatio Seymour, Governor of New York State.

Nicola Morris
Dublin, 2008.

Preface
1898

HAVING SPENT MANY YEARS OF MY LIFE in America, in my young days, when I emigrated to that Country in the year eighteen hundred and forty nine. Contrary to my expectations, I enlisted in Uncle Sam's little army. after a number of years service. and trough the great Civil War, in eighteen sixty one and sixty five, I returned to Civil life again. after some knocking about I went to work, with a will to see what could be got out of Labour. dureing my Millitery Career before th ewar I served in the great wild west from Texas to Arazonia [sic], as it was then one vast wilderness from Kansas River to the Passific [sic] Ocean. it was this particular chapter of my life which induce me to write this very imperfect Book, which has been a Source of pleasure and pastime to me in my Idle time. and having kept a diaary and some notes which I saved from time to time enabled me to go trough my whole history as Brief as Possible Confineing myself Princibly to what I saw and expearienced on my way trough life from child hood to old age. When my Wanderings were over and my History growing dull I stoped there.

Andrew J. Byrne

Chapter One

Monica, Monica where art thou?
I often times be thinking,
Misfortune made your memory dear,
in all my wanderings far and near
and yet no pleasure in it.

ഇ

'Thoughts of the Past'—Andrew J. Byrne

Clan Ranelagh

MY GRANDFATHER Andrew Byrne a County Wicklow man came to Dublin some time previous to the year Eighteen hundred. A Bricklayer by profession he married Miss Dun of Kilmacud Co. Dublin. My father John Byrne son of Andrew married Mary Gillam. Daughter of Patrick Gillam Dublin. Andrew J. Byrne sonn of John was born in Dublin in the year Eighteen hundred and thirty. February the twenty-second in Church St. number thirty two nearly opposet Old St. Michael's Church in the Parish of St. Michael. when I was three or four years of age I was sent to school. where I was out of the way and out of dinger (danger) for the greater part of the day. the most notable event of my young days was when I received Confirmation from Archbishop Murray in Old Church St. Chapel this to me was a great day and the honour of been stroked on the cheek by the great man. I always remember. […] As I grew up I was of an enquireing turn of mind and would ask my father many questions concerning his past life his travels abroad and how he went to sea when a boy. here is one.

The copper kettle

One day (in 1811) my father was sent with a Copper Kettle for water to the fountain he met some of his playmates who were playing marvles (marbles). leaving the kettle down near the fountain his attention was taken away by the excitement of the game and forgot for a short time all about the kettle which had disappeared. when he found the kettle was gon his amassment and grief were very sore. he was afraid to go home where a severe chastisement awaited him. to be trashed with the end of a rope was more than his youthful hardihood could bare. he wandered about for some time but the loss of the kettle was too strong on his mind to face home. turning down along the Quays looking at the ships and vessels loading and unloading, he bethought of his Brother James then serving in the British Navy. he would give anything to see his Brother. His immagination ran high. when he came to a full stop where a number of persons were looking at a Man of War Tender lying near the point of the wall. [...] that evening the Tender was sailing down the River with John Byrne on board Bound for some Naval port in England. on his arrival there he was shipped on Bord one of the King's Ships.

I am not going to enter into all the particulars of his Life for the three years he was at Sea. Cruiseing in the Atlantic and other parts. Fighting the French or Life on Board Ship which was very Interesting to me at the time. My Father made all enquiries about his Brother but of no avail. not knowing the name of the vessel he served in. this made it very difficult for him. at one time his ship and another British Man of War Lay Close together in some Foreingn Port for Several Days. when the other ship parted Company and Bore out to sea my Father afterwards learned his Brother was on Board that vessel the next account was of his Death in the West Indies. No longer having any expectations of meeting his Brother he thought oftener of home Father Mother and Sisters and longed to return to them once more and be a good

4

Boy for the future. at the end of three years he came Back fresch and Breezy with a purse of money and was the talke and admiration of all the Neabors. My Father was a good man everyone said so he was very social in his relations among his friends and companions this often led to excess spending to many of his Evenings Out. Dresed well too free with his money generous to his Mother too easy and not watchful anuff as a parent he Died 1857 adged 57 years. May he Rest in Peace.

School Days, Politics & The Repeal Movement

At an early age like any other good little Boy I commenced going to school. I could not understand why I should be shut up in a schoolroom during the Best part of the Day doing nothing as I thought and lots of other little Boys playing outside on the Flags and in the Sun enjoying them selves to there harts content so little did I care for going to school that trets (threats) and foarce had sometimes to be used. going from one school to another I made very little progress though my Lessons ware fue and Simple when Compared to what some of our Boys are able to do now in the Christian Brothers and the National Schools, which were then fue and fare between. a very large number of the working Class People of Dublin sent there Children to a certain class of schools very much in use at that time. private schools of a very humbler order held in some Court or Back St the Scholership was easey and pleasant. a Poor man would rent one or two rooms gather a number of Boys around him paying a fue pence a weeke the poor master eaking out a misorable existance he should be quiet and humour the boys if not the schollers woud soone skip away from him and go to another school in the next street. this old fashioned way of Keeping School creped into existance after the Repeal of the penal Laws. Previous to this all the advantages of a good Education and other necessary training was withheld from us and the Celt was trampled in the dust and degraded. [...]

OConnoll was now in his prime as Agitater and Leader of the Irish People the Question of Repeal was well keped (kept) to the front by holding Monster Meetings in all parts of Ireland his Popularity was immence his name was Constantly before the People. My first remembrance of him was when a Child going to one of his meetings with my Father and Mother to the Coburb Gardens. Then an open field where the Royal University now stands that was the commencement of my political thought for Ireland which waxed stronger as I grew up as an humble follower of the popular Leaders of Ireland to the present day. In 1840 I went to a trade Political Meeting Held in the Corn Exchange. Children as well as men were allways ansious to see the great Tribune. if I remember rightly he made one of his promises at the meeting that Day that wee would have the Repeal of the Union in three or four years it is hard to say whether he was serious or not this was responded to by a great cheer. it apears he promised various times when Addressing the People that wee would have Repeal of the Union in a fue short years. […]

OConnell's Meeting at Tara the largest he ever held. when some hundred thousands of People assembled on the old Historick Hill to hear again the hopeful pronouncements of the Liberater. I was a very young Boy. thirteen years of Age. the Evening before the Meeting numbers of Persons left Dublin for Tara taking The Road to Dunshaughlin. it was fine Summer weather at the time. The meeting was expected to be the Largest Demonstration ever held in Ireland. The talk of the People completely carried me away. So making up a plan with two more boys wee started for the great Meeting to be held next Day. a fue pennys to take us There and Back was all wee posesed. we were Boys then and in our youthful simplicity the long journey before us did not deter us. The Evening before the meeting we started off as light as a cork the road was getting tronged with men making there way to Tara on foot. wee had plenty of Company good humour and lots of fun going along the

6

road all night. when we got to Dunshaghlin we were terid (tired) out. after resting awhile we got to Tara looked around us and saw the Croppies grave we sat down some where and fell asleep oblivious of the noise and Cheers and everything around us. When wee woke up the meeting was over and wee were alone on the Hill. After a Day or two wee got Back to Dublin Hungery and weary. Such was the spirit of the times the hopes of the People were at its highest the promises of O Connell and the hopes he inspired in his followers. The[y] were ready to do and dare anything in the Cause of there Country. [...]

The goverment at last decided to move against O Connell and proclaimed the Meeting to be held at Clontarf and Dispatched a large number of Troopes to the place of Meeting this was a great damper on O Connell and compeled him to hold his meetings in door. In 1843 it was decided to Build a large Hall on the Burgh Quay called Conciliation Hall at the same time O Connell was arrested by the Goverment charged with Declamatory Language and Sedition. He was tried and found guilty and was sent to prison. after a short time he was released by the Decision of the Law Lords of England [...] after this he held his meetings in the Conciliation Hall. [...] The Repeal Association was formed a large number of young and tallented men became members and the Hall resounded with eloquence of Meagher O Brien and and [sic] many others who ably assisted the great Tribune in the cause of the country. [...] *The Nation* newspaper was Established and conducted by Thomas Davis the great National Poet of Ireland, Gavin Duffy and John Blake Dillon and others, there writeings were most Inspirating fraught with hope and cheer to the down trodden People who wished to be free. a change now came over the young Bloods of the association the[y] believed O Connell had exausted all the means and everything that coud be done within the limmets of Constitutinal adgitation in Ireland. he was getting old and his Bloodles pollicy roused the spirit of the opposition which was rising up against him the young Irelanders after some angry Debates seceded from Conciliation Hall and formed the Confederate association of Ireland on Revolutionary princibles which spred very rappetly trugh (through) the Country.

Young Ireland 1848

In the year 1848 when Europe was ablaze with the Revolutionary Movement which started in Paris. At the same time famine was devastating Ireland. Caused by the failure of the potato Crop, and the almost total dependence of the People on it as an article of food.[...] It was intended a Blow should be struck at the end of the Harvest. But the goverment aware of the intention of the Confederates, would not wait for there time, tooke steps at once to put down the movement. Proclamations were Posted up all over the Country offering a thousand Pounds reward for the Apprahension or Information which would lead to the arrest of Smith O Bryan Thomas Francis Meagher and several Others charged with rebellious purposes and so fort[...] there was a large number of Clubs in Dublin at that time got up by the Confederation each Club was Called after the name of some Distinguist Irishman the Curn (Curran) Club used to meet in Queen St. I was a member of the Club at the time and attended all their meetings one night the Reverent Docter Yore of St. Paul's Church Arran Quay a worthy and venerable Priest attended one of our meetings and tried very much by force of argument to change us from the cource wee were pursuing. he was Listened to with the greatest respect, but failed to convince us. wee had no faith in moral force which wee believed a failier. Each Club had one or two flags one in Particular drew my attention the Irish triecolour green white and yellow or orange with a real steel Pike fixed on the head of the Staff. These were to be our Battle Flags But the[y] never waved in Battle Line or Marching Column to the tune wee 'il have our own again' or 'Paddys evermore,' but alas were laid aside or became the Property of the Castle, when the collaps came with all its Mellincolly results and disappointments. The Battle for Ireland was once more lost or deferred [...] The sad state of the Country at this time was deplorable. O Connell Dead and the Leaders of a movement compriseing the Best men in Ireland, transported or in exile. The Prospect was very gloomy, Hunger and Emigration were Dooing the worke for England without the Loos (loss) of a man or a Bullet. Sad is thy fate oh Erin

THOUGHTS OF THE PAST

I often on the corner stood,
George Burns and I together.
An only son of humble birth
Who lived down in the cellar.

Our conversation wasn't much
Our business not progressive
But George, I'm sure, knew more than me
And often went a peddling.

Across the street a maiden lived,
In social state above me,
Her anxious gaze I sometimes met,
Which gave me cause to wonder.

Alas! One evening at a dance,
I often used to go to,
The boys and girls were neighbours all
Good humoured, gay and sociable.

Then was the days of gigs and reels
With ordinary people,
Who did not aspire to the grand quadrille,
And waltzing seemed so silly.

The fiddler then struck up the tune,
Perhaps the Rakes of Mallow,
Or Tatter Jack Welsh just as good,
Or the Wind that shakes the Barley.

Miss McCloud was not forgot,
Nor the Rocky Road to Dublin,
The hare in the corn of course as well,
And follow me up to Carlow.

One night a blooming maid came in
Accompanied by another,
Whom I had not seen before,
And wondered where she came from.

In a rustic way she moved about,
Until she got quite near me,
And put an apple in my hand,
My way of introduction.

That night I saw my dear one home,
Thinking it no harm,
I though her fine and still kept on,
A dallying with my charmer.

Still on the corner George and I,
Our simple stories telling,
For boys were boys in days gone by,
With little were contented.

Then the girl over the way
At the window slyly peeping,
For me she looks if signs be true,
As plain as A B C Sir.

George one evening said to me,
I have something for to tell you,
While strolling in the Park today,
I met a nice young lady.

She spoke to me, I though it strange,
As we were not acquainted,
She blushed and asked me how you were,
And said she wished to see me.

In the Park at half past four,
On tomorrow evening, in the hollow near the Zoo,
This will be our meeting,
Then waved her hand and said Good-bye hoping for tomorrow.

Now to the Park I did not go,
I was a silly Billy and leave the other girl alone,
I was so tender hearted,
I oft times thought what might have been had I missed my charmer.

Now the girl over the way,
A ward of her rich uncle,
A sort of Nabob so they say,
Who made his money on corn and hay and other things productive.

Monica, Monica, where art thou?
I often times be thinking,
Misfortune made your memory dear,
In all my wanderings far and near
and yet no pleasure in it.

The tide will come, and the tide will go,
Casting its flotsam on the shore,
What 'ere they be, has no thoughts for me,
But past mistakes in life remain
A mingling of sorrow and of pain.

A. J. Byrne 1830–1911

Chapter Two

On the broad expanse of the ocean wild,
In a tiny barque we sailed,
An emigrant band to a foreign land
And Dixie far away.

∾

'Off for the New World'—Andrew J. Byrne

Thoughts on America and How I Got There

IN THE EARLY PART OF THE YEAR 1849, when the ceaseless flow of Emigration was Draining the Country of what our English and ante Irish friends called the surplus Population, who were going away for the good of the Country I often wished I could go to America. But as I had no means of getting there I tryed to content myself and wait my oppertunity. Many times have I stood on the Quay at the Custom House curiously gazeing at I may say those strange looking People numbers of them from the most distant parts of Ireland ruff and smood in there native garb going on Bord some antiquated looking Hulk newly tared and painted formerly a Brig. But recently converted into a three master by sticking up another Pole near her Stern, she was then advertised by the shipping agents as the splended American Built Bark of such a Burden having splended acommodation for so many cabben and stearage Passengers, stearage Passage £3.10s. will sail on such a date from the Custom House Quay for Quebec or New Yorke, perhaps the Bottom of the sea if not a slow missarable Passage across the Atlantic. I was then an apprentice with a very imperfect

Knowledge of My Business. I could not make known my intention of going to America with any chance of success to my Father and Mother for the price of a passage ticket because my Mother allways treated me as if I were a Big Child when ever I mentioned the subgect of going away saying that a roleing stone gathers no moss and that I was of a roveing disposition. This was true to a certain extent as I afterwards learned to my cost. when a little fellow I was very fond of rambling hear and there and everywhere as my fancy lead me, long distance walking, and pokeing about delighted with everything, a race or a hunt if not too far.[...]

In the month of October eightenn forty nine I finished a small job which I got a lump sum for dooing. My chance was now come as the proffits out of my little contract enabled me to get my Ticket to the promised Land then somuch spoken about as the New World. The Beacon of hope The Land of Milk and Honey. what Beautifull Pictures I Painted to my minds iey (eye) the Castle I was Building in the aire always looking to the Sunny side. I may say [k]nowing nothing of the realities of Life. After Showing the Passage Ticket to my Mother she became reconsiled and thinking it might be the mains (means) of Braking off my aquaintenship with a young Girl whom I had been Keeping Company with for some time all preparations was then made. My sea store Provisions such as it was ware put in a large Box, many little things that were nesessary were left out. In them Days passengers shoud find there own sea store Numbers of Persons not bringing anuff to last dureing the voiage, especially if the Passage was a prolonged one. this did not concern mee much. All I wanted was to get on Board and get away before my Father Mother and Friends Discovered I was after getting Married. I was of a very shy disposition I did not want them to know anything about the matter till I was gone. I made a fool of my self, this marrige was my first Blunder. Married I often wished I could have recalled that word, which was the cause of so much misery to me

Sails for America

On the 2nd day of November 1849. The Day after my marriage I sailed in the Bark Confidence 450 Tons Burden from the Custom House Dublin for New Orleans U.S. America. she was a new vessel after making her first voyage. Built in America. I had only a few shillings in my pocket yet I was going away Cheerful and full of hope and spirit in the future. After Biding a hasty good by to my Father Mother and Friends my mother unexpectedly handed me a Soverin. I thought I had now ample funds on my arrival in America, where money was to be had almost for the asking of it. How very airey and light my thoughts were then I will leave you to guess [...] there was Bustle and excitement on board. looking at the Emigrants some ware grave while others were gay and some weeping faces ansiously looking at friends on shore while a fue tardy Devil may-care-fellows were scrambling over the side of the ship as the plank was hauld away and the Tow Boat ready to take us out in the Bay. *let go that hawser slip off that rope* and away we go down the river greeted by the parting cheers and lamentations of friends on shore waveing their handkerchifs and wishing us god speed.

> *To the West, to the West, To the land of the free.*
> *Where the might Missouri Rolls down to the sea.*
> *Where a man is a man, If he's willing to toil,*
> *And the humblest may gather The fruits of the soil*

As this was my first voiage at sea short or long I tooke a great interest in evary thing i saw on Board ship, the ropes spars, between Decks and and [sic] all over the vessel. I allmost fancyed myself a sort of Christofer Columbus on a voiage of Discovery or adventure, while fondly gazeing on the distant Shore of Dublin Bay. the old Adeline Tug Boat was slowly pulling us out into the deep clear water smoking and splashing on its foamy way. Clontarfe with its crescent tall trees and glistning Houses the Castle and the Bull wall terminating with Dear auld Howth and the Baily light presenting a most charming shore line on the Northern side of the Bay. On the South the indulating and gently sloping Mountains of Dublin with the sugar loave Mountains in the Back ground flecked with green and Brown. The shore line dotted all along to Kingstown with numerious houses villages and small Towns with gardens trees and Terraces looking fresh and Beautifull. Kingstown with its pretty Harbour, Dalkey and Killiney Hill with its picturesque Rocks and Clifts and rugget shore line. Now becomming more dim and distant to the view The shades of evening coming on and closeing ore us a few sails were spred to the wind and the Tow Boat parted with us and returned to Dublin. Wee now commenced our lone long voiage over four thousands miles to New Orleans night coming on the steerage was made lively by the strains of a violin and the notes of a flute played by two amatures who unexpectedly turned up among us making things a bit Cheary on our first night on Board and a calm sea a number of Passengers enjoyed themsefs Dancing singing and other amusements. the steerage was dimly lit by a lanterin suspended from the upper Deck of this rude looking apartment now become our home for some time to come. Quadrilles jigs and reels made up the simple programme of the nights entertainment. while some of the stallwarts made the Deck rattle to the lively tunes 'the Rocky Road to Dublin' and 'the Green fields to America'. for my part I was in a more Contemplative Moode though I felt somwhat of the enjoyment going on from where I was seated in my Box at my bunk [...] I felt a strange sensetion come over me at the thought of Been married so young and unprepared for such a state. I was not altogether pleased with myself a fue days ago I was single and free but am now married why it seamed like a dream to me but as an old song says

Youth and folly make young men marry,
Youth and beauty will soon decay,
What can't be cured must be endured,
So farewell darling, I must away

The next day wee were going down the Channel Weather favorable and made Cape Clear in a fue days. Wee were then speeding our way over the Broad Atlantic a mere speck on the Ocean wave, without a mark or Bound with a wild waste of water before us. the sea now became ruff and adverse winds set in. Nearly all the passengers myself included were sea sick. Oh how misarable I felt and how I suffered from violint and constant reaching loss of apatite my spirit gone, and every other discomfort experienced on Board an Emigrant Ship. our course lay Southt West we were nearing a warmer latitude. When about fourteen days at sea we passed one of the Azore Islands looking Bright and Cheerful in the distance. the steerage and second cabbin was getting very dirty although some attemts at cleaning was made every day [...] yet there was allways a strainge sickening smell. Tar cloride of lime and other foul smelling stuff made the steerage most unsavery and unplesent to be in, and my sickness worse. when about four weeks at sea a young woman and a man died. the man had a wife and family in Ireland. The[y] wear tied up in a piece of canvas and sliped over Board. Wee ware now getting near the West Indies and expecting to see land every day what a pleasing excitement it causes after been tossed about on the bosom of the deep for weeks without the cite of a single sail. land once more Saint Domingo is seen looming up in the distant horizon. All hands on deck every one ansious to see Land any kind of Land it breaks the monotony. After a favorable run wee neared the Island and had a fine view of its Blue Mountain sides with patches of green hear and there well timbered and most pleasing to looke at. the weather was then getting a little more mild and warm my health improveing and my apatite fairly good but I had then very little to eat and that of the most meagre quality. the mild warm weather and a land Breese now and then reliefd me from that horrid sea sickness and compensated me for my long sufferance and made life much more pleasent to me on Board during the most interesting part of our voiage.

After passing Saint Domingo wee met a very large shoal of Porpoises skipping in and out of the water as fare as we could see them up and down you would think the[y] were racing one another which afforded us much pleasure as the[y] shot out of the water describeing part of a circle with as much ease as a Cat would spring at a mouse. after this wee saw a number of flying fish skipping and flying lowly over the water for a short distance. then take to the water again. the weather continued to grow more warm and the wind favorable. an od turn at the pump was good exercise for us. our vessel was a Bit leakey we had to pump very often but it caused no uneasiness wee now saw land again a small speck I think one of the Bahama Islands and then the Island of Cuba stretching along on our Port side for a bout five hundred miles. […] comming near the gulfe of Mexico the water became very much changed in colour to a light drab or mud colour. The weather was extreamly Beautiful and the sun very warm while I lounged about the deck. Delighted with the weather and this in the latter end of December. Wee were becalmed for a fue days the sails were hanging loosely and flapping against the mast and the water as smood as glass and glistning in the sun like a sheet of gold. one of the Passengers a queer fellow from Dublin thought he would try a Cooler so divesting himself of his cloase (clothes) all to his trousers, jumped over Board and struck out a short distance from the vesel. he was an expert swimmer but he ought to have known he was in strange waters and in Dainger of sharkes. after a fue turns round the vessel a rope was lowered to him, with a fue steps and hand over hand he was on Board again very much refreshed with his first swim in the gulfe of Mexico. it was then very close to Christmas and many were longing to meat there friends who were long separated from them. at lentht about six o clock on Christmas morning a Tow Boat came in sight and was Bearing down upon us very rapetly eveary one felt delighted after a long and sometimes Boisterious passage of about fifty two days of misery and hunger. In a short time the tug came along side after a short parley with the Captain. the Confidence was made fast to the tug a Powerful vessel of her class nothing else would do. it is a long pull up the Misissippi against a six [k]not current. our vessell was made fast to the side of the tug like a twin ship and was luged along very lively. in a short time I was aboard the tug and found hir a very different craft to what I saw to home She had a good many deck hands and firemen all Irishmen. The[y] were very friendly and making all sorts of enquieries about the old dart. Some were very thin and worn looking though well feed as was evident from the superiour quality of the food which was served out to them in abundance and shareing with some of the passengers who had not a square meal in a long time. We now reached the coast or mouth of the Mississippi River the[y] call it the Belieze. The land was low flat and sandy apearing above the water for a time and are washed away again by the cease-less flow and rappet current of this mighty river. the Mississippi somtimes called The Father of Waters. trunks of Trees lay scathe-red about on the threacherous sandy shore and shallow Banks. some of them half Buried in the virgin soil. vegatation soone takes root and more ground is added to the shoreline. before the use of Steam Boats on the River I have been told numbers of Alligaters might be seen sleeping and sunning them selfs on the logs under a Broiling sun stretched out in a state of sleepy watchfulness. near the moutht of the River is pilot Town a fue one story wooden Buildings Clustered together The temporary homes of the Mississippi River Pilots. Here one of the Pilots came on Board and tooke charge of our vessel up the River to New Orleans 105 miles. The Mississippi and Meisouri [sic] is the longest River in North America, four Thousand Miles from its source to the Gulfe of Mexico and navigable for large Vessels for some distance above New Orleans. As wee assend the River its low desolate shore on either side attracts attention the home of alligaters snakes misquitoes mud Turtles Bull frogs and innumuerrable insects the halfe submerged Land composed of loose soil of a frail sampy nature and totally unfit for habitation or reclamation Subject to Inuridation when the river rises. On either side nothing is seen but a jungel of Cane Brakes growing fare and wide along the River Bottom. This was veary novel and new to me coming from Ireland with its Picturesque Shore and Iron Bound Coast. we now arrived at the Commencement of civiliseation and cultivation. The ground is higher and more firm plantations now and then appear along the river side where the tall sugar cane grows and Bussey Slaves are working in the fields.

There are two Forts one on each side of the river Fort Jackson and Fort Philip. hear wee ware joined by a large ship with German Emigrants on Board. The vesel was made fast on the Port side of the Tow Boat in this way wee went slowly up the river again three a Breast the Tow Boat in the Middle moveing along with steady and apparent ease. I was soone on board the German vessel taking stock of the Passengers there modes and ways. as I went among them the[y] all seemed to be very happy and in good humour the[y] were very sociable People among them selves smoking there German Pipes singing and playing Musick while a fue partners were waltzing round the deck. there was a great deal of clatter among them. as evearyone of them seemed talking together at the one time. The[y] were a very healthy looking people Dutch Build. the Woman wearing close fitting frocks short skirts and short waisted which added to there clumsey apearence and strong made stumpy shoues (shoes) on there feet looking like that of the Peasent class.

As wee go up the river the land on each side is more improved and Houses of a Better Class apear along the wide embankments which gird the river and keepes it from overflowing and inundating the plantations, and flooding a large section of the State of Louisiana this has often occurred by the Banks or levies yielding in some weeke spot to the force of the water. which rushes in making the Breach wider and flooding the country in all directions for miles before the Breach or crevas is repaired. The plantations along this section of the river are generaly owned and worked by discendents of French settlers the state of Louisiana formerly a French Colloney But in Napoleons time was ceeded to the U.S. America by purchase Those People still talk French very fluently and are French in manner. The most of the clloured (coloured) Population the Negroes speaks the same Language and are all slaves working on on [sic] the plantations. some of the planters Houses looke very nice Built of wood with Brick chimlys the[y] are all painted white with green lattis shutters to the windows looking fresh and Bright. in there gardens in front are tropical plants mixed with orange and fig trees haveing a most pleasering effect with The somebre looking wood or forest in the Back ground. the trees are of naturel growth some of them old and decayed. Branches of the swamp oak and other kind of Trees are stranngely draped with hanging moss which seams to grow downwards in Clumps and strings, and creeping vines the only bit of fresh green to be seen in these ugly Forest Swamp Lands. Back from the river up to New Orleans, along the River at certain stages are wood piles for the Steamers for firing up purposes the tow Boat drew nar the Bank for a supply of wood opposet a planters House. when the boat was made fast, I went ashore for a short time and walked up to the house to take a looke. a merry laughfing croud of the household servents Big and little came out on the verranda Black white an[d] yellow to looke at the greenhorn while some of the field hands were leaning over

21

the fence close by. a lot of mean looking huts for the use of the slaves. The[y] were all Chattering in French. looking at me while I curiously surveid every thing round about me and retired to the vessel again humming a Negro mellidy. 'Old Dan Tucker.'

Some were Black and more was Blacker
And some was like de colour of chawed tobacker

New Orleans

At last we arrived in New Orleans on St. Stephens Day after a voiage of 52 days. it was early in the night and the City lights were flickering fare and wide along the River a darke mass of tall masted vessels two and three abreast were Berthed along the wodden warfs. heaps of Merchandise lay about and River Steamers passing up and down were all lit up by the Bright and pleasing lights of the caben windows. what a delightful feeling it is to most People after a long voiage or even a short one when the[y] come in cite of the Harbour lights, even if it be in a foregin land. when you feel the solid earth under your feet. I did not concider America a foregin Land Where so many of my Country men had made there home I stoped on Board that night, but was ansious to get a looke at the City by gass light I went ashore acompanied by a young man a fellow passenger like myself wee crossed a wide open space of ground cauld the Levee stretching along the river side. Bales of Cotton, Barrels and all kinds of merchandise were in heaps in all directions. I Concluded that New Orleans was a Bussey Place and a most important Centre of trade and Commerce. on the other side of the Levee was a long row of plain looking Houses shops and stores dimly lighted by the feeble rays of the gass lamps. ruff looking men were passing up and down the sidewalk, princibily Sailors Steam Boat men long-shore men and nigers lounging about. many of them after there days work very Independent looking fellows, droping in and out of the many lowclass Drinking Saloons and Boarding Houses which are principily patronised by men of this Class along the river. at one place our attention was attracted by the clink of an upright organ or hurdy gurdy as we used to call them in Dublin played by a good looking German girl in one of the saloons. as we were Both lovers of Musick even in a small way we stood for a while looking in at the open door of the Bar Room where all was open to the Street. a lot of Red shirted and Blue shirted fellows some with Red or Blue Sashes tied round the waist were sitting at small round tables Drinking or playing cards while a Couple of hard looking fellows were having a Buck dance waltzing round the room to the musick of the organ while another fair looking girl tambourine in hand was going round collecting all the small change she could get from her ruff patrons.

After the Dance there was a song by the Girls the Bold Privateer and a Negroe Melody 'oh Susanna dont You Cry for Me' was enjoyed very much by the company.

When I go to New Orleans There I'll look all round
And if I find Susanna I'll fall right on the ground
Oh Susanna don't you cry for me
I'm going to Californy with my wash bowl on my knee

After this performance wee continued our walk along the Levee untill wee came to a large open structure or shed sueported on Iron Collums. This is the French Market the moast popular resort in the City where evearything neseseary in the food line is sold. there are a great manny nice Coffy stands or stalls on the Levee side of the Market where a light repast can be had for a fue cents. Myself and partner sat down at one of the stands partaking of a Cup of coffey a small cake one eg[g] and a little round dot of Butter nicely served. it went down very well after our long fast on Board ship. near us was a small stand full of cigars. wee tooke one each, and paid our Bill which amounted to the small charge of five cents each a picaune the smallest coin in circulation in New Orleans at that time. wee lit our cigars and started Back to the ship as this was my first time to use tobacco, I thought I was doing it grand and so very cheap I went Back quite pleased with myself. but I had not yet felt any disagreableness from the cigar til I got on Board when I suddenly became very sick my mild cigar was tomuch for me I got very weak what an abominable sickness it is to be shure I was crestfallen. it is a right up and down double action stomack head and sistam sickness, a disaraingment of all the parts, the cold perspiration ouseing from my forehead Weak and feint I thought I was going to die. were it not I knew my punnishment would not last very long.

The next morning all the passengers ware leaving the ship there was a good deal of hand shaking and good Byes among many of the passengers perhaps never to meet again. There was one thing about our dispersion which made me feel a slight pang of sadness and loneliness. A good manny persons came there to meet there friends whome the[y] had long wished to see greeting them warmly on there safe arrival. Bringing them to good homes or where the[y] might rest a short time til the[y] got employment and learn the ways of the City I thought that was very nice and encourageing I wished it was my cace. I picked up my traps and making my way across the Busey Levee trough Cottin Bales Barreles Boxes and drays going to and from the Levee I walked about for some time til I procured a lodgin with an Irish famaly who keped one or Two Boarders.

After Breakfast I spent the remainder of the day going trough the principble part of the City which Contains about eighty to one hundred thousand Inhabitants princibly composed of French, Americans, and Negroes of various shades and creholes (creoles) while a large number are Europeans mostly Irish and German. almost everything was a novelty to me and therefore pleased me for a time. The ground is nearly on a level with the river and of a swampy nature with a dry crust on top. the City is low flat and liable to inundation. the River Sometimes Breaking trough its Embanqments which run for miles on the lower Mississippi and New Orleans for a few Days I rambled about Sight Seeing in the City and along the river its numerious shipping and large river steamers trading to various parts of the Mississippi and its numerious tributeries from one thousand to fifteen hundred miles to the various Towns and Citys situate on these great water cources.[…] Many of those river steamers are very large painted white and of a novel construction no where seen but in America there splendid saloons and good attendence and sumteious fare eagual to the Best Hotells in the city. notwithstanding this pleasant and comfortable way of travelling it is not all the time free from Danger to life and Limb. Now and then an exploxion occurs on one of these Boats making matchwood of her Timbers and dealing Death and Destruction among the Passengers heads legs an[d] arms flying about some of those pieces of anatomy to parts unknown. The Big Saint Louis one of the finest Boats coming in to New Orleans. Blew up a short time before I arrived there. Two or three hundred passengers were on board. […] I was told all or nearly all met a most lamentable Death. […] The enginere had gone of[f] the Boat for a short time previous to the explosion. he was concidered very much to Blame. Then there is the dainger of fire which sometimes happen with great loss of live from bein Burnt or drowned on the River. Many causes are assigned for the frequent disasters which occur on the great Western Rivers. Snags are a great Dainger which at one time were very numerious in the Mississippi River a snag is a sunken tree or log with one end in the sand and the other sticking out of the water and not easily perceived in the night time which make them more Daingerous […] Card sharpers are plentiful on the Boats looking out for the least skilful and unwary whome the[y] might entrap in a game of Poker or Seven up. who are shure to be fleeced. Murder at times frequently occur as the result of this gambling as many lawles persons and adventurers travel up and down river or are employed on the Boats. Now all these evils which I have mentioned and the terrable disregard for life which are preventable in most cases is not as bad as it used to be. but People hear are so bent on money making trade and speculation the[y] apear not to have much time to moralize or think over these things. The helter skelter sort of life so different in dear old Dublin and to which I was not used to surprised me I began to think that New Orleans was a pretty hard sort of place with its mixed population and Southern ways the constant flow of river men from all parts, the distant West and neabouring states returned Calofornians with more or less Bright nuggets of Gold from that far off Terrotery which was then the craze and talk of evearyone. with regard to crime and immorality in New Orleans I have not notised anything very remarkable except there Dance Rooms or as the[y] are cauld hear Ballrooms open every evening to the publick by paying halfe a Dollar for admittence. there are plenty of partners to Dance with if you be so inclined. But it is all clap trap and a snare. I was surprised at the licence giving to such places and many other things as well and the very loose way of observing the Sabbath the taking of life and other forms of crime and many other things caused me to think and dispell many foolish notions which I had about America when I was in the old Country. Yet I felt from the moment I landed I was in a great country the land of the stares and stripes and the refuge of thousands of the poor and down trodden of my Countrymen. And that I was free and felt more of a man then I was under the Union Jack.

Enlists in the U.S. Army

Winter in New Orleans is the most Bussey time of the year the seasin is so mild and spring like. a large number of visaters speculaters and persons seeking employment come hear every Winter and leave again in Spring. in a short time I Began to feel somewhat serious about my prospects. My Bit of money after paying a weakes board was very small and failing to find employment I was getting very uneasey but as I allways had a fair share of hope I thought the next day I might do Better. A very large amount of work is done hear by slave labour which is a Bar against white foalks of the labouring or artizan class comming hear or to any of the Southern States who at that time were slave states. had I went to New York, Philadelphi [sic] or Boston with there neabouring and growing Towns where the Negro Population was small and did not seriously effect the employment of white men my chance of employment woud have been altogether Better. I had no means of going westward up river or by rail I had not a friend and so short a time in the Country I knew very little about it. Going from job to job I was surprised to find all the bricklayers were Niggerrs and the boss or foreman were gentlemen of colour. I was one of the poor white trash not wanted in the South. on the levee there were Black gangs and White gangs all working separately. Some Steam Boats had Black crews and others White. I was in a nice fix somtimes meeting an unfortunate greenhorn like myself and telling our expearience to one another and wishing ourselves out of this Nigerrish place. [...] I was getting weary and tired my last shilling was gone. I sat down on a Bale of Cotton near the Steam Boat landing thinking over in my mind what was best to do when I saw a young man aproach me with a pleaseing looking countenance dresed in a smart looking sailor suit. I did not recognise him untill he came nearer to me. he was my old ship mate whom I spent my first night with in New Orleans and smoked my first cigar. he sat down beside me when a mutual conversation took place relating our expeariance to one another and a little adventure he had on a sugar Plantation which he related to me in a humerious and witty manner which lifted up my spirits for a short time. when he finished his story I asked how he came to be a sailor. I am not a sailor yet said he. I me a lansman (landsman). Maybe Ile (I'll) be a sailor after a while. he was disappointed like myself and having very little money when he landed. he was told By a friend if he had no obgection to go to the United States recruithing office in Lafiyet St. [sic] that the[y] wanted men for the Navy. A goverment surveing Steamer was in New Orleans at the time and required a small complement of lansmen on Board for general work to serve for a fue years. My friend was execpted and sent to the survea ship and became as fare as apearence a full fledged sailor a veritable Jack Tar to look at. he was very much pleased with his new job. after telling me all he said there might be a chance for me I consented very readily as I thought it would do very very well for a while and take me out of my difficulty. when I arrived at the recruiting office I was told I was one day too late but the[y] were enlisting men for the army. I thoutht only of the present and concented to join uncle Sam army. I Enlisted in the U. S. army January 16th 1850 seven of us were brought before the Docter for examination I passed the other six were regected. I was then served with a jacket and trousers of a light Blue grey Collour Trimmed very lightly with white lase (lace). The white lase Denotes the Infantry Branch of the service. Red for Artillery Yellow for Cavalry Ornge for the Enginers and Crimson for the Ordnance Corps the full dress uniform is not worn except in a fue Posts or stations of importance and is not issued to Troops on the frontere or distant stations where ornamentle Soldiering is not required And are not adapted to work that is done in many of those lonely Military Posts. After I dresed myself in my Suit of Blue I was sent to a Boarding House in the City. where I found a number of recruits most of them Irishmen In charge of the recruiting Sergent. The Goverment paid our Board which was of very good quality. I knew wee would not be hear long and that as soone as the Detatchment was made up to the required strength wee would be sent away. I did not dislike my new situation I was fairly Contented[...] My term of enlistment Was for five years. this seemed to me a long time to look a head. I began very soon to feel the inconvenince of my unfortunate marriage, while I so young and unprepared. however I thought there was no use Crying over Spilt milk. [...]

Nothing to do but sightseeing rambling about from one place to another along the shell road or out in the Woods killing snakes. now and then examining some strange insect life and the great large Black Beetles Two or three inches long while now and then casting a searching glance about for an Alligater which might get a little out of his way while I might by chance get too near one of those ugly monsters lyeing low in some swampy hole or creek waithing patiently for anything he could prey on. I never went out much in the evenings it was darke and lonesome except in the vicinity of the Teathre (theatre) or the principle Hotells and places of amusement with there Bright lights and People on pleasure Bent. The rich planters and Northern Business men who are travelling in the South to escape from the Cold riget (rigid) Winter of there almost Artic homes, fill up the Hotells and places of amusement all Winter. Dan Rice the great American Clown was hear he had a very fine Circus Company at one time but got Broken down by a dishonest agent as he said himself Robed him of eveary Cent. he was then trying to build himselfe up again with a one horse show. he was accompanied by another famous English clown Wallet.[...] altogether there was no lack of amusement New Orleans is a fillibustering sort of a place.[...]

After spending about three months in New Orleans and seeing all I thought was worth seeing and the warm weather coming on our detachment of recruits were transferred to New Orleans

Barracks about three miles down the River we were attached to Capt. and Brevet Major Pembertons Co. and 4th U.S. Artillery then dooing duty in the Barracks our detachment was assigned to a large roome The Second Storey in one of the Barrack Buildings. during the night we suffered terrably from Musqitoes we had no Musquitoe Curtan on our Bunks. wee were assailed on allsides by those venomis insexts making furious darts and lighting upon our faces or arms with a Buz and a Sting that was viscious and penatrating. [...] The[y] had the Best of the fight. all night the[y] continued to annoy us in the most spiteful manner there was no escape from them at lenght the morning dawned upon us and our little tormenters departed leaving us alone a degected looking lot after our nights surprise. The next night we were Better prepared for each bunk was supplied with a Misquitoe bar. Wee had a good nights rest and the next morning at Revalle we answered Role Call in good spirits very much refreshed. [...] Our duty then commenced Learning the school of the soldier wee were drilled twice a day 1st the position of a soldier our faceings squad drill the manual of arms, the field gun and Company drill. In the morning for a short time wee done what the[y] call Police duty sweeping and picking up bits of paper or any little rubbage wee could find round our quarters and the parade ground. I soone had to take my turn on guard and all other duty in regular form which I learned quickly and with a soldierly air and freedom which was notised by some of the old vets in Complimentery terms to myself a bit flattering to be shure to a young recruit. [...] our duty hear was light and pleasent varied with light Artillery drill which I like very well. after a short time I was Relieved of all duty by order of the Commanding officer of the Post and put on extra duty working at my trade Bricklaying in the Barracks. it was then Summer the sun was roasting hot and almost unbearable I was wishing to get away I had anuff of this place. [...] July the 4th the Day of all Days in this Country is clebrated with great spirit and enthusiasm it bein my first 4th of July in America as an Irishman and a lover of my country my thoughts went Back to Ireland when will wee have our 4th of July our Independence Day when Emmets epitagh (epitaph) will be written. [...] But as wee cannot allways be thinking of those things, I Honoured the day like the rest of the Soldier Boys feasting and Drinking and amusing our selfs in various ways dureing the Day at 3 o clock on the morning of the 4th the orderly Drummer Beat the assembly the men answered the Call and turned out very promtly. after Roll Call three Brass field guns ware hauled out on the Bank of the River and a salute of thirteen gunes were fired one for each of the Old Thirteen States of the american union, and one gun eveary halfe Hour till sundown. at 12 o clock a National salute was fired, while the Boomeing of the Cannon Citywards announced the cellabrations had commenced. wee had a grand Dinner with plenty of wine and Brandy for Refreshments several Boxes of Cigars lay about for anyone who chose to use them the day passed over very quietly and nice. And everyone well pleased and Proud of the Day, the Declaration of Independence July 4th 1776.

Our Detachment is ordered to Texas

August the 4th 1850. our little detachment numbering about sixteen men went on Board the steam ship Galvestin [sic] for Galvestin [sic] Texas en route to San Antonia [sic] Headquarters of the 8th U.S. Infantry our voiage across the gulf of Mexico was very warm yet pleasant. the sailors and stokers of our ainchient (ancient) and wonderfull looking Craft were all nigers slaves I presume the[y] were a jolly lot allways laughing singing and poking fun at one another in the most good humoured manner one Big greasy looking niger as Black as a cole (coal) with a large mouth, and teeth like ivery, would give vent to his musical powers now and then while seated on top of a barrel singing

Fare de well my own true love Fare de well I go
Fare de well my own true love I'm bound to Mexico
Some body in the house with dina, Some body in the house I know
Some body in the house with dina Playing on the old banjo

On the thired or fourth day we arrived in the City of Galvestin [sic] the commercial capital of Texas Galveston is a Small Town all frame Buildings but is growing very Rapidly and has a prosperous future before it. The weather was intensely warm the Boys decided on taking a Bath. we went along the sandy Beach til we found a quiet and secluded Spot. In a short time we were splashing and tumbling in the heavy warm surfe which was washing and foaming along the shore for miles as fare as we could see not a house or a human bein were visable along the low Barren sandy waste at lentht (length) a sollitery Boat man made his apearance seated in a light smart looking Boat with a small sail well filled stearing rappedly towards us the Boat man shouting at us. I say boys, get out of that there are sharkes about hear in a moment there was a panic among us every man for him selfe Such tossing tumbling and floundering about in the great surf, til we came out on dry ground again, a frightend shakey looking lot we were we thanked the Boat Man who warned us of our Danger. we went Back to the Town and abard Ship and were Soon off again steaming for Indi[a]nnola and arrived there the next morning. We remained hear fue Days when we Commenced our March for San Antonia [sic], one Hundred and forty miles up the Country. There was no Railroad in Texas that time it was I might say a vast wilderness of immense extent with a fue settlements between San Antonio and the Coast. our first days march was about twelve miles a cross the prairie very sandy covered with coarse Sun Burned grass. The sun was Blazeing hot some of the men put their handkerchifs under there caps the end falling down covering the Back part of the Head and Neck and side of the face which afforded a slight Protection from the scorching rays of the sun and fanning our face and neck when a Breath of air came along how Delightful it felt even for a moment. our feet warm and heated by the hot sandy nature of the soil which yielded under our feet at every step making our march very labourish and trying on us, there was no water or shady spot to sit down and Rest our selfs and Replenish our Canteens which were soone empty or unfit to Drink. The next day we marched about twenty six miles to Victoria. a Small Settlement on the Guadalupe River and arrived there about one Hour after dark Completely played out, after our Days March and the constant exposeoure to the Sun. We sufferd very much through the want of water our Thirst was so great a pool of water more properly Called a mud hole was a welcome sight and was made use of by some of the Men as ardently as if it was out of the purest Spring. One of our men a young Irish Man from Carlow was so Completely Prostrated by the heat and unable to continue on the March droped out and lay down in the shelter of a small Bush. we were unable to do anything for him and were reluctingly obliged to leave him behined. Our Wagon which was a conciderable distance in the rear in Charge of a fue men when it came up poor Murphy was dead. The escort with the wagon remained with the Boddy that night and burried it the next morninig. we had no coffey that night as our Rations and Cooking uetintials (utensils) were in The Wagon. we were very hungery but bein somuch fatigued we lay down on the Bank of the River and sleeped sound til the next morning when the wagon came along we heard of the Sad fate of poor Murphy. after about Seven Days marching such as I have described from the Coast and about four miles from San Antonia [sic] we halted at a fine Clear Running stream of Water we stoped hear for about Two Hours and Refreshed our selfs in the Cooling waters and Bathet and scrubed our warm and dirty skin, which refreshed us very much and revived our sistim (systems). We started on the road again with Renewed energy as we were near the end of our journey, and Comming in view of the little Town of San Antonia [sic]. it was a most pleaseing Sight to us after our scorching weary little March from the Coast the white Houses and green trees and the old Spanish Church apearing over all formed a most pleasing picture but as distance lends enchantment to the view and Comming to the end of our Journey we longed for a Square Meal Something more palatable and Better than what we had on the March, and to Replennish our stomach more emthy (empty) then full, and enjoy a needful Rest. entering the Town, we passed through the Main Street to the Plaza, near the old Spanish Church which looked so Bright in the sun shine with its lime washed walls and green Trees. at one end of the Plaza, a Bare unsightly looking place are the Temporary quarters of the Soldiers a row of one storey Houses of the Mexican style a very tall Flag Staff Stood in the middle of the square with the Stars and Stripes floating from the Top. a lot of Soldiers were standing outside the Buildings eagerly looking at us and making all sorts of enquieries about Certain places, New Yorke [sic] and down East. after a fue days Rest we were assigned to Co. B. 8th U.S. Infantry stationed in San Antonio commanded by Capt. and Brevet Colonial (Colonel) I.V.D. Reeves. Three or four Days after my arrival hear Resting myselfe on my bunk, I was seised with most voilent cramps and pains in my limbes I was taking to the Hospital and detained for a fue Days and returned to duty again Two Soldiers who came hear with us Died a short time after. It was seposed (supposed) it was from the effects of the March.

Our regular ruetene (routine) of duty hear was light and not of a showey Character and concisted of Guard duty, Drill onst (once) or Twice a day and some fatague duty. Texas comprises what the[y] call Eastern and Western Texas, and is devided from Mexico, by the Rio Grande River. at one time it was Part of Mexico, but had seperated from that Country by Revolution, and became an independent Republick. afterwards in 1846 it was annexed to the U[nited] States whose Goverment at onst (once) tooke up the question of the Boundery line between Texas and Mexico. Which resulted in a war between the U[nited] States and Mexico which lasted Two years from 1846 to 1848, and ending in the Defeat of Mexico, and the granting of some very valueable concesions to the U[nited] States by giveing over to this country New Mexico and Calofornia [sic]. I have been very much surprised and impresed with the number and extent of the great Teroteries (Territories) in the United States so little Known to the White man, who are steddely pushing westward from the great long frindge of Civilizeation into the unknown Wildeness Braveing every Danger and discomfort and exposed to attacks from Hostile and Cruel Indiens [sic] who Inflicts apon there captifs the most Crueal Torture. Texas is the largest State in the American Union the summer is veary warm but the air is clear and light. Winter is Mild and spring time is fresh and green. one great draw Back is the long droughts which sometimes sets in The heat Burns up the Crops and the rank wild grass of the Prairie. The ground where it is of a loomee (loamy) nature cracks and opens in various Directions in long narrow seams going deep in the ground when the Rain comes it Pours some times acompanied by the most vived flashes of lightening and the loudest thunder I ever heard. The cheapest article of food in Western Texas is Beef when I came hear it was selling at Three Cents a pound, [...] game was fairly Plentifull, Deer, Wild Turkeys, Prairie Hens and Rabbets. Wolfes are veary numerous and often make themselves heard in the night time Barking and Howling.

San Antonio is a small town with about five Thousand Inhabitants about one halfe Mexicans, the remainder Americans and Foreigners. haveing a fair share of time and leasure I soone made myself aquainted with the place and what was to be seen in and about it. Like all other Frontier Towns in the Southt West and along the Mexican Border are many honest men and

Industerous Traders. But gamblers and murderers and Texan Rovers who who [sic] spend most of there nights gambling and at the Fandanggo (a Mexican dance) with a class of Mexicans no Better then Themselfs. [...]

My soldiers life became very monotonus and dull when off duty. most of my leisure time was spent in reading. I longed for a change and would like to go on escort duty, as I wished to see more of the Country Beyoned the Boundles Prairie to some other fare distant Post, to se[e] who was there and what was going on. once more in the Peaceful wilderness with its Death like stillness in its Primative nature free from restraint and where the hardy Pioneer and venturesom setler has not yet planted his foot. All this had a great charm for me, on the march or escort duty. floging as a mode of punnishment in the American Army Surprised me very much. one morning we were ordered to parade on the Plaza in front of our quarters. When three Prisoners were Brought out of the guard House. The[y] were then tied up by the wrists and received thirty lashes each and there he[a]d shaved and Drumed out of the servise.

After six months servise I was promoted Corporal the Captain questioned me very much with regard to the duty and my fitness for the rank. Soone after I was Detailed for escort duty with Three Privates under my charge to take a Waggen load of Barrels of Flour to Fort Martin Scott a journey of seventy miles, and allowed three Days to go there and three days to come Back. I was delighted at the chance. Some of the old Soldiers said I was going on a Picknick trough a nise Country with plenty of game But the smallnes of the escort was a surpris to me. one Corporal three privates and a Teamster in the Country of the Comanche Indiens allwaise hostile and uncertan. The[y] were not on the War Path this time when we commenced our journey. after proceeding a fue miles the ceanery (scenery) of the Country concisted of low Hills and valleys covered with Misqueit, grass, Clusters of live

Oak abound in the low grounds while The hills are Bare of Trees. in some places the road is ruff and stoney [...] As we proceed the prevailing Timber is live oak till comming to the Sabine Creek on the margin of the stream large Cypress Trees were growing. after Crossing the Creek and ascending the ruff stoney ground in front Bits of prairie Land apeared before us with clusters of Trees fare and near Breaking the expance and looking if I may say so the only signe of life in the great camb (calm) peaceful looking wilderness around us. Wee encamp allways in the evenings a short time before sundown. The mules are watered and hiched to the tongue of the Waggon and receive there allowance of Corn. A fire is made and supper prepared, Coffey Bread and Pork. Some times in place of Bread warm slapjacks a sort of ruff and ready pancake arraingements are then made for the night and an early start next morning. The three privates form what we Call a running guard No. one going on post soone after sundown keepes moveing about round the Waggon and mules keeping a sharp looke out in all directions espiscialy in the night time and paying the strictest attention to the slightest noise or rustle in the grass. the mules are very quick to perceive the slightest movement at the least sound, the[y] will cock there ears and look stedely in the direction any alarm, whatever way it comes. I was told the[y] have a great dislike to Indiens the sentinel if he thinks there is anything suspiscious about will quietly waken up the rest of the men who at onst get on there feet and grasbing there musquits (muskets) which are allready loaded with Buck and Ball. if there is no cause for alarm the[y] then roll themselves up in there Blanket and stretch themselfs on the ground for another nap.

Soone after crossing the Gaudaloupe River we Proceded trough a very nice valley thick with Trees and most refreshing to looke at we passed a small village onst a Mormin Settlement which the[y] abandent and is now in ruins traveling for a conciderable distance after passing this lone village wee arrived at

Fort Martin Scott. I reported myself to the Commanding Officer of the Post and gave him the invoices of the goods witch I had brought with me. after looking at the papers he smiled and in the most pleasing manner said well Corporal you have brought me Something else besides Flour. In eveary one of the Barrels of Flour witch you brought hear are a Certain Number of Colts new Revolvers for my men who will be delighted to get them. he asked me did I know anything about them. I told him I did not that I felt very much surprised to hear that, But was very much pleased that they were safely delivered and from under my charge. The[y] were the first Revolvers issued to the united states Troopes on the Frontier. The[y] were worth about forthy Dollers a piece rather heavey But very much in quest by all sorts of Persons who would give almost anything to procure one of them. After parthing withe the Commanding Officer and crossing the Parade ground, I unexpectedly met an old school mate of mine from Dublin [...] Flyn was a Jolly Humerious sort of a fellow who tried to make eveary thing agreable and as pleasent as Possible for me. he was not long hear till he was found out for his Musicle Tallent as a violin player with fair vocle abilities. Of course my friend became a great favorite in his Company and among the soldiers stationed hear compriseing a fue Companyies of Dragoons and Infantry. an amature performance was givein that night I got a front seat on a ruff Board or Bench. the performance was of the variety carricter my friend Flyn took the Negro part and in all the glory of Burnt cork with which his face was smeared. he wore large collar and long cuffs. he was received with great applause singing several of the Poppular Songs of the day [...] which helped to make up the variety of the entertainment for the evening. the next morning we started on our return journey for San Antonio, after Bidding good Bye to my old friend, at the crack of the Teamsters Black snake whip who was alredy in the saddle We were on the road again. that night we had a Bit of a scare we were all asleepe when the Sentery on Post woake us up and pointing to an obgect not very far of[f] about the sise of a man like an Indien. the night was Darke and the obgect was Barely discernible. The Sentery was a German, naturaly very nervious, he said he saw it move. Looke looke he said to us with his teeth chattering in his mouth. One of the escort Pat Doolin an Irishman fixed his Bayonet and Clutching his musquet firmly darted to the front. Devil take it said Pat when he came Back its nothing But an old Burnt stump. these stumps of Trees when seen at a long distance by the unprac-tised eye might be taken for a man [...] these stumpas are the remains of Trees Burned down by the prairie Fires from time to time which destroys everything Consumable in their course. The second day on our journey we met with very good sport game was plentiful. In the morning I had a fue shots at some wild Turkeys but the[y] were too far away and constantly on the move. Though I [k]nocked fire and Smoke out of a Rock close under one of them which farely lifted him off the ground then I saw a big wolf sitting down who seamed to be watching our movements. as soone as I attempted to move the gun to take aim he was up and and [sic] away going directly to the rear for a conciderable distance. He would then turn round face me again looking right straight at me. I closed on him for a short distance and was Bringing up the gun slowly to the shoulder when he scampered off again as before he turned round and sat down on his hunches looking towards me like a Philosopher. I thought that fellow was two [sic] old for one I then gave him up. That Eveaning when we halted for the night and had partaken of a hearty supper which wee relished very much wee ware reclineing on the ground near the Brink of a small valley with a fue spare Trees dotting the opposet or riseing ground in front of us when we saw three or four Turkeys going along in the direction of one of the threes. wee stretched our selfs flat on the ground and remained motionles for a short time watching there movements and night comming on the[y] flew up to one of the Trees to roust (roost) for the night. wee tooke particuler notice of the Tree. about one hour after dark I went down the Hollow with Two of the men moving very slowly towards the Tree till we got quite close to it. I saw three Black round lumps which we suposed were the Turkeys each man took aim and fired at onst when to our great delight and merrament down tumbled three Turkeys on the ground with a thud that told of there weight and not a kick in them. on the third day one of our men wounded a Deer slightly as we coud not pursue him he made his escape in the Evening we arrived at the Alamo after a pleasant and most enjoyable trip of seven Days.

Deserts from the Army

At this time my Company was stationed in the Alamo [...] Comfortable quarters and very little to do, and close upon Two years servise. I had made up my mind to Desert, and only waited a Letter from Dublin to make the attemp[t]. while my mind was most occupied thinking and planning what was best to do. I did not dislike the Service As I would still be a very young man after Completing my term of five years. I then could make a new start in life with about four Hundred Dollors in my pocket to begin with. after fairly concidering evearything for the Best there was nothing left but secure my escape. At lenght the expected Letter came to hand. I told one of the men in the Company whome I knew I could trust, what I was going to do he was an Irishman named Jerry Spillane a Corkman, who was of very great service to me a plan was arranged (arranged) and the night appointed to take french leave and trust to luck. On the night of the 16th January 1852 I went to the Padre a Spanish Priest who had one Hundred Dollors belonging to me I told him what I intended to do he felt great sympathy for me and gave me my money. I then knelt down and he gave me his Blessing I took my departure and going through a fue Back Streets was soon out of the Town where I met a Man with a horse and Cart at a certain place who tooke me to a farm about ten miles out from the Town. I remained there for a weeke dooing some light work and amuseing myself in the Evening hunting rabbets in the Shaparel or Bush. I watched eveary strainger who came along which made me timorous and uneasy. At the end of the Week in the Night time I came into Town where I had apointed to meet my friend Jerry who had been up to time waithing for me. after a warm shake of my hand and a fue words now said he you are allright now. Wee had Bloody murder since you left. you were not long gone when Seargeant Smith all in a splutter went to the Captain and told him all about it. The Captain gave Smith an order with his compliments to the Quarter Master for three good Horses and take two men along with himself and go down the Road to the Coast for for [sic] fifty or sixty miles if nesescery. you were not long gone at all said Jerry again While I waited ansiously for eveary word that dropped from his lips. Seargeant Smith got the Horses from the Yardmaster but trough some mistake or other got two of the Generals Horses which he thought a great deal about. The next morning when the[y] were missed there was an Infernal row the yardmaster was discharged Smith came Back after four Days the Horses looked Bad and wore out he was very much disapointed and got as Drunk as the Devil. Oh I could tell you a lot more said Jerry you may go now said he it is near Tattoo and for the life of you dont come back hear again. we parted I felt very lonely, one hundred and forty miles lay between me and the Coast and must walke it in the night time beset with Dainger and hardship which had to be faced. The night was darke when I set out across the plain when I struck the right road the lights of the Town soone vanished from my sight and no House on the road with a friendly light for many a mile before me. with the light of the stars I was able to keep the road, a narrow pale streake beneath my feet. I had a light shabby suit of clothes on me. The Night was veary cold with a keen Blast Blowing trough the spare Trees. I keped (kept) plodding along on my way with one comforthing reflection that I dodged my pursuers and was on the same road which the[y] had been a short time before me. on my right I heard a party of Mexicans going towards the Town singing 'San Te. Anna' [sic] a favourite song of theres. But I keped clear of them. during the night I heard one or Two packs of wolfs Howling and Barking the[y] were not very far from me. The[y] seemed to be in opposet directions and repeted there howling and Barking as if answering each other I keped moveing on. I felt very curious I was alone, unarmed thoughts crowded on my mind I was helpless if attacked by these hungery ferocious Brutes. No House or Ranch near me with the Bark of the watch Dog to keepe them off nor a Tree that I coud take refuge in. I Bethought of the good Padre who gave me his Blessing. I listined attentively to the sounds of the answering Wolfs when to my great reliefe the[y] ware moving away from me...as there Barking and Howling was becomming less faint untill it died out in the distance. The night was far advanced how I wished for morning. a light appeared before me a long way off I quickened my pace till comming near it I stood still for awhile, a wood fire was Burning brightly four or five men sat round about it, some of them asleep. I recognised one Man I [k]new in San Antonia [sic]. he gave me some hot Coffey which I needed very much. he then pointed to a log hut whare there was plenty of hay and remain there till morning. These men were working for the stadge Company, which runs betwn San Antonia and the Coast. as soone as I got into the hut, I Burrowed myself in the hay. I coud not sleep it was to[o] cold. When Daylight came I started on the Road again in the eavening I stoped at a Farmers House where I assumed the Name of Tom Rogers from New Orleans. I stopped there all night til the next morning, and resumed my journey again. dureing the Day I met Two men on the road going to San

Antonia each of them had a gun after an exchange of a fue words we parted. in a short time I came to a road which Branched of[f] slightly from the Road I was on. unfortunately I took the wrong one which Brought me to a lone House after Walking six or seven miles out of my way this was a hard pull on me which I felt sorely. I stopped at the House a short time and procured something to eat and some Coffey which warmed and refreshed me. I then struck out across the Prairie a small herd of wild Horses made there apearence who stood for a short time looking at me veary attentively then cocking there mains and switching their tails the[y] plunged and jumped in in [sic] the most friskey manner. Away the[y] flew as free as air and was soone out of Sight the[y] looked veary veary slick and hansome and were in fine Condition after walking for sevearel miles I struck the Right Road again, but my feet were getting sore which caused me to limp. at lentht I got to Kings which was Cauled the Half way House where the stadge stops to change Horses and refreshments for passengers. not been able to walk any farther I decided to stop hear a fue Days and take the stadge from San Antonia, for the remainder of the journey providing all was right. I paid Six Dollors for an out-side Seat on the Coach with the driver. I had now about Seventy Miles to go in a veary exposed situation on top of a Coach without an over Coat or Rug to keepe me warm. the journey was veary tedious and unplesent. the Coach upset the Day after we left Kings. myself and the Driver Thumbled of[f] the Box. I came to the ground Bottom under fortunatly I was not hurt, I was severely stund, comming down on the ground like a lump of led. there were four or five passengers in the Coach who were in a Confused heap all mixed up together. no one was hurt in a short time we had the Coach righted again and Resumed our journey. for the greater part of the way I had to walk. The Cut up Prairie track was very soft after late rains. At times the wheels were Sunk to the hubs all the passengers would then have to assist getthing the

43

Coach out of the hogwalla. At lenght we arrived at Port Lavaca about twelfe o Clock in the Night. all was Darkness not a light to be seen except one in a House Called the Planters Hotell the little street was ankel deep in mud. I knocked at the door and was admitted along with a Burley old Texin [sic] a strainger. My Stars said the old fellow as he stamped the ground with his heavey Boots to get rid of the Black muck which the[y] were Covered with. in a short time myself and partner were Shown into a Roome with one Bed and a fue other things. if there is anything I hate more then Sleeping in Bed with one of my own sex I dont [k]now what it is. the old fellow was veary Chatty and a fameliour sort of person which relieved me of some of the embarisment which I felt. he had a large sum of money in a Canvas Bag which he placed under his pillow with a loaded Revolver in the most unconcerned fashin as if I was an old frind (friend). he said he was going to New Orleans to Buy a couple of niggers to work on his Farm. I sleeped soundly after a missearable and slavish jour-ney til morning when the tinkling hand Bell of the Host called us for Breakfast. Port Lavaca is a small unsightly little Town, of modern growth wooden Houses, one and two story high I expected to get a Steamer hear for New Orleans but was very much disapointed after waithing a weeke with the loss of time and money which Required great Care and Management, as I had a lot to do with the small sum of money I was owner of. I went down to the Wharf a Small Sail Boat was takeing some pas-sengers for Indienola [sic] Twelf Miles from hear with the expec-tation of getting the Boat for New Orleans. between Rowing and Sailing our little Craft got to Indienola [sic] about Sun down. the next Day I had the good fortune of gething clean away out of Texas on Bord the Steam Ship Cincinnati. She was a Chubby lit-tle Boat veary strong, a most fortunate circumstance as she was Put to a veary severe test after wee left Indienola [sic], Crossing the Bar before we entered the Gulf of Mexico with its Daingerous shoals. it was low water at the time a foaming tossing swelling streak of the sea streached out before us a stiff Breeze was Blowing at the time. [...] we did not have long to wait when our vessel struck Bottom and Rose again with the heavy swell which carried hir forward and let hir down again on the sand Bar which made hir shiver. the passengers began to feel uneasey. Some who were in great spirits and of lude (lewd) manners but a short time before, became greatly frightened took out their Bibles to Read and looking Pale with fear our vessel still thumped but Riseing quickly Bounded onward on the summit of the waves then plunging downwards strikes Bottom again with great force shaking the vessel from stem to stern anuff to knock you off your feet. It was then decided to lightin the vessel as the only means of gething across the Bar safe. a Large number of Barrells of Sugar of large Demensions were on Decke. fifteen Barrels were Rolled over Board still she Bumped. fifteen more were consigned to the Waves at lentht wee got Safely over the Bar. the Steamer became unmanageable hir Rudder was gon. this Caused some delay a Temporery Rudder was fixed in its place. we Called at Galvestin [sic] and tooke in some freight and arrived in New Orleans after a passage of Seven or Eight Days veary slow sailing with a make shift helm which Could not be depended on. I stoped in New Orleans about Two Weekes, As I could not procure a passage for Liverpool anysooner. I was Compelled to wait for a ship that was loading Cotton for that Port who had acomodation for a small number of Passengers. I felt veary lonesome the time passed very tedious as I was obliged to act with the strictest economy [...].

Sails for Liverpool and Thence to Dublin

At the Begining of February 1853 I took my departure from New Orleans on Board of the Ship John and Lucey Bounded for

Liverpooll with a cargo of Cottin and about sixteen passengers Men and Momen. I paid thirty Dollors for my passage and found in cooked Provisions, of a kind furnished to the Sailors. I was veary much pleased at this arangement. Besides the John and Lucey was a much Larger vessel then the Confidence. I thought I would have a more favourable passage home, then I had comming out. We were towed down to the moutht of the River. A dense fog obscured eveary thing from viue (view) at about a ships lenght. a great number of vessels of all Sorts were mooveing about in all directions in veary close proximity to each other and doing Some Dammage to there Ropes and Spars catching in one another causing a great deal of Confuseion. a Merchant Steamer collided with a small Barke pushing hir over almost on hir Beam ends. at lenght the fog lifted and a favouring Breeze Sprung up. we were soone out of our entangelment and were Speeding our way trough the Gulfe nicely. a large steamer from San Francisco passed veary Close crowded with Passengers a veary ruff looking lot of Men Returning from the Gold Digings in Calofornia [sic]. the gold feaver was then subsiding I sepose some of them made there pile and more did not. I had a Berth in what was called the second Cabben on Deck. the first Night on Board I Lay down in my Berth to have a sleep in a short time I had a most Disagreable sensation as if something of a grain like nature was droping on my face from the Boards of the Cabbin above me in a short time I began to i[t]ch the place swarmed with Bugs The annoyance and disgust which I felt was Shocking. I was getting pretty well used to what the[y] Call Ruffing it But I could not Battle with these Beastly insects I got out on the Deck as soone as I could the night was fine and I sat down on the main Hatch, thinking what to do and Condole over my misfourtune all the Berths were in use eveary available place where one or Two Bales of Cotton could be stowed away was made use of. I was obliddged to Remain on Deck during the whole of the passage and put up with what shelter I could find in some hole or Corner about the Ship. the Captain was a veary ruff, a hot tempered Sort of person who would stamp on the Deck in Bad weather and curse and dam the wind because it was not favourable. he wondered veary much [why] I was going Back to such a poor impoferished place like Ireland. for four or five weekes wee had very ruff and unfavourable weather. I suffered very much from the sea sickness the food was of the ruffest quality and very unpalitable. even the Sailors found fault with it and grumbled very much about it. After about six weekes at sea we had some expectations of seeing the Irish Coast. one Dark Night the sea was a little ruff with a good Breeze on our quarter the sailor on watch saw a glareing light ahead the Fastnet Rock light seemed to be directly in front of us and veary near us the crew were on deck in a jiffey the ship was put about in a very short time the light was now astern the Dainger was past it was a very narrow Shave as we were about Two lenghts from the Rock. [...]

Day light comming on, the Iron Bound Coast of the old Land was looming up before us with its lights and shadows of Purpel and grey the great indents and Bold Cliffs, with a speck of green hear and there. Now and then a warm glow of Sunshine Brightning up the Cean (scene) of the great Coast line spread out before us which made my hart glad to be near home once more. we made Cape Clear and tacking about up the channell we passed the Tuscar Light and at last made Hollyhed [sic] where we Lay allmost motionles in a Dead Camb (calm) on a fine April morning I had a good vieu (view) of Hollyhead [sic] and the Welsh Coast, the weather was warm. my health was perfectly Restored the soft bamey air off the Land invigorated my Sistim (system) at length we were taken in Tow and hauled up to Liverpool after a passage of fifty Two Days. It was in the Night time when we arrived in the Mersey. the Anchor was let down. I Remained on Board till the next morning, and then went into Dock. this was my first time in Liverpool. I stoped for a fue Days to have a looke at the

Town and the Docks which I had heard somuch about. the Broad River has a very animated apearence with a number of vessels of all sorts Lying at Ancher up and down the River. Steamers and Sailing vessels outward and inward Bound [...] the miles of Docks which fronts the River filled with ships and Sailing Crafts of all Nations are a Curiosity alone worth seeing. there is nothing Remarkable about Liverpool, except as a vast Commercial emporiam for eveary Class of goods Both Foreigne and domestic. the Town is dingy looking well Built, possesing many fine Buildings the Post office the Exchange and Saint Georges Hall. [...] after stroleing about Town for a fue Days and seeing anuff to sadisfy my Curiosity I started for Dublin in the Old Dutchess of Kent [sic] a small chubby Dirty old cattle Boat belonging to the Dublin Steam Packet Company. I left Liverpool about eight o clock in the Eveaning. the Night was very fine. it was a glorious April morning as I crept up the hatchway of the old Boat to have a good looke at Dublin Bay under the most favourable Circumstances. the sky was of a pale Blue tinged with a golding glow of the Riseing Sun. the water was like a sheet of Pea green glass with a golding flicker Dancing on its Surface while the old Dutchess [sic] was gliding along like a duck. It woud be unnesessery I think to Discribe Dublin Bay on such a lovely morning as this was whose Beauty has been so often told. But I could not help saluteing the Bayly [sic] and the old hill of Howth and the Pool Beg Light House and The Sand Banks where I gathered shells in days before when I was a little chap, and thought there was no Place like Dublin.

About nine o clock in the morning I landed safe and sound Back again in Dublin after an apsence (absence) of Two years and a halfe I had Breakfast in one of the eating Houses near hand and put on my American Suit of cloas (clothes) which I Bought in New Orleans. when I had done with myselfe and looking pretty sleek my apearence was quite a yank of the Southern type. as soone as I steped of[f] the Boat the first thing I notised was the Jarveys the[y] were a Red faced good natured looking lot of fellows tipped with a Brogue peculiar to a large section of the Dublin People the nixt thing I noticed as I came along on an outsider was the dullness of Dublin. In a short time I arrived at my Fathers House the[y] did not know me at first til I told them who I was. My funds were very low. I gave My Mother a fue gold pieces whitch were very exceptable. after a Short Conversation, I took my departure promiseing to Come Back again in the Evening.

OFF FOR THE NEW WORLD

On the broad expanse of the ocean wild,
In a tiny barque we sailed,
An emigrant band to a foreign land
And Dixie far away.

Our steerage was full it could not hold much,
In a four hundred and fifty tonner,
It was a dreary month and a dreary year,
For us poor 'Forty niners.

From Halpin's Pond we sailed away,
Towed down by the 'Adeline',
An ancient boat from the Clyde, worn out
Good enough for Dublin Town.

Beyond Poolbeg on an evening grey,
And a wintery look in the sky,
The tow line was slipped and the tug went back,
Leaving a spray behind.

A sort of loneliness soon we felt,
In the disappearing land,
And the shades of night coming on,
The golden spears and all we held dear,
In poor old Ireland.

Then down the mysterious hold we went,
Our first night altogether,
In twos and threes and family groups,
We all sat down where 'ere we could,
Around the grim apartment.

Two lanterns hung from the deck above,
Which shone with a feeble light,
On a mixed-up set from City and Town,
And far off country-side.

Then the tramp of the sailors over-head,
As they spread more sail to take the wind,
And square the yards and belay them tight,
And the barque went on like a thing of life.

Then the sound of a fiddle and flute was heard,
Sent a thrill of pleasure through us,
And a rattling jig an Irish reel, roused our spirit,
And quickened our heels with dance and song,
We felt relieved until the midnight hour.

Then all went well 'til off Cape Clear,
And felt the force of Atlantic waves,
Nearly all were sick and worn out,
With a tortured stomach and aching head.

Day by day was much the same,
Until we came to the Azores,
The weather cleared and the sun shone bright,
On the little Island called Saint Marys.

It was a short respite to the sick on board,
Who crowded on the deck,
Up from below the foul smelling hold,
Who enjoyed the scene like a rare show,
Then dimly faded out of sight.

For weeks we sailed and no sign of a sail,
While we searched the horizon round,
'Til at length one night a ship passed by,
Like a phantom ship not a sound was heard,
Though her lights were burning bright.

The sea the sea the angry sea,
How our vessel tossed and rolled,
On the crest of the wave and down again,
Labouring hard to keep afloat.

While the wind blew strong and screamed in delight,
On our little barque with all its might,
Persisting in its grand uproar of wind and water,
And tempest shock and the flash of lightening round about.

Thank God we are saved, the storm is past,
There's a mournful scene on board,
Two emigrants dead, a short prayer is said,
Then over the rail dropped into the sea,
To the fathomless depths below.

Then the weather grew fine and a softer blue,
The clouds were not racing along,
When the man on watch shouted out "Land ho, Saint Domingo,"
It was a magic sound that filled us with joy,
And gladdened the heart within us.

Some pleasant sailing now we had,
And watched the porpoise play,
And flying fish with finny wing gliding o'er the water,
Then Mother Carey's chickens were flying round about,
As if to say your welcome to the sunny South.

Then warmer grew the sun and the sea was smoothing down,
When we came to the Bahamas where pirates used to hide,
And Morgan the Bold Buchaneer, who knew the islands well
And robbed the Spanish Galleons and got drunk upon their wine.

Then on the Coast of Cuba we got into a calm,
Our vessel lay quite motionless upon the glassy tide,
Our deck was dry and seamy and the pitch was oozing up,
Until it came monotonous we thought we had enough.

Someone whistled for the wind sure enough it came,
But oh, the gentle breezes merely kept us moving on,
If we were pleasure seekers how delightful it would be,
To sit and lounge about the deck upon the summer sea.

Then in the Gulf of Mexico we slowly sailed along,
Until we met a tug boat before we saw the land,
The tow line fixed, she pulled through the tawney coloured flood,
To the mouth of the Mississippi where it enters in the Gulf.

Then up the mighty River one hundred miles or more,
With clay banks on the water side to keep it flowing o'er
The low long lying bottom lands on each side of the river
Where tall canes grow in patches big,
On the sandy flats and lonely shore.

Where primeval trees grow rough and tall,
In the gloomy swamps draped in moss,
And creeping vines round hoary trunks
And rotten branch and sapling twines,
Like a thing of life it seems to waste,
Where ere it clings in its foul embrace.

At last we arrive in New Orleans a very niggerish sort of place,
Half French, Americans, Creoles and Blacks,
And many natives from foreign parts,
A busy mart alive with trade,
Cosmopolitan in all its ways, built in a swamp,
No better site could be found higher up or lower,
Yet looks as if some day it might sink into the River.

A. J. Byrne 1830–1911

Chapter Three

The tide will come, and the tide will go,
Casting its flotsam on the shore,
What 'ere they be, has no thoughts for me,
But past mistakes in life remain
A mingling of sorrow and of pain
ॐ.

'Thoughts of the Past'—Andrew J. Byrne

Returns to the Building Trade

I ARRIVED VERY UNEXPECTEDLY at the Home of my Motherinlaw [sic] where my Wife Resided since I went to America. my Wife and hir Mother were present. it was a very curious meeting I could not very well describe my thoughts. I was naturally of a shy disposition, and not impulsome anuff to open my arms and make any great demonstration of Love or affection I stood at the parler door. my Wife when she saw me went Back a fue paces until the wall stoped hir, as if a little Bit overcome. I was observeing hir closely I thought there was Something Cool and Suspisous looking about hir I felt taken back a little, But did not Show it But as I allways looked to the Bright side of things, the cean (scene) Soone changed. my first thought was to commence House Keeping I was in a fix and considered myselfe Sold. But I was young hopefull and willing to make the Best of my Self. I soon found employment and went to work at my Business. [...] In Eighteen Fifty Three, I was employed by a Dublin Builder to go to the Queens County to Work on a new Mansion in Roseinalas (Rosinallis) for a Country Gentleman. I passed trough Mountmellick a fine Country Town well Built. a con-

55

ciderable amount of Industry was carried on hear at one time. But now very little is left of its former Prosperity. a Beet Rute [sic] Sugar factory was in full opporation in the Town. It was Market Day and looked very lively. from Mount Mellick [sic] I Continued my Journey on foot to Roseinalas (Rosinallis), about three or four miles, near the Slieve Bloom Mountains. after a fue Weekes hear Learning all about the County and what was of most Interest in Sight Seeing. one fine Sunday Myself and fue Companions started out for a strole up the Mountain, to Kippards Demesne and othere parts of picturesque Interest. the Day was Camb (calm) and the Sun Shineing with an even mellow glow which gave a Rich softening tint to the Surrounding landscape. on the Mountain Side Black Berries were very plentifull and good and aforded us a good deal of amusement as we went along now and then stoping on the way to pick some Berries which were very large and Ripe and looked very temting to us. we arrived at the gate of Kippard a beautifull Domain and proceeded along a smood well keped Road which led to the House. A plain substantial Building of cut lime stone with very large parlor windows arnomented (ornamented) with Rich hangings and Blinds. In front of the House a Beautifull green lawn sloaping downwards to a plantation of young trees full of Rabbits. From this point a very fine view opened out before us. On one side looking down on a waste of Barren Bog Stretch-ed aut (out) before us, Called the Red Bog. in another Direction an immense expanse of ground well Cultivated Dotted with Black patches of Bog in various directions with a net work of green hedges and Trees scathered cabbens (cabins) and white comfortable looking farm Houses, with fields of yellow Corn with a golden sheen of the Bright sun making the landscape vearied and Beautifull. In the distance the Towns of Mount Mellick [sic] and Mary Burrough [sic] an[d] Behined a Blue Mountain rainge Completed a Picture most Delightful and pleasing. after Roaming about for some time on the heath Covered Mountain and down by a small ripling stream we rested for a short time and returned to the village well pleased with our trip on the Mountain. […]

In the Spring of Eighteen Fifty four I went to Liverpool along along [sic] with a man of my Business who had tramped a good deal of England. he induced me to leave my work and go with him. I was growing discontented at my wifes habit of Drinking otherwise I would not have gone I had a very Dirty Passage of Seventeen Hours going over. I was Sea Sick nearly all the way [...] I had very little money when I arrived in Liverpool and started on the Road for Bolten [sic]. My Companion seamed to know all about this part of the Country as we went along, now and then stopping at a way side ale House for some Refreshments and Resting oursefs for a short time. we took the Road again, passing through several smalls Towns on the way. Every Town Village or Hamlet had its Factory or many Factories with there tall smoking chimlies and near hand Comfortable and well Built Cottages cleanly keped with no Signe of Dirt Squaler or Poverty about. what a Contrast to Poor Old Ireland with its lonesome Roads Deserted Mills and disapearing Industry. We got into Bolten [sic] about six o clock in the Evening, after a Tramp of thirty one Miles. Bolton is a Hive of Factories princibly in the cotten Bussiness. the Factory People were leaving off work. the roadway and side walks, was crowded Male an[d] females everyone of them wearing Clogs the patter and noise of Hundreds or thousands of feet clad in this way Sounded very strange to me. The next Day we started on the Road again for Black Burn [sic] about twelfe miles from Bolten [sic]. Blackburn is a stiring Town full of Factories and well to do shop keepers the Houses are all new or very modern looking nothing old save a small Stone Church, Black with smoke and age with a plain Square Tower. while looking at the plain and unpretentious looking Edifice a Merry Peal of what I thought the Sweatest of Bells Broke forte from its old and Crumbly looking Tower whitch Surprised and Delighted me, been allways fond of sweet chiming Bells when properly Rung. I Bethought of Home and Christ Church Bells, on many a Christmas Eve in Days not very long a go, when I was young and free from care and trouble.

The merry bells are gladly pealing
Sounds of joyful tidings bring
To my ears in tuneful changes
Happy Christmas to us bring. (Byrne)

[…] I went to work along with my Friend at the new Town Hall then Building. Sathurday [sic] Eveanings hear are very pleasint and lively all the workers are out on the streets Shoping and about the Market. Buying and Selling goes on very Briskly. all kind of Cooked meat are set out before you Black Puddings and sassiges (sausages) steaming hot are sold veary freely you would immagine some of these People were eating their Dinner on the streets with a Black Pudding in one hand and a grain of salt in the other eating as the[y] went along doing there Business. […] I did not Remain long in Blackburn, about two weekes when I came Back to Dublin again. one Day My Employer asked me would I like to go to Connamara [sic] to work and take charge of a job that would last for a bout Three Months. I thought the terms were very favourable and that it would give me an opper-tunity of seeing the Western Highlands so little none (known) to thousands of well to do Irishmen who chose to go to other parts aut of the country, more fashinable and snobbish then the grand and Romantic wilds of Connamara [sic].

[…] Docter William Wilde of Dublin became owner of a Small Bit of Ground called Illen Roe Lake Navara Connamara [sic] for the purpose of Building a fishing Lodge on the little isleand near the Lake Shore. I was to act as foreman the Docters stewerd was to suply me with evearything I wanted for the Building. one fine morning I started on the Seven a.m. Train from the Broad Stone [sic] accompanied by the Gentleman who employed me for the

Docter. He was to Pilot me to the job and see that every thing was all Right for me this was very encourageing and sadisfactery to me. we got off the Train at athen Righ (Athenry) and drove on to Tuam, County Galway where we changed Horses. we stoped hear a short time and picked up a fue passengers and Drove on again passing trough the Town. I had a look at the fine Catholick [sic] Cathederal presided over by the great Arch Bishop John McHale, whome O Connell called the Lion of the fold of Judia [sic]. we were now on our way to Castle Bar [sci] County Mayo passing trough a Bleak poor looking Country we arrived at Hollymount, a nice place with a fue Cottages and a Police Barrack. I bethought of the French General Humbert who at one time occupyed this place and the Races of Castle Bar [sic] and what might have Been. But the Continual driving and change of cean (scene) Soon Banished these mellincolly thoughts out of my mind. we arrived in Castle Bar [sic] and changed Horses again and started for Wesport [sic]. [...] we passed trough the main street a long crooked thourafare lined with Houses Two Storey high, and Terminated by mud Cabbens. we were soone out on the Country Road again Joging along nicely thanks to the fine weather as I was beginning to get tired of the autsider and the continuaty of the journey and the Bleak poor looking aspect of the Country which we were passing trough. It was long after Dark when we arrived in Wesport [sic], and put up at a very comfortable In[n] til the next morning. after Breakfast having a fue short Hours to spare I set out to have a looke at the nise little Town and its surroundings, and Lord Sligos Demain. the old fashioned Quay or Harbor with Two or three small schooners moored at the wharf and Some fine old warehouses with nothing in them. It was very quiet and sleepy looking. Nothing but decay. the morning was Sun Shiney with a clear Skye the Bay of Wesport [sic] stretched out before me Croagh Patrick on the left the great Hudge Peak Towering upwards to a great hight from the fringe of the Bay with its Green Cambe (calm) Water silent and motionles and in the distantance Clare Island. I returned to the In[n] and took my Seat on the Care and was soone trotting along the road again for Kilemore [sic], Passing trough a country full of Huge stones and patches of Bog. I had about Twenty Eight Miles to go to my destination after fourteen or fifteen miles we arrived at the Killeries a long Winding Lake as I thought til I was informed it was an arm of the Sea with grand old Towering Mountains Rising up from the edge of the Dark and deep looking water lone and Beautiful. at the Harbour I saw several nise comfortable looking Small Houses. We stoped hear a short time and changed Horses there were Several young gentlemen about who belonged to a fishing party. five or six young Connemara Girls were sitting down near a wall kniting stockins of various Collours. the Girls were nearly all of the Brunet or Spanish type so frequently met in Gallway [sic] and the West of Ireland, with there long Darke tresses parted in the middle of there Forehead and expressif eyes of darke Blue or Grey I bought two pairs of stockens. The[y] were so attractive and Comfortable looking. I sau (saw) very fue tourists it was the fall of the year. The effects of the late famine could be seen on my way hear in the ruined Cabbins and desolated Hamblets. After a Short Drive from the Hotell we came in viu (view) of a Beautiful Lake nearly surrounded with Mountains of a very Romantic Caracter. near the Northern Shore is Ilan Roue [sic] a small Island of Bog and rock in the Hart of Connemara, Near Joyce's Country. [...] after making an arraingement with the steward for the Commencement of the work, I Crossed the Lake in a small Boat to a Cottage occupied by a herd, where I lodged til the termination of my work. Having very little time for pleausure or Sight Seeing in this Land of Wonder with its Mountains Crags and Peaks, except on Sunday's weather permiting, then going to mass three or four miles away, up hill and down hollow, the People comming in Twos and threes along the

Road, or by some wild mountain Path. Mas[s] was said in the little chappel every fourth Sunday the priest had to attend at one or Two other chapels alternetly. the sermon was generaly preached in Irish. after mass I took a strole trough the Country or along the wild sea shore. I allways loved the Sea Side wheather in its placidity or in its mighty swell Booming and tossing along with its white crested waves dashing against the rocks. By the sad sea waves I listen while the[y] moan. another time climbing a high Mountain in order to get a vieu of the Surrounding Country. In the West the Boundless swelling Atlantic with Clare Island and Achel [sic] Island in vieu then sweeping Round to the South and East a vast Reagin of Ruged mountain seanery (scenery) is spred out Before you. the twelfe Pins, Numbers of small Lakes and poolls, Patches of Bog and verdent spots of Green with a grey thiney smoke curling up from some fare of[f] aboad which are fue and fare between. any one comming from the plains or low Country might immagine him self in another part of the globe when sojurning in Connemara.

One Bleak afternoon the weather looking uncertain I started out to go to Letterfrack, a part of the country I was unacquainted with for the purpose of procureing articles of under cloathing which I needed, and my desire to see all I could of Connemara, while hear. Letterfrack is about eight miles from Lake Navara and the nearest place for me to get what I wanted. The Evening was a shade gloomy and the ground moist from late rains. leaving the Road I crossed a fue low hills for a short cut. I made nothing of that But a wet stocking and a lot of climbing up Hill and down again til I got on the right road again. I passed five or six cottages Newly Built and a large one storey House intended for a school. [...] on my way a dark close mist of rain came down srouding the Mountain tops as I was passing along by Kilemore [sic] Lake which the Road skirts for five or six miles the opposet side of the Lake was Bounded by high Hills Bare and unattractive on my Right Rising up from the side of the Road great Towering Mountains of a Preciptious apearence stretched along the Road for several miles. in some places Huge mases of Rock overhanging the face of the Cliffs looked very tretning (threatening) and Daingerous as you pass along the narrow Road under neatht. I was feeling damp and uncomfortable when the mist and fog began to clear as I neared Ballinnakil [sic] In a short time I entered the little village of Letter Frack [sci]. the sun shone aut Brightly for a short time with a rich mellow glow imparting to the face of nature that Beautiful Collouring which pleases the sight and makes the Hart glad. Hear I noticed some signes of improvement which shows what can be done in a poor Mountain District like Letter Frack [sic]. A Family of quakers settled down hear some time after the Fammin in the Poor little village and at onst (once) set to work making improvements Building and Reclaiming a large Section of waste Land and tilling the ground. the little village was put in order and looked very neat and comfortable looking. the[y] opened a small country store or shop and were doing a good Business. the people came far and near to deal with them finding them honest and Real Benefactors to the place. I did not stop long hear the Evening was fare advanced and a long road before me and the weather chaingible and uncertain. It is a very lonesome Road to travel you might not meet a Single Person on the way. when about halfe way I came to a poor lonely cabben a short distance from the Road I was very dry although there was plenty of water in the Lake along side of me and more over Head ready to come down any minnut. I asked for a Drink of water the Woman in the House was very friendly when I told hir who I was and where I was going to she went into a little Dark Room and returned with a glass Tumbler in hir hand halfe full of what I though was water. take this she said it will do you more good than water. she said this with an expression of kindness I all ways Remembered. it was the real mountain dew Potteen Whiskey as clear as cristle (crystal) with that peculiar smokey flavour which I coud not doubt. she said it was Parliament. But I knew very well it was not Parliament I offered hir Payment which she Refused. I thanked hir very much and came out on the Road again. Night was Comming on. I crossed the Hills and sloppy Mountain Slopes till I neared the edge of the Lake which I was hard set to make out when a faint light in the caben where I lodged apearing farther on I made my way to it. after my journey my feet was wet and muckey I was pretty well tired out and a pinch of Hunger gave me a relish for my Supper. as I sat by the glowing turfe fire which was resoded I soon found myself very comfortable, after my wild and lonely adventure. early in November the walls of the House were up for the roof my part of the work was completed. I set out on my journey for Dublin, taking the road to Cliftin [sic], in company with two men who worked on the job with me and were returning to there Homes in the Town, about sixteen miles from hear. the weather was gloomey and rainey looking. on the way I found my Two Companions were very intheresting and good Company, knowing eveary part of the Road and the People as well, droping in now and then on the wayside to a poor lone Cabben to light there pipes and chat awhile withe the good People of the House. when we Reached Letter frack [sic] it commenced to Rain lightly and Night coming on I began to feel very ansious about the rest of the Journey. but my friends did not seem to mind it. Never mind said one of them I think we will get something in the next House that il warm us I think a small drop of the crather wont do us any harm. after some time we came to a house and went in with that old time salutation in Irish *God save all hear* the Bottle was Brought out and the glasses were filled and handed Round. then with a kindly parting wee started off again it was getthing late and I wished to get to Cliftin [sic] as soone as I could the rain was Comming down hevey when we arrived in the Town. I was soone along side of a good fire in a very Comfortable old fashioned Inn. After Supper and a glass of Good punch I retired to rest and slept soundly that night. In the morning I felt very much refreshed and in good form. after Breakfast I took a strole trough the Town, while waiting for Bianconys [sic] Car which was to start for Gallway [sic] in a fue hours. after dooing the Town, I came Back the car was redy with a full compliment of Passengers for Galway, about fifty miles from Cliftin [sic]. what if it would Rain I thought my friends on the car were well rapt up and looked very comfortable. I had a light suit of working Cloase (clothes) on me and no [w]rap or over Coat the weather was chilly and gloomey while we Rattled along the Road at a very smart pace there were many sights to be seen from my seat on the car. the Twelfe pins of Connemara and Later on Ballinahinch Lake and Castle. Night comming on and the Twinkling Stars now and then apeared in viu (view) some of the bright and lustrous one's with an apearence as if to say looke at me and tell me what I am. after a long weary-som Drive we Came into Galway I felt a bit Cold and stiff. But was soone Comfortably Housed and all my wants Supplied. the next morning after Breakfast I was stroleing about the old streets of the City of the Tribes with the most eager Curiosity the fine old Spanish Houses are a remarkable sight nowhere else to be seen in Ireland well Built of cut lime stone. [...] I remained for Two Days in the Town, at times stroleing round by the Harbour or among the Cladah [sic] Fishermen and many other parts which interested me. on the third Day I started By Rail for Dublin.

The Crimean War

The Crimea War was a Reality and formed the princible topic every where I went. Politicks was Dead and the Millitery athority's were veary Busey Sending off Troopes to the seat of War. Some of the Redgements marching along the Quays to the North Wall and to Kings Town were very Enthusiastic, singing 'Annie Laurie' and 'Cheer Boys Cheer' Two poppular Songs of the day, and all for a Shilling a day and British glory. Some of the English Malitia (Militia) Redgements were sent to Ireland, to take the place of the Regulars. many persons looked at them with as much curiosity as if the[y] were Turks or Cassicks [sic]. [...] the Irish Malitia was Raised for the first time in a good many years. as a force the[y] were almost forgotten Three of the Redgements in Dublin, Two in the City and one in the County. the Dublin Artilery was the most favored and promised to be a very smart Corps. the men were Superior in point of Phisic (physique) and character in a general Sense to that of the City and County Dublin Redgements of Infantry which was composed to a large extent of the very worst characters in the City so much so that old Granny Latouch [sic] Coloneol of the one hundred City of Dublin Militia, Said if his Redgement could not take Sevastopol, the[y] would steal it. [...] I was disconted and troubled for reasons which I do not care to explain. I joined the Dublin Artillery Militia not for love of the service which I hated as an Irishman should. In a short time I was promoted a Bombardier and from that rank to full Corporal. Nearly all of our officers were of the Aristocratic Class Country Gentlemen and a fue retired army officers the Redgement was Commanded By Coloneol Hancock, Lord Castlemain rather an ornamental Coloneol But I sepose good anuff for the Malitia.

As fare as outward apearence the[y] left all to the Adjutant a very efficient officer a good man well liked by the men. Our Redgement was distributid trough the different Barracks in Dublin, the Pigeon House Fort was Head quarters our uniform was the same as the Royal Artillery with a very slight difference, a Busby, Blue Tunick and Pants of the same Colour. Our arms a short smoode Bare Musquet (musket) and Bayonet and Black Belts. The uniform was very neat looking. As to the Colour Blue I preferred it to the Red, a Colour I allways Dislikid. Our duty was not heavey as we had no horses to attend to. when at the field guns we allways used drag ropes. In the Parke on fielddays wee were allways well up. In chainging Position and Coming into action we commenced firing nearly as quick as the mounted Battery of the Royal horse Artillery. this if cource allways delighted the Adjutant who Complimented the men and felt proud of the Redgement. Sometimes he would say at Batallion drill now men March like Irishmen. Yet I never coud make out which of the three Countrys he came from but in apearence and manner I would take him to be an Irishman with a fine old Scotish name Charles McCallam. we allways called him Charley he was a good friend of mine on many occasions. I was stationed in the Pigeon House Fort. It was my turn for orderly Corporal for the week and consequently coud not leave the Barrack except on duty and going to the Town Majors office Royal Barracks onst a day to take orders. one Evening when all was qui[e]t I felt a Bit lonesom a good many of the Boys recived Passes and were going into Town some to see there friends or to Cramptin [sic] Court Musick Hall. three pence to the pit, you retained your Ticket which would procurea Point (pint) of Sloppy Porter when you weint in side. This evening after thinking over what to do and felling a bit reckless I told one of the men to tell the Sergeant I was going into Town and that he would find my orderly Book in such a place. now this was a very serious offence But I walked away with as little trouble as if I was going to a picknick I went into Cramtin [sic] Court But I was no sooner seated when about a halfe Dozen of Tin quarts and Pints of Porter was held up to me, *hear drink Byrne, take some of this, a go on,* and such like manifestations of good will from men of my Redgement. That I was obliged to dip a little into the cans or pretend to, as a recognition of good fellowship. There was a fue War songs sung that night in the Musick Hall style. the glory of the great deedes of our army in the Crimea at the Battle of Alma and Inkerman. a good many of the Red coated Regulars were there. Some of them must have felt there Martial Spirit Rise listning to a very Bombastick Song imported from England. But as I thought like Micky free in Charles OMalley, *Faith its little for glory ied Care.* The next day about noone I was going along the Pigeon House Road to the Fort I could not exactly say what my thoughts were like after my foolish escaped (escapade) the night previous. I think the[y] were a Bit mixed, with a small grain of indifference. I heared the Clatter of a Horse trotting along the Road Behined me. I did not look behined, as it struck me it might be the adjutant. If he speaks to me what shall I say, yet it turned out very fortunate for me in a short time he came up with me and Brought his horse to a walke now said I to myself ime in for it. When at onst he spoke to me. hello Byrne what is the matter with you are you mad. I said no Sir I am not mad do you know said he you have left your selfe liable to a Court Martial. I listined quietly and with respect because I [k]new he was a good humane man with non of that aragance which we see so much of among British officers. he was inclined to talk. I have been in the service said he since I was a Boy and had many trials and temtations But I got away from all those things and worked myself up step by step by hard work an persavearence . He seemed to be a Bit Concilliatery with me. Now said he if you promise to me that you will mind your self in future I will do all I can for you. I thanked him very much. he then galloped on before me and concidering one trouble anuff at a Time I concidered myselfe fairly out of this one. as an Irish man I did not like the Queens Service neither was I inclined to make unnecessary trouble for myselfe. as regards promotion in the Lower Ranks I allways looked upon it as a right without been (being) mean or cringing. I walked into the Pigeon House Fort a bit unconcerned and went about my Business without any interruption. I keped to myselfe the Conversation I had with the Adjutant on the Road. I was not placed under arrest. Some of the non com's did not know what to make of it most of them were not of my style ex police men and Pensioners Sons, and fellows who came to the Redgement when it was forming with Letters in there Pocket and looking for promotion in preference to others, , and looking after or something in the[y] thought was going to be permanent. a fue days after I was made full Corporal. this was a surprise to many who were aspiring to be a Sergeant as there was a vacancey at the time in the Redgement a fue months after I was appointed Sergeant to the surprise of some of the non coms who had there eye on the vacansey. the Redgement was ordered to the Curragh. we made a Brave show marching trough the Town to the Kings Bridge with our Germain [sic] band playing in front of us it was good fun for some of our Boys But our officers looked as serious looking as if the[y] were Marching to the front but I sepose that was for the purpose of Discipline. on our way we were followed by a great crowd of Sight Seears it is allways easy to collect a Crowd in Dublin. there are so many Idle People and many who are in no hurry at all, every little thing attracks there attintion. Mothers and Fathers were parthing with there truent sons some of there Dear Boys was only Relieving them of a Burden perhaps for a Short time. Well we got to the Curragh Save and Sound. it did not apear to me like Camp live (life) the[y] were all large wodden huts laid out in squares and streets the Troopes were composed of regulars and Malitia. Drilling and field days was the order of the day. a Call was then made for folunteers (volunteers) from the Malitia to the Regulars to fill up the depleted Redgements in the Crimea great indusements by the way was offered to join the Regulers. a large number of the Irish Malitia of all ranks responded to the call a fue extra pounds and a good Drink and away the[y] went. I stood firm and remained where I was. I privately gave my vieus (views) to a good many of the men not to leave the Redgement and that at the termination of the war which might not last long the Redgement would be disbanded and that we would all return home again to

Dublin, in full Bloome like the Enniskillen Dragoone, and be free to go where we liked. the war at last came to an end and the allied Troopes were leaving the Crimea after a strugall of about two years. The Malitia was disbanded and returned to civil live (life) But would be Called up at stated periods for the purpose of training until our term of service five years was completed. I was Paid in commutation and part of Bounty a small sum of money which I did not wish to slip away from my fingers. I resolved on going Back to America again. I could not stop hear my money was small and must act quickly this was a dreary land without a speck of hope or reward and my domestick trouble still existing I longed for freedom and lost no time. I went down to the North Wall steped on Board a small Steamer and started for Liverpool. this was not done with a light hart yet I did not to trouble myself about the future. No Thommy no Mickey or Bridget to Bid me welcome on my arriving in New York with a Bare Shilling in my pocket after paying for my passage was not a very pleasant reflection. Well if the World frowned on me the Sun shined on me.

Chapter Four

In the great lone West on the borderline of San Antonio,
A frontier town, close by the River near the Bridge,
Where the Alamo stands can tell a tale
Of Crockett and Bowie of Texas fame.

✆

'Who Knows'—Andrew J. Byrne

Back Again to America

IT WAS A FINE SUMMERS DAY July 1856 when I sailed from
Dublin and arrived in Liverpool after a very sea sick passage I
procured a Passage on Bord of an American ship of the Black
Ball line the Collumbia was taking out emigrants to New York.
My sea store was very little but I did not mind trifles so long as I
was on my own hook. I was anxious to get away and commence
our voiage and settle myself down once more in my ocean home
away from my tormentor and Ruff it out the Best way I could.
after a fue days I sailed for New York with a motly crowd of emigrants. English, Irish and Germans the wind not bein favourable
for going down the channell the captain desided sailing north
about trough the Irish sea this cource suited me very well as I had
sailed south about going trough Saint Georges Channell on my
first voiage to America. I would now have a oppertunity to see
some of the Northern Coast line of Ireland which I new nothing
about. we were sailing well and passed the Ile of Man with the
dim outline of the Scottish coast eastward. On our left the Irish
Coast stretching along before us. The green fields and pastures

of Down. The Copeland Isles and the Antrim Coast till at length we were plowing away trough the wild and bleak Atlantic we now began to feel the misery and discomfort of an emigrant ship in the old sailing days with a ruff captain and ruff weather and nearly everyone sick on Board myself included. About as bad as the worst of them. After about five weeks sailing we came in sight of Sandy Hooke my sistem improved and my appetite revivid which I had to bear with. passing Sandy Hooke the land closing in on each side but still leaveing a broad spacious passage which is called the narrows with long Island on the right. and Fort Hamilton and Lafyet [sic]. also called dimond battery guarding the passage on that side. On the left Statten [sic] Island with its Forts and pretty houses with the Jersey shore and Jersey City. at the mouth of the river New York on Manhattan island with the Hudsin [sic] river on one side and long Island Sound between New York and Brooklyn the harbour looked very beautyiful in the glare of the hot sun and the hansom cottages and large houses of an armamentil charracter on Staten Island and dotting the shore all along on each side of the Harbour. Numerious Merchant ships and war vessels laying at anchor.and steamers small and large going hear and there. The City Wharfs were lined with shiping while a large number of vessells lay along side Brooklin and Jersey City. The Harbour amid the splendid water way round New York, presented to me a most annimated picture of every material interest that go to build up a great and prosperous City. The Stars and Stripes the red white and Blue was waveing from a tall flag staff on Governors Island remineded me that I was once more again in a free land and from under the controle of the Union Jacke and away from poor hapless Old Ireland, all the passengers were landed at the Castle Garden depot for emigrants. There lugage was examined by the revenu officers while I was allowed to pass out in a short time. i was accompanied by a young Irish man whome had become aquainted with on the passage out to New York and who very kindly asked me to go along with him to a friends place who kepet a grocery store in the City he told me I would be all right for a day or two. This was a God send to me as I had only one shilling in my pocket. I put a Bold face and apeared to be happy which I was not, going to a strange place to People I did not know. However I was treated very well I had plenty to eat and drink. I stoped there til the next morning. I bid goodbye to my friend whome I thanked very much I made my way to Broadway the great central artery of the City and there among the Bussey Trong and the roar and noise of traffic I commenced to inspect the Buildings, the various modes of traffic in the street, the tall houses that lined the sidewalks, the marvel and Brown stone fronts and red press Brick the most Beautiful I sepose in the world, the hurry skurry of the People on the sidewalks, there pale yellish worn look, all nearve in quest of the almighty Dollar. I passed Trinity Church, Barnums Musseum, the City Hall, park and notable places. Till I found myself after a long walke at union Square.

Enlisted in US Army

I ritreased my steps back again down Broadway. and sat on a wodden Bench under the shade of a Sun Burnt tree and commenced to muse over what I should do. My condition was very trying. The fall of the year was near at hand too more months of fine weather and then a long cold Artic winter before me which I was not acustamed to. with all its drawbacks for out door Labour, which I was not prepared to meet. My case was so eurgeant I made up my mind to enlist again in Uncle Sams Army and not to bother myself any further. But how was I to do this. I was a Deserter from the army now. Four years ago since I tooke my leave. I was smood faced. But I now wore a mustach perhaps that might help me if I should meet anyone that [k]new me, I prepared to face the musick, and the next morning I presented myselfe to a recruiting officer in Chattim [sic] Street and enlisted and was sent to Governors Island New York Harbour. I was put along with the recruits in Castle William a large circular Fort casemated. And near the water facing the Harbour I was not long there when I was transferred into the permanent party on the Island which are composed of two Companies well drilled for the purpose of garrison duty and drilling the recruits. Which are sent away from time to time to various redgements in the army. after a short time although I never pulled an oar I became one of the crew of the Bedlos Island Barge composed of eight of a crew and the kockswain. I received extra pay Twenty five Cents a day and exemt from all other duty . The oars were long and heavey but I soon learned to pull very well. the Barge made sevearel trips during the day between Governors Island and Bedlos Island. Which a small place and contains a Fort and a Goverment Hospital for Soldiers. There was a number of sick and wounded Soldiers in the Hospital who came from Florida where they had some trouble with the Indians. After about tenn days Service with the Barge the little garrison on the Island was withdrann. a New Campaigne was about to be commenced in Florida against Billy Bow legs chief of the Seminoal Indians who was very troublesom and not inclined to go on a reservation. I was then reported for duty with my company I was not sorry for this I was gething tired of the Barge. It was hard work sometimes in ruff weather pulling against wind and tide. There were two soldiers on the Island who I knew very well in New Orleans Barracks in 1850. The[y] used to eye me very sharply at times almost stare me out of countenance whither the were shure of me or not I could not say But I never budged, I was made a Corporal. in a short time after I was promoted to Seargent. It was very dull on the Island when off duty and when looking across the water at the great city of New York with its joys and sorrows incidentle to

74

city life. its riches, its pleasures, and its wicketness I did not think my lot an unhappay one. Were it not for one thing alone my old trouble allways a subject of thought and humiliation to me but not wishing to dream over my misfortune I done the best I could do in the hum drum sort of a life on the island with a Bussy World all round about me. I could not leave the Island without a pass which was granted at certain Periods. One evening after retreat the first sergeant an Irish man named Gannon a Galway boy with the twitch of the old time sportive way of the gentry of that county disclosed a little game to me. A quiet spree in his roome after tattoo half a dozen of the boys were invited Minto, a Scotch man who had seeamed to me like a man who had been in a better position at one time than a high private in Company V on Governors Island. The soldiers called him Lord Meinto he was to be one of the company he was fond of the sup when he could get it. But being well seasoned to the stuff could drink more than many without loosing his balance. One night after taps. Lights out we were all assembled in Gannins room a Brown Army Blanket was fastened against the window so that no light could be seen on the outside. The night was very cold I sat near the fire and soone found myselfe very warm with the closenes of the room looking round I saw a small suspisous looking keg in one corner of the room partialy covered by Gannins over coat. I smelt powder at onst. Surmiseing what was in the keg. I wished myself out of it as I was no lover of drink and wished to avoid trouble. yet not wishing to make myself disagreable by leaving the company which might be construed as a breach of trust or bad manners. I remained where I was Gannin uncovered the keg and told us all about it which we were to keep secret. that morning early after revaille Minto was taking a walk on the beach near the graveyard and found a small keg of Brandy which he hid in the sand till night came along. When it was smugled in to Gannin room. The drink went round pretty freely and being nearly all

75

amatures in drinking. in a short time it took effect on us. We soon passed from grave to gay and getting a bit lively. We were under bonds to keep quiet. another drink a little more talk, the very Mild Brandy deceved us. Some of the boys were beginning to get dizey Tim Daly went backwards off the stool he was siting on and brought little Fauset with him. Joe Byrne stagerd a few steps and collideds against the Seargents bed and dropped in to it Our fun was cut very short Gannin took me over to the Barrack roome the rest were not removeable untill the next morning. for three days after I was very sick I could not eat anything frequent vommiting of a severe nature and throwing up stuff of a greenish colour and bitter teast this continued for three days which made me feel very week the vommiting ceased. I was soon well again. I would have passed over this trifeling incident were it not that it had a most beneficial result on me in regard to my health. For a long time my bowls were very much out of order. I was subject to costifnes which lasted for several days. I was then attacked with vrilent in the stomach. Perhaps in the middle of the night followed by a number of irreguler passages which lasted to the middle of the day this misarable condition continued alternetly from time to time. The vommiting after the Brandy which continued at intervils for nearly three days and eating nothing was so severe that it broke and expelled from my stomach some foul matter that was the cause of my trouble and poisening my sistam I was completely cured and restored to a natureal condition of good health and regularity.

The winter of 1856 and seven was very severe in New Yorke. ice everywhare and intence frost which continued all the winter. There was no spring time in the middle of June the trees were bare looking. til Summer allmost burst upon us in July the heat was intence and almost overbearing there were a great many sunstrokes. in the evening after sun down was the only enjoyable part of the day. I was getting tired of the Island and longed for fields more green and pastures new. In the summer of 1857 after serving about nine months on the Island I received a letter from my Wife I made up my mind to send for hir and my Daughter Maryan. a mere Child. I saw it was a venture as far as my happiness and peace of mind was concerned. I tried to dispell my doubts and let things slide for the present In the month of June or July 1857 my Wife and Child sailed from Liverpool in an emigrant ship the Tuscarora bound for New York. after being at sea for eight days the Tuscarora collided with another ship the Andrew Foster in the nighttime bound for Liverpool the Andrew Foster went down her crew was saved. the Tuscarora was badly dammaged and returned to Liverpool. My Wife then came out on the ship John Bright and arrived safely in New York.

Soldiering in New Mexico and Arizona

About one week after this I was a prisoner in the guard house. Tormented in mind I gave myself up as a Deserter they would not believe me at first and thought I was acting very foolish. The Commanding officer on the Island Major Baccus was very friendly and sent a Lieutenent to me to question and advise me he told me what to do. I was a little bit surprised at the cource of events. The friendlynes of the officers and the interest the took in my cace I was pardoned by Lieutenent Genneral Scoot the Commanding Genneral of the United States army and to be sent to my Redgement the first opertunity to complete my term of service three years. having served two years when I deserted would make the full term five years. about the later end of August 1857 a large detachment of recruits was going to New Mexico. My old company B of the eight Redgement was stationed at Fort Stanton. I was sent with this Detachment. The Post Band playing us off to the tune of The Girl we left Behined us. at Jersey City we started by rail for St. Louis Missouri about twelf hundred miles from

New York. passing trough the states of New Jersey. New York. and Pennsylvania and Ohio one of the most productif States in the Union. On the way we passed a number of Small Towns and villages principaly composed of Wooden Houses. at Cleaveland a large town near lake Erie one of the inland Seas of America, we changed cars and passing into the state of Indiana we arrived at Indianapolis the Cappital of the State which apeared to be a young town in an unfinished state and in the proces of Building up and spredding out which made me wish I was droped there.

We stoped three or four hours hear and then started on our journey and were soone crossing the plains of Illinois after three days we arrived at the Missouri river. opposet to the City of St.Louis we crossed the river on a steam ferry to the city. our time was short hear and was soone on Bord the Cars again for Jefferson City about one and fifty hundred miles from hear. we arrived there in the night time and went on Board a Steamer for Levenworth Kansas. Our trip on the Missouri was pleasant and sometimes exciting, it was low water in the river it Been the fall of the year great care and good piloting must be observed. the land on each side was low and flat and covered with trees. on the way we passed several small towns the most important is Kansas City. after four or five days we arrived at Fort Levenworth in the night time. We encamped outside the Post for two days. on the tenth of September we marched out about three miles when everything for our journey across the Plains was arranged and put in order. the next morning after a hurried Breakfast we took up the line of march westward ho depending on shanks mare with hundreds of miles before us through a wild unhabited conntry stretching out away Back to the Rocky Mountains and the Pacific Slope. we had a large number of Waggons with us each drawn by a six Mule Team the were loaded with supplies and ammunition for Fort Union New Mexico the whole forming a large Carravan with the battalian of Soldiers made up of different ditatchments

78

about eight hundred strong and a number of officers.

We moved slowly along through a thinly settled country sparly timbered on the Eightint of the Month we crossed the Kansas River. a fue civilised Indians of the potowatiny Tribe had charge of the ferry a large flat bottomed Boat worked for hire we passed through there village and was surprised at the comfort of there homes and cultavated grounds well fenced in. a large Log Built school House full of young paposes ran out to see the soldiers the were catholicks and had there priest I was glad to see them so happy and contented, you may make Catholicks of some sort or other of the Indians but Protestantism is a failour.

After crossing the Kansas River it commenced raining comming down in torrents upon us. we were in a woful plight wet to the skin. draging our feet out of the Black Muckey Soil as we went along. it was impossible for the waggons to move. we then halted for the night. the rain ceased and the fires were lit the camp kettles were filled with water. In a short time coffee was served out to the men. the weather cleared and the sun shone out again making the earth Steam. and the heat of the fires we were soone dry again after a few days we were out of the settlements and on the vast and Boundless plains. without Mark or Bound Buflows ware numerous some of them would come very near us walking along with the command. I was told the were attracted by a small herd of Beef Cattle which we had along with us.

we generaly marched all day from water to water which was very scarce and sometimes not anuff. our thirst compeled us to drink the water out of pools and mud holes which acumalate after late rains. when we stoped for the night at the end of our days march a number of men were sent out to collect Buffalo chips, dry dung composed of vegatable matter which made a fine fire. after sic or seven weeks we came to the Arkansis River where we halted for two days to rest ourselfs and clean our Sweltring Body in the clear and refreshing water of this lovely river. which we neded very much after a long and toilsom march on the Desert plains. A small party of Chean Indians came into our camp. The were powerful lookeing fellows who would think nomore of takeing your top nott or scalp then the killing of a fly this is done by scoreing the skin round on the top of the hed about the sise of a saucer with a scalpeing knife and tair the scalp off with their hand reeking the blood of their victim. The Indians pretended to be in friends with the white man and wished to trade with us. The had some very fine Buffalo robes which the[y] exchanged with the officers for some coffee and sugar. One old villian had a captive Woman along with him she was a Mexian dark skinned very pretty But worn and sorrowful looking. She at onst aroused the simphaty of the soldiers who would have taken hir away from her Brute Capter were it not that the officers had strict orders not to meddle with the Indians only in selfe defence. Poor thing, she was unable to walk from the cruelty and ill treatment which she was long suffering hir shin bones which were not covered bore the marks of many a scar inflicted on hir by hir Crueal Master for reasons of his own which he afterwards explained. Two light poles of Hickory or some hard wood was fastend to the sides of a poor halfe starved Indian Poney the other ends rested on the ground. Between the two sticks a piece of raw hide was made fast on this primative yoke she was seated with hir limbs gethered up in a heap. not able to speak English she implored us by hir looks to save hir an agrement was then made between the Commanding Officer and the Indian for the sale of the girl for a Bucket of Sugar and a Bucket of Coffey. The old Indian in order to convince them that he was a good Indian produced a tin Box with some doccument very carefully rolled up within it for the officer to read it but which the Indian did not understand. It was giveing to him by a former Union States Officer as a Passport for his good behaviour it read thus looke out for this fellow he is a damn Thief. The officer handed back the paper and said it was munch a waino very good.

The Indian smiled grimly and was much pleased. The then left our camp and departed to parts unknown. The Mexican girl told hir sad tale she was taker away from under hir own ruff in the province of Sonara in Mexico hir Father and Mother cruelly murdered by Indians she was taken across the Rio grande River into American Terrotery hir person outraged and sold from one tribe to another scared and bruised untill she could scarcely stand. hir joy was unbounded the poor creature shed tears of delight for hir freedom after six years of captiveity.

From Fort Leavenworth to the Arkansas River we had marched about seven Hundred and fifty miles. After resting the two days we resumed our march again to Fort Union, New Mexico two or three hundred miles west we proceded along the left bank of the river passing by Old Bents Fort a large Adobe house built with sun dryed Brick very strong now looking Desolate and lonely. I heard it was an old trading post or fur depot dateing Back to the early years of the present Centuary. the old building no doupt could tell some strainge tales of its former and adventures traders. we crossed the River and got into a mountainious regen. after toiling along for a number of days we arrived at Fort Union where we stoped for five days the recruits for the Eighth Redgement were to proceede to Fort Stanton and a company of the mounted rifils in Command of Lieutennant Lane. another march of about two hundred miles had to be acomplished before we got to our destination.

It was then gettin late in the fall of the year when we started on the road again it was very cold after marching about twenty miles we came to Los Pecos a small Mexican Town it was then dark and a light covering of snow lay on the ground. we stopped hear for the night And the next morning we were on the road again. after eleven days marching from fifteen to thirty miles a day through a wild barren Country of Mountain and Plain we arrived at Fort Stanton after a march of at least twelfe hundred miles from Fort Leavenworth Kansas. my old Company B. of the eight Regiment was stationed hear the Captain gave a very strange look at me going Back again after my Desertion four years ago but did not question me. I mist the old famelior faces that I knew then and my Dear friend Jerry Spillane who assisted me in making my escape. the were all gone but two who reenlisted and their places filled by new men but as halfe of them were Irishmen I did not concider them straingers to me.

Fort Stanton is nicely situated in a valley which runs Back to the White Mountains with tall snow caped peaks while a pretty little stream or river is trinkling down along the low ground called the Rio Boneta which supplies the Post with pure and wholsome water. the duty was light pleasent and Climate good part of my time I worked at my trade and received forty cents per day in adition to my regular pay of aleven Dollars a month. while i was away the Army was increased by several Regiments which were badly needed owing to the small number of troops stationed in the great Wild West at long distance apart the home of a large number of hostile tribes of wild Indians. scouting after those devils are very laborious and sometimes dis-apointing when you dont meet with success. a scouting party went out of here after some Indians who had made themselfs troublesom they were out about six months without having a chance of a shot at one of them who would not be surprised and retired to the mountains playing hide and go seeke with the troops till at last the halfe starved men and horses and pack mules gave up the hunt and returned to there different Commands tired out weather Beatin Bearded and raget a sight to looke at.

October 12th 1858 Donatos Commet was Shineing Beautifull in the Heavens. It had a long large nubelo with a long tail sligtly curved. It seemed to me to be pointing in a South West direction. The Indians had a superstitious fear of the commet. that it prodicted War and all sorts of things. Night after night it apeared in the Heavens and so near the Earth according to the common understanding made it apear more remarkable untill it faded out of sight.

82

After serving about twelfe months or over in Fort Stanton my Company received orders to procede to Fort Buchanon Arazona [sic] in the South West near the Mexican Border about five hundred miles from Stantin. The men of the Company were delighted to get on the road again notwithstanding the very long march before them across the Rockey Mountains. There was no Pasific Railroad then it was not even thought of. early in the Spring of fifty nine we commenced our March some of the Boys singing snatches of Songs on the first day out. I remember a fue words of one of them in particular which used to be sung or humbed by every white marawder or Devill Skin who loufed about Santafee and Albuquerque.

Oh Johny Cox a weino Commadante
Lives in Albuquerque in an old dobe Shanty

We proceded ina Southerly direction for Fort Filmore marching trough a ruff mountainous Country one day a small party of our men seperated from us and following an Old Indian trail believing it would be a short cut to our next camping ground. We halted in the late afternoone. But the party that left that morning were absent. The following morning the came into our camp but three of there men ware missing. The joined us in two days very hungery and thirsthy. The sleeped very little fearing Bears and Indians and subsisted on crabs. There was no water to be had at lenght the discovered the road and followed the trail of the Company till the joined us again and were the subject of much merriment among there comrades for going astray The next day we were encamped near the Dog Cannian in front of a wild and steril plain stretching beyond the limmet of our vision. lone vast and soltitery. A fue distant Peakes and the tops of mountains were visable on the Border line of the great plain. All was as still as Death no Song Bird no chirp or chattering of the feather tribe to Break the awful stillness round about us. I was becomming acustomed to those things and did not mind. Close to our camp stood a long ruged rainge of mountains in the Centre is a Chasm or pass called the Dogs Cannian. it is a ruff narrow passage with great cliffs of hudge rocks standing almost straight on each side of the narrow pass. it then opens into a Broad and fertile valley of a considerable extent Surrounded by rocks of a preciptous nature a good cover for Indians and in vieu of the great Plains Streched out before them.

Wee Crossed the Rio Grande River at Mesilla. a small Mexican Town in such an out of the way sort of place sandy and hungery looking I was surprised to think that any Civilised Bein could live in such a remote and daingerous situation. We had then about three hundred and twenty miles to march to Fort Buchanan. We passed on though the Mesilla valley and crossed the Rockey Mountains trough Doubtfull Pass. The Mountains and Rocks had a scorched apearence as if done By the action of fire ages ago in the dim and unknown history of this truely wonnderfull Country. Water was scarce and very fare apart. At one time wee marched over fifty miles to water. How the mules did roar as we nearid the place the seamed to get new life and energey as the tuged and pulled the Waggens over the rough road when nearing the water.

A mirage and opticle illusion which are some times seen in this part of the Country on the Sandy and Saline Plains. One day on the march we were all very thirsty and Canteens emty. On one side of the road a short distance from us wee saw what wee thought a vast lake or sheet of water as smood as glass and as soft and placit looking as the Sun and air could make. The men looked and looked and yet though wee doubted the reality and existence of a lake in this part of Arozona. Still the illusion was so perfect and real to me I walked out as fare as I thought the edge of the water. But in this cace the water was gone yet it had

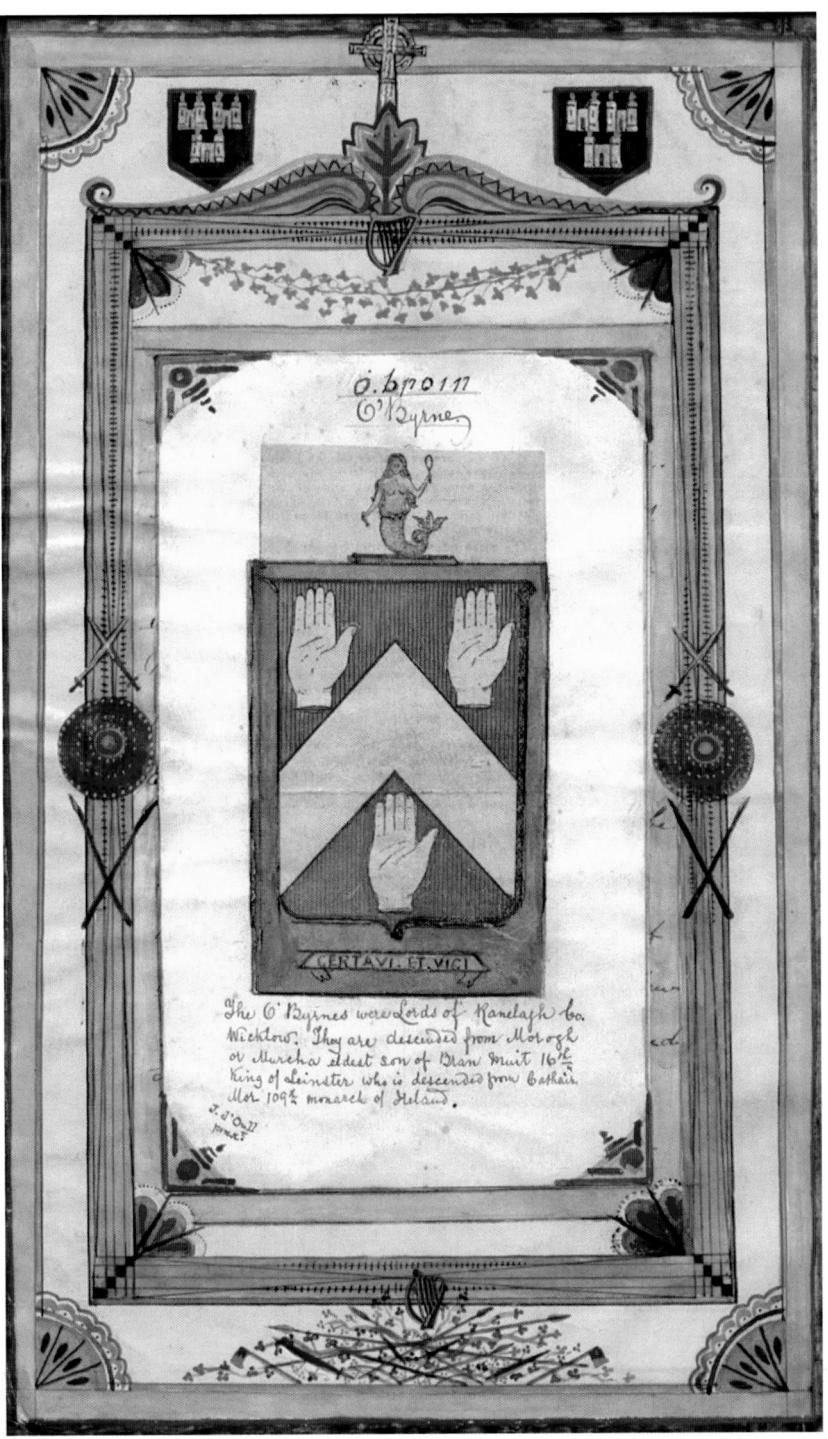

O'Byrne clan coat of arms.

Lieut. Andrew J. Byrne (1830–1911)
65th New York State Volunteers
(August 1861 to February 1864)

Flag display, USA.

The barque *Confidence*, Custom House Quay.

Confidence on her voyage to New Orleans, 1849.

The Planter's House, New Orleans area.

Mississippi steamboats.

Stacked arms, Colours and Drum.

Barracks—Sentry, New Orleans.

Off for Texas—Steamboat.

The Mission of the Conception, Texas, 1851.

Comanche Indians.

On the road.

The *John and Lucy* bound for Liverpool, 1853.

The Mersey, Liverpool.

The Great Industrial Building, Leinster Lawn, 1853.

The Trade Picture, building.

Head of Killary Harbour, Connemara, Ireland.

Street in Galway.

The Road to Ruin. Public House scene.

Poolbeg Lighthouse and South Wall, Dublin Bay.

The ship Collumbie in tow, passing Fort Hamilton, New York Harbour, 1856.

Infantry US Army, Uniforms, 1856.

Crossing the plains, 1857.

On the march to Arizona, 1859.

Street in El Paso.

Going up the Ohio River, 1860.

The ship *Dreadnought* passing the Bull Rock.

Derry City, 1861.

The ship *North Britain* keeping clear of the icebergs.

Notre Dame de Lourdes, Montreal, 1861.

hand. My arm hung by my side as if merely held
by my Coat Sleve I was loosing Blood fast. I told the
Colonel who was near me I was wounded. I walked to
to the rear a short distance and growing very weak
from the loss of Blood I sat down Behined a tree for
a short time. Bullets from the enemies front were
Passing me very lively and over a large open field
which I had to Cross in order to get out of range.
Zap Zap went the Bullets into the tree where I sat

The Carried me to the Surgeons Camp

I could hear there Compact
very well. yet i must
cross that field to get
out of range if able.
I stood up again and
and made my way to
wards an old wordden
Barren a short distance
from me. I passed a Number of wounded
men lying on the ground. a Battery
of artillery was shelling the
enemy over our front line.
there Shells Bursting
in the woods beyond our
Barren.

front. the shades of evening were Comming on & sat down behined the
Barren growing weaker all the time. one of the artillery men Collected an
arm full of leaves of Corn for me to ly on & thanked
him and felt very gratefull for his Kindness. I then Crossed
the open and came out on a Road where a large Number
of wounded soldiers were lying down on the side of the Road
and others hobling along to the Reare in quest of the Surgeons head
quaters. I was now in a very weak Condition my eyes a Bit hasy
I was terrable thirsty and would give anything for a drink of

Page from original journal.

On the 19th of July a large number of ambulances assembled in front of the Libby prison in the early Morning. four or five hundred union prisoners all wounded men. thees were anxious moments for me. as I did not know I was going. all those who were able to walk fell into line. I was put into an ambulance not been able to walk it was a sort of a funeral like procession as we passed trough the streets to the Petersburgh Railway Depot. a lot of half beaker wasted looking Man. after a very slow Ride we arrived in Petersburgh. on the James River about thirty Miles from Richmond we changed cars hear and was put into old freight waggons. after jolting and joging along for some time over a worn out Railroad we arrived near Harrisons landing. Two large

Part of Fortified Camp at Harrisons landing. July 1842

River steamers flying the stars and stripes were laying along side of an old wooden Jetty. partly Burnt. the joy we felt at the sight of the flag and the glad and cheerful faces of the Ladies and gentlemen of the sanitery association who were there to receive us. we were the first prisoners that came from Richmond. No time was lost getting us on Board after Been duely turned over By the Confederat officers in charge of us. I went on Board the old vanderbitt Steamer which used to Run Between New York and Abbany before the war. what a Change. the kind Ladies

Page from original journal.

the same allusive appearance the Mirage had receded or apeared to me as fare away as ever. I moved forward again and again the result was the same I looked down on the ground and saw nothing unuseual but the hard dry ground under my feet I gave up the Will o the Wisp Chace after the seposed water and returned to my Company a wiser man.

One day some friendly Apache Indians came into our Camp acompanyed by a young wolfisn looking Dog of a dirty white colour I was told it was a cross between a Wolfe and a dog. The mixture seamed very traceable with its reddish ies long hed and mouth he looked wicket but soone became very friendly with mee. in a short time he paid no attention to the Indians. I gave him a bit of meet he would not go away from mee. Wee moved on again after our repasts. In the maintime I lifted the Dog into a Waggon he was quite contended and soone settled himselfe down in a corner among some emty sacks and remained quietly till the end of the days March. The Indians mist the dog but thinking he had roamed off somewhere and would come back again but Chip which I named him was no fool he prefered the white man who treated him more kindly then his savage master.

On the way we passed some of the Stations on the Butter Field Stage line a very remarkable enterprise recently established. running Stages for Mails and passengers from St. Louis to San Fransisco a journey of two thousand seven hundred miles the longest Stage Line in the World. At last we arrived at Fort Buchanan after a march of at least five hundred miles from Fort Stanton New Mexico. A Company of Dragoons ware stationed at the Post when wee arrived there who would now be free for any offensif movement against the Apache Indians when called on. The soldiers quarters were of a temporary construction Built of timber and mud one story high with earthen floors and flat slopeing roofs. The post is situated in the valley of Santa Cruise. A small stream of water runs trough the valley. On the opposet side great Mountains lifts there bulkey forms in the centre is the great Santa Rita Mountains riseing on a series of gravelly hills and Hollows. A fue dwarf Trees are scathered about the great Mountain Slopes in some places dark patches of timber relieves the eye of a sombre aspect till it terminates in a great tall Peak. Pierceing the Blue Skye and overlooking the vast and sollitery reagens surrounding it.

One night after I arrived hear the Mountain presented a most Dazeling and interesting spectacle it was on fire which spread fare and wide on that side of the valley. I have seen the praiery on fire sweeping onward for miles with a huge trail of black smoke fringeing its Border of fire and leaveing nothing but the Black chard earth behined. The Mountains west of the Post in the night time were all illuminated by tiney streaks of fire up and down three steep sides and running in all directions in some places looking like an illuminated Town with the Camp fires of a vast army surrounding it.

Wee were not long in Fort Buchanan when several of our men got Chills and feaver. After a short time they were very fue who escaped this miserable complaint there seamed to be no cure for it it was Seposed it was caused by bad water that sprung from a rotten lime stone bottom. There were several Deaths it was thought the Post would have to be abandoned. I was the last man in the Company who was attacked by this Blighting and weekening sickness. Sometimes well and Sometimes ill with a Pale yellow sickly look from the constant use of quinine.

We had very little trouble with the Indians though they were hostile and Daingerous. Two Discharged Soldiers and there Wives with a waggon and team of horses going to El Paso were murdered and robed a short distance out the road. Dragoons were sometimes sent out on a scout through the Mountains while four or five Infantry Soldiers supplies with rations would move out opposet direction in the hills and concealing themselfs in a

Commanding Position as a looke out party for the Cavalry who might pass that way. In cace of dainger the were to steal back to the Post giveing any information the posest to the Commanding Officer on there return.

Arazona [sic] is the land of the Cactis of various sorts which is common in South America it is a singular tree or srub of purely vegatable matter. The prickly Pear so called on account of its thorns is a wilde peculeour fruit about the sise and shape of a small pear of a purplish colour which grows on the edge of its great green flat leaves and when ripe are plesent to teast and good to eat. Arazona [sic] is the home of Scorpions Santapedes and that great wicket looking hairy spider the Tarantala.

Religeon in the Teroteries (territories) I may say is a thing unown there cannot be churches were there are no people. Since I left New Yorke nearly three years I had not one singly opportunity of hearing Mass or attending to my religious duty. I had not seen a Clergiman but one when I was in Fort Stanton New Mexico. A French Priest visited the Post and stoped a fue Days.

Discharged from the Army

In the month of May 1860 a waggon train arrived at the Post loaded with goods for the quarter Master. I had only two months to serve. I was discharged consequent on a oppertunity to reach the Settlements. The train was going back to San Antonio Texas about one thousand miles from here May the twenty seventh I was Discharged and started with the train going East to El Pasa on the Rio Grande River. it was no pleasure trip for me it was a long wearysom journey across the Rocky Mountains. My intention was to try and get to San Antonio where I expected I would get worke. The Waggon Train did not belong to the goverment the Waggon Master was owner of the Train and worked for hire I concidered veary fortunate he was a white Man though a Mexican he was a pure Castillian he had no Indian Blood in him the are the Dons of Mexico let them be poor or rich the concider themselfs fare above the real natives Mexicans the Darke Race who has too much of the Indian in them to be trustworthy the Teamsters were of the latter class and all talked Mexican which I did not understand this made mee feel lonesome and suspiscious

I had over a thousand Dollars on my person and carried a loaded revolver all the time day and night. I sleeped very little except when overcome trough fatague how I sleeped many a time I could not tell the ground was my couch my rest was short as I allways wanted to be up and about. I tooke veary little interest in the strange aspeck of the country on my way. I amused myselfe with an ocasional shot at some wild Birds or snakes which ware near at the hand and keeping my shooting iron in order by firing one or two chambers of my revolver and reloading again. I shot a veary rare snake about four feet long of a white and green colour it is called a Milk Snake it is not Poiseness. I was told it would coil itself around a cows leg and draw the milk from its elder. after two weekes travelling wee arrived at El Paso. There was some signe of civilisation here it is a veary sandy place you would sink to your ankel in the dry Powderly Sand. It must be almost intolarable when the wind is blowing strong and the clouds of Alkali dust and sand is flying about in all directions. The Rio Grande runs by hear and forms the Boundery line between Mexico and the United States and continnues on to the Gulf of Mexico wee stoped two days in El Paso and started on the road again for San Antonio about six hundred and fifty mills from hear another wild stretch in Western Texas.

After six weekes travelling we arrived at the fringe of civilisation and comming in sight of the white walls of the Town so fameliour to mee. I felt my hart lift while a cloud of uncertenty hung over my mind. I could not picture to myselfe future joys and prosperety under the conditions I was Laboreing under in relation to my

Spouse who Blured my understanding and impeded my efforts in all i could do. I soone found employment and commenced working at my trade the Presidential Election was much talked about which resulted afterwards in the Election of Abraham Lincolon the Republican Candidate as President of the United States.I notised at this time there was a great deal of Speculation with regard to the result and of such a nature as made mee Suspiscious of comming events like the rest of the South the Texakins [sic] ware all Democrats yet it was not much of a Slave State.

A New Volunteer Company was then forming in San Antonio called the Alamo Rifils. I was asked to join them and certain inducements ware held out to me which ware very encourageing some words passed which aroused my suspisious even more than I had allredy felt. yet there was nothing unuseual in getting up a Millitery Company for it was only in harmoney with all the growing Towns and Cities in America. After a very short stay of a month in San Antonio private reasons compelled mee to leave hear and pitch my tent in some other place. I resolfed to return to Ireland. I had a long weary journey before mee with an uneasey mind and eveary discomfort to face, and a loss of money as well it was not with a light hart I left San Antonio on the Stage Coach for the Coast and then by Steam Boat for New Orleans. On my arriveing there I prefered to take the River route to Pittsburgh Pensilvania and from thence to New York by rail. I started up river on a stearn wheeler which went puffing along against the strong current of the mighty River making good hedway. After several days we arrived at Memphis Ten. a small City standing on a high Bluff which slooped down to the River we stoped hear for a fue Hours to take in freight and started again for Cairo at the Mouth of the Ohio River a large but much smaller River than the Mississipi and one of the most beautyfull Rivers in the United States. At Louisville Kentucky the Boat put out some freight. It is a very nice City on the Bank of the River with Steam Boat connextions with various parts from Louisville to Cincinata [sic] we had a most exciteing Race with another Boat our Boat creeked and groand from Stem to Stern panting and puffing like some great Monster. The two Boats at times abreast with each other and very close this was very dangerous amusement which often times ends in the most callamatous manner I wished myselfe off of the Boat till I arrived in Cincinata and started on another Boat for Pittsburgh and from there by rail to New York. Passing trough the great and Prosperous State of Pensilvania. On my arrivil in New York I lost no time. I procured a Passage for Liverpool in the famous New York Clipper Ship The Dred Nought.

Return to Ireland

In December 1854 the Dread Nought made the quickest Passag on record from New Yorke to Liverpool in thirteen Days and Eleven Hours. Wee had a very ruff passage coming over but the ship saild well, under a terrable stress of Canvas, which I did not like. I was getting to be quite a sailor at this time and knew very well when the wind was strong or Blowing a gale that she was Carrying to[o] much sail when almost Lying on hir Beam ends tearing away trough the huge waves and passing a Ship whose cautious Commander had taken in nearly of hir sails. Captain Samuals of the Dread Nought was not this kind of man it was Hell or Liverpool, as soone as he could get there. at last wee sighted the Irish Coast to the great joy of the Passengers. wee passed near the Bull and Cow Rocks. The[y] are very remarkable looking and must have Been much more exstensif at one time then the[y] are at present owing to the tremendous sweep of the Atlantic Ocean which has Beatin against those frail looking Rocks for ages with a fury and force at times anuff to sweep them off the face of the Ocean. wee arrived in Liverpool after a very quick passage of twenty one Days. two or three days afterwards I Landed in Dublin. Which looked about the same since I last left it in Eighteen fifty Six.

After Lincoln was elected President of the united States, Publick opinion in the Southt was growing stronger. the Southern People were very much displeased at the result of the election and were growing angry and from that to tretning (threatening) and as time went on assumed a Bullying aspect. The North which included the West remained passif and firm. [...] Seeing the turn of things had taken since I left the united States, I watched with interest news from America in hopes that War might be averted. the attack on Fort Sumter in Charlestin [sic] Harbour By the Southterns at onst settled the question of war or peace. discontented and tormented at home, I then made up my mind to go back to America and in a quiet sort of way Buckled on my armour My sympathy were for the North the lawful Government, and the old flag the stars and stripes under which I had served and remembering the famous words of the Irishs American President Jackson at one time, "when disunian treatened the country the Union must and shall be preserved."

WHO KNOWS?

What might have been had I not wed,
Is far beyond my knowledge,
A maiden fair with wavey hair,
Had set her eye upon me.
It was not her looks, I though her fine,
When she an apple gave me.
No thought had I of harm then,
Unless my youthful folly
Led me astray on the serpentine way,
And many long years of sorrow.

What might have been in that far off land,
Which I trod in my early youth,

91

On the Texas strand and the prairie wild,
With a burning sun in its vault of blue,
Where the Rio Grande flows down to the Gulf,
The hunting ground of the fierce Commanche,
With scalping knife and bow and arrow,
And sharp light spear beside,
And stripped to the waist on his fleet Mustang
He scans the country round.
If out for a raid his companions are near,
In a live oak glade or shaparel brush,
Lay wait for the signal what 'ere it be,
Like hungry wolves no pity in them
For the hapless victim woman or man.
In the great lone West on the borderline of San Antonio,
A frontier town, close by the River near the Bridge,
Where the Alamo stands can tell a tale
Of Crockett and Bowie of Texas fame.

What might have been when I finished my time
In the fighting eight of the dough-boy line,
Here was a place to settle down and help to build the little town,
And look at it growing all round about
No surplus labour far or near,
No place for tramps, no railroad near.

What might have been, when the War broke out,
I would have to go and fight for the South,
Perhaps leave a wife and family,
A house and lot and all my store
And renege the flag, I love so well.
For the stars and bars did not suit me,
And the bonny blue flag they used to sing
And Dixie land might do for them,
I knew no North, I knew no South and a Rebel I would not be.

A. J. Byrne 1830–1911

Chapter Five

And the boys with whom I marched and fought,
The boys who wore the Blue,
In old Virginny and Chickahominy swamps,
When the sun poured down on our weary ranks,
And the boom of the cannon was heard in the front,
Then into line and fire at will,
The rest to God or night would come.

∾

'Musings'—Andrew J. Byrne

Journey to Canada

IN THE LATER END of June Eghteen Sixty one, I Bought a trough
ticket for myselfe and my six year old Daughter on the Allen line
steamers from Londondery [sic] to Quebec and from there via
Montreal to New York This was a round about way but it afforded
me an opportunity of seeing a very large and important portion
of Lower Cannada [sic] and shaped my cource so to avoid trouble in getting away I set out by rail to Londondery [sic] where I
stoped for near two days.

On the twenty Eight of June I started down the Foyle on Board
a steam tug with a large number of passengers to the Allin [sic]
Line Steamer at Movil [sic] about sixteen miles from Derry on
the way down the River, we had a very fine prospect of Country
on each side and some pretty river scenery til we arrived in the
Broad expanse of Lough Foyle. at Movill [sic] we went on Bord the
North Brittin a screw steamer and started on our voiage. [...] Late
in the eveaning we passed Tory Island with the iron Bound coast
of the North on the Port side. Night comming on the gloomey

93

Coast, where the Restless waves were dashing against the dark masses of Rock was fast disapearing from our sight. after six or seven days sailing we passed several small fragments of ice there numbers increased as we proceded, and of larger dimensions. night comming on and the ice becoming more dense the steamer was stoped. the sea was Calm while she lay almost motionles but the jaring and cringing of the ice on the ships side made a very disagreeable sound in the stearrage and prevented many of the passengers from sleeping while a large number of them felt very uneasy. The next morning, we moved ahead slowly. a fue weeks Previous to this, the steamship Cannadian of the same Line was Buldged in by ice and sank in halfe an hour a large number of hir passengers were lost. In a short time after starting we were moveing trough a great field of ice fortunately for us the weather was calm and the ice a Broaken mass of sheet ice. the weather was clear and very cold. after some time we got into the open sea again a large number of ice Bergs were floating about in all directions But there was plenty of sea room our vessel was put to full speed we passed great heapes of ice some of a Cliff like form Riseing out of the sea, others of various shapes and forms which your fancey might take to looke like many things some of the ice Bergs look-ing like islands about three times as large as the ship. July 7th we were sailing trough the Straits of Bullisle [sci]. Labrador on our Right Bleak Barren and Mountainous looking, with patches of snow hear and there and no signe of life on its Dreary aspect. on the left is the Coast of New foundland looking no Better than Labrador, wintery lone and sollitery looking. I was disapointed in this as New found Land was so often Boomed a good place for Irish Emigrants to go. now in the middle of Summer it looked noway inviteing to me. after passing trough the strait we entered the Gulf of Saint Lawrence, about five hundred Miles from Quebec. the weather was now getting warm and comfortable a most agreable Contrast from of a fue days ago. [...] we passed Anticosti Island looking as if covered with a dence forrest of Trees. going up the Saint Lawrence for a Certain distance it is more like an open sea then a River. [. .] higher up the River we got a closer viue (view) of the shore the Houses ware numerous and cultivated patches of ground and trees make up the whole of the seanery along the Border of the great River we passed some fine Islands thick with trees but the weather was Cold and gloomey. Not favourable for Sight Seeing on the Deck of a Steamer. before arriving at Quebec the River is divided by the large and Beautiful Island of Orleans the weather was getting warm again and the seanery along the River much improved by the Rich glow of the warm sun. The Deck of the Steamer was Crouded with the Passengers everyone ansious to see a Bit of the New World. The shore line becomes more Bold and Picturesque as we near the Falls of Montmorencey on the North side of the River. The falls are 250 feet high and eight miles from Quebec at lenght we arived there after a cold and Dangerous passage of twelfe days. as I did not land at Quebec I saw very little of the Town, which consists of an upper and lower Town. [...] passengers for Montreal and other parts were Landed on the other side of the river at the Station of the Grand trunk Railway.[...] we Crossed the Great Victoria tubeler Bridge at Montreal. It was late in the evening when I got there and put up in a small Hotell which was very Comfortable and home like without been snobish. It is the largest and most Populous City in Canada. A fine growing Town, has a good trade and plenty of Business. it is well situated on the left Bank of the Saint Lawrence River an immence water way to the Gulf of Saint Lawrence. it has one draw Back it is ice Bound in the winter when navigation ceases until Spring. Then the ice Brakes up and Business resumes its most Cheerful aspect, after a long dreary winter, Snow Bound and ice Bound. The most notable Building in Montreal is the Cathedral of Notre Dame de Lourdes it was then the largest Church in Canada and the united States. I was impresed by its size and the solidity of its construction. It must have Cost a large sum of money and speakes well for Catholick zeal in Montreal. The Victoria tubeler Bridge is a remarkable structure its great lenght about two miles long and the large number of its Cut Stone Piers Built to resist the pressure of thousands of Tons of ice which is carried down the River in the Spring and packing against the great Piers of the Bridge in huge masses and Bursting its way trough the intervils, cringing Breaking and Mounting upwards in its course. having Seen anuff of Montreal, I set out again By Rail for New Yorke. Crossing the Saint Lawrence again going trough the tubeler Bridge a long dark streak we were soon in the open again. forty five miles from Montreal the train stoped at Rouses Point the Boundary line our Bagage was examined by the United States Custom House officers, which caused some delay we came down along by Lake Champlain, a fine sheet of water 143 miles long, passing on our way some pretty Towns and vilages. Comming trough Vermont the numerous white marble quarries attrack your attintion piles of white shingle and the walls of the Quaries glistning in the sun large blocks were laying about ready for transportation to all parts of the United States for various purposes.

I arrived in Troy a small City on the Hudson River at the hed of Navigation about one hundred and sixty eight miles from New York in the evening I started on the night Boat for the great City five miles down the river, we passed Albany the Capitol of the State of New York. it was then night and nothing could be seen but the flickering lights of the Houses on shore or some passing Steam Boat. I paid fifty cents for a sleeping Berth in the grand saloone a very large apartment nearly as long as the steamboat carpeted and well furnished with Cushioned seats, the sleapeing Berths ware arrainged on each side of the saloone, draped with curtains which could be drawn to one side or the other by the occupants of the Berths at there pleasure. The next morning I found my Boots polished ready to put on me, no charge for this.

I mist one thing, the Charming vieu (view) of the Hudsin [sic] River Seanery which has often been descrbed by tourests and travellers the most Beautiful River in America.

Early in the morning I arrived in the City of New York. I had breakfast in one of the Cheap Resterants which are very numerious along the River side. Recruiting for the Army was very Brisk thousands of men of all classes in the country were entering the Ranks of the Volunteers for the defence of Washington and the preservation of the Union. Business was very Bad in New York in consequence of the Breaking up of trade between the North and Southt thousands of men were idle yet thousands of emigrants ware landing every week in the Castle Garden. Some of the new Redgements had very fanciful names and catching uniforms. The wifes and familys of Soldiers in the City were provided for by the Munisiple Counsel that along with the money sent by there Husbands would keepe them comfortable if Properly laid out.

Enlisted in the 65th New York Volunteers

Having selected a Redgement and provideing for the care of my Child, I enlisted in the 65th New New [sic] York Volunteers then known as the 1st U.S. Chasseurs, head quarters Palace Garden, fourteent Street. We remained a short time hear when we were shifted to Willet's Point on long Island about twenty one Miles from New York. while hear we passed our time very pleasantly when off drill, fishing and Bathing in the Sound better known as east River. Some would go clamb gathering a sort of shell fish very good to eat when Stewed which is called Clamb Chowder. we were served out hear with our new uniform which looked very well when properly fitted. Short blue tunick with ornamentle Braiding french Cap and lose grey Pants and white legins Some of the Boys thought it great fun. $11 Dollors a month with food and clothing, and $100 Bounty at the end of Three years or the termination of the war, and Discharged from the service. little we knew of the long terrable weary war before us which lasted four years and the great loss of life, which no one thought for a moment would be the result of the hotheaded Braves of the Southt who thought the[y] were going to do away with us in a short time. the[y] were going to wipe there feet in the Northen Mud Sills. Mud sill a name giving by the Southt to there Northern Brothers whome they dispised. [. .]

Seven days after I Inlisted I was promoted Corporal, a fue days after I was made Sergeant. [...] at Millets Point the Chassurs were presented with its first set of Collours two in number the National flag and the State flag two Collour Bearers were chosen from the Sergeants of the Regiment selected by the Coloneal for there Millitery Bearing Disciplin and good Conduct I was selected to carry the State Collour and a young Welsh Man named Jenkins for the National Collour. Our Regiment might be said to be Cosmopolitan in its Composition, about half American next Irish then German with a mixture of English and Scotch and other Nationalalitys. yet we got along very well with one another there was not the slightest friction between us at last we start for Washington. Moving out of our Camp and stretching out on a sandy road we marched for about three miles to a Steam Boat landing and went on Board a steamer for New York amid the plaudets of a lot of People assembled at the wharf who gave us a harty good By when the steamer moved out into the Sound. Some of our men kissed ther hands to the fair sex on shore who were entusiasticly waveing their hankerchifs as we sped away on our journey.

Oh my love he is a zu, zu, zu,
Now don't you think he ought to
For he's going down to Washington
To fight for Abrahams daughter.

[...] we arrived in New York and were warmly Received as we marched down Broadway in open Colloum of Companys, our guns at the sholder and our drums Beating a march. the side walkes were lined with People who clapped there hands and cheerd us on our way I and my friend Jenkins Bore our Colours aloft and marched as Brave as any man there was many an iey (eye) on the Colours so we thought ourselfs no small potatoes that day. at the lower end of Broad way we went on Board a Steamer and started for Southt Amboy, New Jersey. It was Sun down as we steamed down the Harbour and passing a United States Friget a loud cheer went up from our men, which was warmly responded to by the Blue Jackets on Board Ship. The crew of the Beautiful French yacht Napoleon lying at anchor close by tooke of[f] there hats and saluted us as we passed in a most friendly spirrit. Night comming on and darkning my vieu (view) thousands of lights were beginning to glimmer along the shore line and on the great City, and flickering round the dark waters of the Broad Harbour. Some of our Boys had, perhaps the last fond look of there Native City which had disapered out of sight. all was still and silent save the noise of the paddels of the Steamer and the splashing waters along the side of the vessel. I felt tired and seated myself on my knapsack in a quiet corner thinking of the past and trying to looke into the future [...] there was a bustle on Board the men ware Picking up there knapsacks and slinging them on there shoulders. A fue corse voices shouted out to someone on shore, then a fue turns of the wheels bacwards. we are at Southt Amboy, from hear we went By Rail to Philidelphia [sic] and arrived early in the morning, in the Quaker City. we went into a large Building where Breakfast was prepared for us by the Patriotick Citizens of Philidelphia [sic]. Coffey meat cheese and vegatabels was served out to us in the most plentiful manner. as soon as daylight came we started by Rail for Baltimore. our Reception there was Better then I thought it would be, according to rumours of an unfriendly nature, which we picked up on the way. Baltimore was full of Secesh (seceeders) at the time and all trough the State of Maryland. it was a Border State next to Virginia which had joined the Confederacy and became the Battle Ground of the contending forces between Washinton [sic] and Richmond.

Arrival in Washington

On our arrival in Washington, wee marched trough Pensilvania [sic] Avenue a large number of People Collected on the side walks looking at the Soldiers some of our men woud now and then cheer as the[y] went along an old Gentleman standing by, hearing our Men Cheer shouted out *Boys dont hollou til you get to the front*. I thought that a dry one with a good deal of meaning in it.

We encamped outside the City. The ground was very damp and muckey after the nights rain. we went into Bell tents and tryed to make ourselfs Comfortable as well as we could straw was served out for each tent at night a Bayonet stuck in the ground answered for a Candlestick. the first night some of the Boys thought it very hard stretching themselfs down on the light covering of straw which covered the damp ground a Brown Army Blanket on top and the napsack for a pillow but the[y] soone got use to this and when things became worse Bore there hardship with great cheerfulness and patience.

We were now Drilled to excess, in Company and Battalion Drill twice aday for six hours each day two hours in the morning and four hours during the hottest part of the day. September 1861 I was taken from the Colours and promoted 1st Seargeant of my Company. This put a lot of work on me all the Orderly duty of the Company making details Drilling and a General Supervision of every Thing connected with the Company I was kept very Bussay and close to Camp. after a Brief stay in our New Camp we receved Orders to cross the Potomack [sic] River and join the main Body of the Army which was protecting Washington and geting ready for a forward movement. The Rebel commanders Johnston and Beauregard were a Bout twenty or thirty miles distant in our front at Manases [sic]. [...] The news Boys kept us pretty well posted comming into camp every day selling the newspapers if anything was gained by our side little or Big the Boys would shout out another Union victory, and would sell out quickly. It was after midnight when we left our camp near Washington and passing trough the City we came to the Chain Bridge which crosses the Potomack [sic] River, a very long bridge. the march was conducted in silence no musick not a sound we crossed the Bridge which was well guarded after bean (being) challenged by a Sentinal in the usual way wee were now in Virginnia [sic] and near the Encampments where McClelland [sic] was collecting a large Army for future operations against Richmond. on the way we were challenged by Sentinals Posted in various parts on the great field of Mars [sic]. Passing a sentinal standing near a Battery of Artillery shouted out *what Regiment Boys, New York Chasseurs, Bully for you lots of New York Boys hear.* Some of the Camp fires were Burning dimly and dieing out at last we reached the place assigned to us. we stacked our arms and posted our sentinals and spred our Blankets on the grass and lay down. early in the morning after a fue hours sleep we were aroused from our slumbers by the sound of Bugals and Drums Beating the Reveille. I arose stiff and tird from my damp couch and with eager curiosity to see where I was and what was to be sean round about me. on a riseing ground and about fifty yards from me a great Earth work Called Fort Eathin Allen Surmounted By field guns and heavey Artillery I did not have much time to looke about me when we were ordered to fall in and sling our Napsacks we moved off to the left of the Fort about two miles and then halted. We had no tents and as we did not chose to wait for them we put up shelters and huts in a temporary manner with pine tops and Branches of trees. the camp ground was Covered with all sorts of leafey abodes and cool shades of every discription. we got on very well for a fue days as the weather was dry and warm. it then rained a good old rain accompanied by wind which soone scathered our toy Houses and temporary huts in a very short time. It rained all Night. we sought what shelter we could get among the trees and groves and groweld and grumbled at our ill luck in not having our tents with us. The next Day was fine and warm, we had little to do. we set to work again and reconstructed our shelters our little unplesentnes soone passed away feeling sadisfied that the Goverment were doing there duty towards us notwithstanding the great demands on the different departments connected with the Army which was growing larger every day. New Regiments were constantly comming from Washington, and disciplin was moulding the Army into shape Company and Battalian drill then movements by Brigade and Division, soone followed, Reviews, then General McClelland [sic] and staff Road along the line the bands playing 'hail to the Chief'. Camp life withe its variety and incidents was in full swing. large parties of men were constantly Building earth works and cuting trenches on each side of the Potomack [sic] and around Washington the Rebel Army was not far off an attack on Washington was expected every day. all kinds of Rumors were flying about. the Brigade which my Regiment belonged to and some others ware in advance of the main Army about five miles from the Enamys lines. one fine Evening some fuegitives rode into our camp pell mell and stated the Enamy was comming in large numbers. in a short time our troopes were on the alert and several Brigades of Infantry, and Artillery were moved to the front, a short distance and then halted. The Regiments then commenced taking up there places in the line of defences allready Described. The Chasseurs were sent to the right to Fort Eathen Allen. Not a shot was heard nor no signe of the Enamy the Confederates were near us but keep close to the woods and could not be seen. The sun had set and night comming on there was no expectation of a fight. the Enamy withdrew, Burning down a fue farm Houses belonging to Union men. The Regiments ware then ordered Back to there Camps and hold themselfs in Readyness that night My Regiment was ordered to return to the City and leave our exciting and troublesom Position in camp advance. winter then set in and all expectation of a forward movement was giveing up. the winter is not near so Cold in this part of the Country as it is further North we got along pretty well in our tents till the return of Spring 1862. thus our first winter camping out in tents showed to our men that this was no holiday soldiering the[y] were engaged in at present the alternet rains sleet snow and slush and the Blowing down of tents perhaps in the middle of the night on there scrambling occupants an[d] the many discomforts of Camp Missery prepared the way and hardened there minds as to what was before them.

The Army of the Potomack [sic] was formed into five Corps [...] General Keys [sic] Commanding the 4th Corps to which my Regiment Belonged. [...] on the 9th of March 1862, our Regiment received orders to be ready to march the next day with a full complement of rations and ammunition a forward movement was about to take place. the next morning not a Drum was heard. the men prepared themselfs silently and fell into ranks the Battalion was formed and the Regiment marched out of Camp. The men ware quietly talking among themselfs over the prospects of the Campaign the resources of the Rebels and many other subgects in relation to themselfs. I wonder where we are going now Boys a simple Sort of an Irishman would say while another Devil may care Irishman answered to Hell or to Connought, Mick. Oh Begorragh I dident care if I was Back in Galway this minuet, Ide be to home the same to you said another then a Laugh. Thunder and Blits says a Dutchman higher up in the ranks and halfe turning round to one of his countrymen *Vot you kick me for*, his rear rank steped on his heil, it was the route step, not steping together. Horse foot and artillery was passing trough the City in the early morning. The head of the colluam was passing over the long Bridge which spans the Potomack and was pushing on to Mannases where the Confederate army held a strong position. The road was Bad pools of water and mud ankle deep in some places untill we got fairly out into Virginia. The knapsacks began to feel heavy and the sun was gething warm we began to looke serious as we now felt shure where we were going to. after a march of about seventeen miles we halted and stood still for a short time. The Rebels evacuated there strong position and retreated with precipitancy destroying everything the[y] could not take with them and placing quaker guns in position which were of a very deceptive nature when seen at a distance Bocas (bogus) sentinals where standing at intervils along the works.

The Peninsular Campaign

The plan of Campaigne was now Changed to the Peninsula the army after resting for about Two days returned to Washington on the march Back it Rained Continuosly we were in a misarable condition we could light no fires and the loss of our Coffey made us dull and cheerless. The Coffey served out to the Army was very good suffisient in quantity and ready for use when given to the soldier, along with a full complement of sugar, for a number of days acording to issue. The soldier mixed his dry Coffey and Sugar together and put it into a small Bag which he carried in his haversack. this along with a quart tin can which the soldiers generaly carried. it was his drinking Cup and Coffey Pot on Campaigne allways ready Buckled to his Haversack which enabled him in a short time to make a Cup of Coffey for himselfe on a small fire. in a very short time it was a source of great comfort to him and a stimmulis at times. I carried a tin of Condensed

Milk when I could get it using it in very small quantities it was so presious and nice it made the Coffey more palatable and Drink more of it and enjoy my frugal repast in a way that People in Civil life and removed from the Seat of War might envey.

When we came Back to Washington we heard a flotilla of steamers on which we were to embark was not ready for the transportation of the troopes. My regiment went Back to the old Camp ground again which looked very tossed and dirty. we remained hear till the 25th of March when we Broke Camp again and marched down to Alexandra where the transports were waithing to take us down the River to Fortress Monroe, two hundred and twenty miles from Washington. after a fue Days we were glideing down the Broad and Beautyful River Potomack [sic] which I enjoyed very much it was so much better then marching. we passed Mount Vernon, a short distance from the House is the tomb of Washington. All eyes were turned towards the hallowed spot where the great and faithful champion of Liberty is intered. Mount Vernon is Beautyfully situated having a most extensif vieu of the River scenery. The House stands on a high Bluff near the River which is densely wooded it presented to my mind a most charming sight crowned by the old Colonial Mansion, the home of the Washingtons. The sail down the River was very pleasent. The weathere was fine and the River side soft and pleasing its green slopes and woods the white farm Houseses. Now and then an old Comfortable looking Mansions of the Georgean [sic] period onst in opulence when Tobacco was king and numerous slaves were working in the fields which are now worn out from the constant raising of the weed, at one time a great source of wealth to Virginia. Looking at the land and the change of scene, my mind reverted Back to the State of War in which I was living the Army of Potomack had done no fighting as yet But it saved Washington and Completed its defences and compelled the Reble army to fall Back from Manasses [sic] for the protection of Richmond.

We arrived in Hamptin [sic] Roads near Fort Monroe at the Point of the Peninsula a very formadable work capable of standing any amound of hard [k]nocks and posesing the largest gun in the United States a 400 pounder called the union gun. a large number of vessels of all classes ware riding at anchor keeping pretty close to land. Several vessels belonging to Navy old class wodden ships who could give a good account of themselfs at one time. [...] after the disembarcation of the Troopes in Hampton Roads McCleland [sic] commenced his forward movement in the direction of Richmond which is situated at the head of the Peninsula which is formed by the James River on the Southt and the York and Pamunkey Rivers on the North. The Chickahominy River crosses this sextion of the Country, running from Northwest, Easterly. [...] on the march, our Brigade passed trough Hampton, which was burnt down. The Inhabatents had left and had gone to Richmond and other parts. it then apeared to me the Commencement of a Bitter struggle on the part of the Confederates who were determined to make every sacrifice sooner then come Back into the Union again. Richmond already with a large population was growing very Congested and a great strain on the supplies General Lee was completing a corden of earthworks round the City, very formadable and well engineered every day was in their favor untill these great works were completed and guns mounted [...]. It apeared there plan was to delay McClelland's march up the Peninsula as much as possible. The portion of the Rebel army engaged in this work was small but knew there work. After resisting all the[y] could the[y] were to fall Back step by step untill the[y] Crossed the Chickahominy River and retire on Richmond.

After passing trough Hampton I notised a small redoubt which seemed to be constructed very hastily. we then halted for a fue days. at this time my Regiment belonged to Couch's Division, a most admirable Officer a Brave Soldier and a Gentleman our

Corps Commander Keyes, was a tin spared wiery looking man a vetern officer of the Regular Army, a good Corps Commander well liked by his men. after resting for a fue days, we resumed our March again in the direction of Warwick Court House, or Yorke Town [sic]. The Sandy Road and the hot sun made the march very Laborious some of the Regiments in front were proceeding slowly some of there men had trown away several articles of Cloathing reducing the weight of there knapsacks. The Rebels were in front of us and were falling Back stedily as we moved forward. there movements could not be observed By us owing to the thick grote (growth) of timber to be met everywhere save now and then a clearing for the purpose of Cultivation. There were a number of Abandined Homesteds som were ocupyed By women and children, an old man who pretented to Be friendly, The woman were very Bitter. The young men were in the Army, or acting as scouts spies or Bushwhackers. we had strict orders not to meddle with those People and to respect the Persons and property who were non combatents. Sometimes this rule was not always observed but as fare as Persons the[y] ware generally carried out and respected. a Negro teamster went into a lone House and insulted a woman or committed an indecent assault upon hir, after a strict consultation he was hung by Order of General McClelland.

We arrived at Youngs Mill and Crossed an ugly little Creek with a redoubt on the other side. we met with no resistance hear. Though a larg Force of Rebels were stationed hear for Some time in comfortable quarters in log Houses Built on a high level piece of land well shaded By tall trees while the Busy Mill suplyed them in flower [sic] and Corn Meal we disturbed there quiet seclusion where the[y] lay all winter and they decamped just about Two Hours before we arived at the Mill. its onst Bussay wheel was motionless and Silent, and its workers cleared out. we Continued our March passing trough the little village of Warwick, which Contained a small Court House, a fue frame Buildings and Some fine old trees. there was no one hear all were fled the Door of the Court House was open, a number of Law papers of various descriptions lay scathered all over the floor the place had a Ramsacked apearence. Some of our men picked up some very interesting old Documents dateing as fare Back as the Reigne of William and Mary, some had reference to the founding of the Collage of William and Mary in the Town of Williamsburgh not fare from Warwick. as we Continued our march we heard the Cracking of Musquetry in our front which became louder acompanied by an ocacional report of Artillery. we then expected we were going to have some fighting, as some of our advance Regiments were already skirmishing with the Enamy. our Brigade at this time had entered a large Clearing and passing trough a fine Belt of Timber we came into a large opening surrounded by a dense wood we then halted and unslung our knapsacks and and [sic] rested ourselfs for a short time still the fireing continued in the woods. it was impossible for us to See But a short distance round about owing the extent and closeness of the forrest. a mounted officer reconnoitreing the woods in front of us was suddenly interupted by the exploseion of a shell Close to where he stood unhurt. Not much notice was taken of this as we were getting use to these things. the noise of small arms and Artillery were now very fameliar to our ears. another shot was fired and a soled (solid) shot came whising trough the air over our heads this Brought the Command to there feet and the staff into there sadels then another shot with a closer range sweped past us. The Command moved Back out of the open field to the shelter of the woods. a gradual descent aforded us protection for a short time yet the Enamy were getting the range of us and there fire encreaseing. we then moved further to the rear and encamped for about Two Weaks among the green pines which abounded in this quarter which made camp life very agreeable the ground was covered with pine tops, like a carpet, to the dept of a fue inches Brown and soft, making a good Bed to lye on when the weather was dry. The rain was very prevalent and retarded the movements of the Army very much. we had shelter tents which are very well adapted for a warm Country, of a light Material each soldier carried a smal sheet of thin Cotten Canvas which at any time at the shortest notice and with the aid of a fue sticks or suspended from the Branch of a Tree and in the cooll shade of his little shelter sleep Sound and heedless of Dainger that even the noise of Artillery at times will not Break his camb (calm) repose perhaps in dream Land. Home once more the Pictures of the past haunts his Brain perhaps his last sleep. [...]

There is a small little insect called a wood tick which was more anoying to us then the Enemy. The[y] attack a person in the Calf of the leg and working his head into the flesh which we never noticed untill iching sets in and causes our attention. embedded in the flesh care must be taken to remove the head as the Body will Brake of[f] and the irratation continues. we were about one Mile from a Rebel Battery's on the oppsete side of Warwick Creek Some of there troopes must have been much nearer to us as we Could hear there men Cheering at times and there Bands playing their favoret tune 'Dixie'

In Dixeys land where I was born
Early on a frosty morning look away
Look away in Dixie's Land.
I wish I was in Dixie hurra hurra,
In Dixie's Land I'll take my stand
To live and die in Dixie.

Dixeys Land means the Southt, and was current among our soldiers when speaking of that Country as Dixey. The Union lines were drawing closer round York Town [sic] a number of guns were placed in position for the purpose of Bom Barding the Town which was well Fortified with Earth works skilfully constructed and stretching Back on the Penensula which protected there rear and keped the Road open to Williamsburgh [sic]. York Town [sic] is situated on the York River. McClellend expected the Cooperation of the gun Boats when a combined attack would be made on the Town. us Soldiers knew very little about all these preparations, were it not for a constant fusilied of arms at times and an interchange of cannon shot, away down on our Right, keped us allways on the alert and expecting a forward movement every time, a Musketry fire would Break out some of the Boys would say well I think we are going to have it now. after a short time the fireing would cease and all was quet and camb again som of us soldiers oftened wondered what was the Cause of the delay believeing almost in the invinsibility of our Army and Confident in our Beloved Commander the[y] wished to push on to Richmond and end the War. later on these delusions were soone dispelled the[y] made up there mind for the enevatable. May the 4th (1862) the Rebels evacuated York Town [sic] in the night time after a fierce Bombardment by our Artillery with the aid of a fue gun Boats on the river. on the Morning of the fift[h] to our great surprise we heard the Enemy were retreating on the Road to Williamsburgh [sic]. we were Soone after them. I was now enabled to get a looke of there workes which were very strong we were Cautioned to keep in our place and at a halt to bring down our Muskets to the ground easely, as torpedoes were sunk in the ground in various places caped so as to expload by standing on the cap a Dainger which we never suspected. a Reble officer who had fell into our hands was compelled to move some of these loaded shells which were of large dimensions there had been several exploseions and Some of our men were killed and wounded a Regiment in advance of ours on the Road lost six men. The Rebels in there heasty retreat from York Town left a large number of their tents which were all cut into sreds were no longer usefull. various Articles of camp furniture cooking utentials and nick nacks lay about and along the Road. we passed one or two old Garrisons Guns the spoks of the wheels were slashed with an ax and were unservable.

In the Evening we Bivouaced in a large open field Recently Plowed, somewhere between Williamsburg and Warwick. The weather was chilly and gloomey our knapsacks and Blankets were left Behined in our Camp that morning, so that we were able to move with more celerity after the Enemy. during that night it commenced to Rain I awoke from my sleepe on the damp ground our fires were extinguished the soldiers sought shelter among the Trees. Daylight came it was still Raining and not a Brake in the murky Skye in some sheltered places our little fires lingerd and Burnt feeble but By dint of patience we Cooked our Coffey and Munched our hard tack with a Bit of Soiled Pork out of our greasey Haversacks. our Knapsacks came along dureing the Night when daylight came we were Busay puting up our Shelter Tents. I got a lot of corn stalks and was spreding them on the wet ground when we got orders to Pack up it was still raining our little shelters came down faster than the[y] went up there was some tall swearing among the men while others Bore with mute patience and shuck there Heads at one another and slung on there Knapsacks and tooke there place in the ranks with meek resignation. [...]

When we Commenced our March a slight sound of cannonading was heard in the distance towards Williamsburgh [sic]. How many miles we could not tell a Battle was going on. it was still Raining the air heavy and close and the sandy muckey road almost impasable and all cut up with artillery and Waggons. a larg number of troopes who had proceded us were then engageing the Enemy and must need our assistence. The Devisions in

Rear were stretched out in long lines on one or two Roads The Artillery and ammunition waggons were geting stuck in the mud and impeding the march of the Infantry our movement was very slow while the Boomeing of Cannon sounded more audable in our ears as the Day wore on we were making very little progress. our Men were very much disperited, chilled with the Rain and wet to the Skin. hunger did not seem to trouble us much, so it appeared to me oftin. Dainger for a time Drives away hunger. The poor horses and mules Suffered very much some times sunk to there [k]nees in the slush and trying to pull the guns and loaded Waggons out of the ruts and quagmire of the Road, while the Black snake whips of the Teamsters cracked across the sides of the poor Beasts, acompanied By the shouts and curses of there task masters *get up ge long* then another lash of the great Whip it was getting late in the evening and a hevey Musketry fire was going on. nearer still we heard the Cheers of our men But faster we coud not go my pants was coated with sand and muck we huged our fire locks under our arm to Keep the locks dry and servisable as we expected to use them before night I now saw a lot of straglers in the woods mopeing about I presumed the[y] Belonged to some of the Regiments in the front some of them were making Coffey and seemed quite unconcerned of the fate of there Comrades in front who were fighting all Day we were then almost on the verge of the Battle field a large strip of Timber dividing us from the Combatents who were fighting stubernly. The Battle was going in our favor as our troops were now receiveing seport forom the marching collumns as the[y] came on the ground wet and worn. Fort McGruder was holding out and resisting all attacks this was the Key to the position the shades of Evening were now closeing over the mellincoly scene the driping woods afforded us no shelter the ground was spungey and full of water we halted awaithing orders our suspence was misarable waithing for one thing or another. The Sounds of Battle had grown less, thank God, untill it ceased altogether. General Keys our Corps Commander galloped towards us and lifting his hat shouted Boys the Day is ours. This news was joyfully recived by our men whou were in very poor condition for a fight. but what about the night we had orders that no fires should be lit I think I was one of the first to pay no attention to that order it seemed inconsistent and might not have come from head quarters I lit a small fire. in a short time others followed which grew Bigger and Biger untill the glare of our fires lit up the Woods and gave them a more Cheerful aspect. The Rain stoped and the Big Blobs had ceased dripping from the green Canopy of leaves over head. many of us thanked our God for his Mercey to us that Day we were still a live and had one more chance in the future. I sleeped very little dureing the night I was princibly occupied Drying my cloas and scraping and Cleaning my Pants which was Coated over betwen my legs with sand and mud like plaster.

With the dawning of the day the dark Clouds disapeard from the sky. The warm sun riseing higher and higher was sending flashes of light and sunshine between the Trees. The Birds chirript and sang and the promise of a fine day cheered us once more. I had my Soldier Breakfast early Coffy and Crackers with a Bit of Pork toasted at the fire on the Point of a Stick. The Rebels retreated dureing the night leaving us master of the field and the Town of Williamsburgh. I was ansious to take a look at the Battle ground a short distance from our Bivouc as I passed trough the Woods great Branches of trees were lying on the ground some hanging down by the paternal trunk trees torn and slashed small saplins were cut in two and numerous marks of shot and shell and Rifil Ball were visable as I went along til I Cleared the timber and came out apon a a [sic] larg opening where most of the fighting was done one of our Guns was disabled and stuck in the mud dead bodys Lay about in all directions in some places the Blue and the Grey were Close together. There was no wounded men about. Those more seriously wounded were carried of[f] the field the Dead lay in all Kinds of Positions on the ground. passing By and among several of the Dead Bodys the Blue with there soild and water soaked uniforms it was remarkable to note the different expresions on there face so different from one another. But as I had not time to go about and in a short time had seen anuff of this human slaughter some of them had the apearance of been killed at onst and suffered little or no pain one of our soldiers was Lyeing partly on his side a faint smile on his face his stomac torn open By a Cannon Ball or a piece of a shell his entrals allmost scooped out of his Body and lying on the ground. Some it would apear must have Died in great agony. passing from one to another I saw a dead Indian whou Lay in a sprawling condition on the ground There was a painful expression on his Brown face he must have Died in great agony he had torn tufts of grass out of the ground which he held tightly in his hand even in Death. The Dead Body of a Confederet fixed my attention a young hansom man he lay on his Back with a Bite of a Johnny Cake in his mouth he received the fatle Bullet before he had time to swallow the Bit haveing sean anuf of the hundreds of Dead Bodies that lay about in all directions I returned to my Regiment very much impresed with what I saw I could not describe my thoughts. The dead were all collected and depossited in large pits in Layers like a Box of Sardines Belts and all as the[y] were Picked up on the Battle Field there was no Ceramony But get them under ground as quickly as possible.

[...] The Sixt and Seventh of May The enemy were in full retreat towards the Chickahominy, closely pursued By our Cavalry, who were Busily engaged picking up straglers and small partys of the enemy. at Noone the Day after the Battle our Brigade was on the march again following after the Cavalry. we passed trough the Centre of the Battle field our spirits elavated By the musick of several Bands as Regiment after Regiment marched off the ground. after going two Miles we entered the pretty little Town of WilliamsBurgh [sic]. the shops wer Closed and the window Blinds down. The Citizens had left the Town some of them locked themselfs up in there Homes not taking notice of anything going on outside. The yankies were marching along trough the main street quietly and unobserved. The new song now and then was heard in the ranks but they did not enthuse much

Marching along, we are marching along,
Gird on your armour and be marching along,
Rebellion may dare us to crush it we're strong,
For God and our Country we are marching along.

[...] Now and then we decerned the Pale face of a young Girl peeping trough the Blinds at the hateful yanks who would rather be friends then enemies and who would like to Bring them Back again as Brothers under the old Stary Banner which the[y] had Biden good By to for ever. The Town had a most ruefull look no one to be seen about But soldiers and the marching Battalions going along the main street hopeful looking and curious. Blankets knapsacks and camp utentials were scathered about in all drections. a number of the wounded Rebels were found in the Houses and were treated with humanity and kindness in a spirrit that was never acted on in like manner By the Enamy during the whole War. The Collage of William and Mary was Converted into a Hospitol. The Blue and the Grey were mingled together and treated alike with Care and attention. Patroles of Soldiers were moveing about trough the Town all Straglers and Rambling Soldiers were ordered to join there Regiments as quick as posible. a fue shops in the Town that sold Cakes and Pies ginder Bread and Candy sold out in a short time, what thou the shop keeper might lose Cast for selling goods to the yankee they liked the old money best.

The army was then in full Persute (pursuit). [...] our opening Campaigne and our march up the Pininsula was very succesful so fare. The Enemy when overpowered and unable to Resist us fell Back but to Confront us again and gaining time for the completion of the defensife works round Richmond and increaseing the strenght of there army Consentrating there, which had Reached formadable dimentions. [...] hevey fireing was heared in our Camps that day many miles in a Northerly directin in the neborhood of the Chickahominy River Rumour Ran wild as to the cause of the fireing when the truth became known it caused some disapointment among us. our eagerness to capture Richmond was so great believing it would end the War But it was very much farther off then we thought.

The Summer of 1862 in these parts was an unuseual wet one which retarted our movements and very severe on our soldiers. Keys Corps to which my Regiment belonged Crossed the Chickahominy River at Bottom Bridge a small wooden structure which was Burned by the Enemy and rebuilt by our enginears in a short time. after crossing the River we Continued our march for five or sick miles and encamped in the woods about six miles from Richmond. The Chickahominy is a wild swamphy River halfe smothered in the gloomey Forrest, an unhealthy looking region girded By wild weeds and tangled Brush wood and Creeping vines. in the early Days of the settlement of Virginia by the adventurous white man Captain Smith a noted and romantick figure in American History saild up the Chickahominy when he was Captured By the Indians Smith was going to be sacrificed to the great Spirit when he was saved by Pocahontas the Daughter of the head Chief this was his hapy hunting ground. one Day on the march I had Pointed out to me the identical tree where Captain Smith was to be put to Death. it was an old ainchient looking trunk of what was onst a large tree in a small inclosuer, surrounded by a Brick wall for the protection of the venerable stump which is held in great venaration by americans and a most interesting Relic to those who read its history.

We were then in a very exposed situation with only one small Bridge betwen us and the Main Body of our Army [...] for several Days we Remain in this position Diging Rifil Pits felling Timber and Building Cordiroy Roads in soft or swampy Places, which is done by Cuting young Pine trees into eauquel (equal) lenghts and laying them on the ground like Railroad ties close together. we were keped very Bussay and takeing our turn on Picket, allways watchful day and night, and keepeing under Cover as much as Possible the Rebel sharpe shooters were allays lookeing out for a shot at one of us yanks, takeing Deadly aim from some tree top obscured by the foilage or Behined a small Bush or lying low Behined the Bottom rail of a fence. The Pickets some times when there was no Danger of an advance from either side, commence fireing on one another, and cause a faulse alarm. Fatague Parties and straglers would fly Back to there Camps then the firing would cease as if By Mutual Consent and every one would want to know what was it all about. Relieveing time on the Picket line in some parts was very Riskey the reliefe party sometimes becomming visable to the Enemy has to run the gauntled of the fire of there sharp shooters and there spiteful Bullets. [...] on the 30th May McClellands Army on the Southt side of the Chickahominy, occupied the following position. Caseys division on the right of the Williamsburg Road Couchs division of Keys Corps at Seven Pines, Kearneys division on the railroad from Savage Station to the Bridge, Hookers division at White Oak Swamp. These troops were in advance of McClelen's Army which had circled round the Chickahominy River on the North side from grape vine Bridge to Mechanicsville north of Richmond. on the night of the 30th of June [the author is probably referring to the night of the 30th of May] a terrable rainstorm acompanied by great Crashes of thunder and lightening Broke suddenly apon us some time after midnight I awoke from my sleep and crawled out of my little shelter tent as the water was passing through it and ready to collaps any minute. I sought what shelter I could get among the treesb it was a miserable situation the night was darke and shadowey forms of our men were flitting about from tree to tree while the thunder Pealed louder and louder and the lightening shot down among the timber splitting some trees down to the ground till at lenght the rain ceased. When Daylight made its apearence the shelter Tents were nearly all down and everything presented a most chilling appearance later on the watery clouds disapeared and the sun shone out Bright and warm making the earth smoke and steam. It was a Bussay morning round Fair Oaks trying to put things in order again little thinking that the enemy would be in our Camps before night. fresh meat was issued to the men and a full compliment of Rashings (rations) for three Days I cut my allowence of fresh meat into small slices and roasted them at the fire on the point of a stick as it would keep longer. Some would cut there meat into strings Mexican fashion and dry it in the sun. we had no Idea of the disastrous Results of the Storm that night else we would concider our position a very Bad one. nearly all the Bridges Crossing the Chickahominy held by us were sweeped away. one or Two Bridges remained temporary Wooden structures in Danger of been carried away also by the riseing flood in the River which was swelling out into large preportions so that we on the Southt side were almost cut off from the Main Body of our Army in cace we were attacked by the Enemy.

Battle of Fair Oakes May 31 and June 1 1862

May the 31st the Rebel General Johnstin [sic] with a Force of Sixty or Seventhy Thousand men were on the move early that morning fully prepared to attack our left wing and cut us off as we might not be able to get seport from the other side of the River. we had not the least expectation of a fight or any movement whatever til about 12 o clock noone, when the Report of a gun Beyond the woods in front of where Caseys Brigade held an advanced Position and the Bursthing of a Shell in the Middle of a Clearing opposet our Camp. we did not mind this much as it was not an unuseual thing to happen. But then another and another Shell Bursting in the air soon followed then a Bustle became visible in our camps then came the Rattle of Musketry and the sound of Cannon. we were no longer deceived we were surprised. Mounted officers were flying about some with orders and others to there different Commands. we had not one moment to spare to get on our equipment on and fall into Ranks. The Artillery men were harnesing and sadaling up and were soone in Battery. Haversacks and Canteans were not thoutht of so great was the hurry. The fire of the Enemy was increasing and drawing near the[y] drove in our pickets and were smashing up Caseys Brigade with great impetuosity and Force. The enemy were gaining ground and the Roar of Battle became louder as the seports came to Casey. great gaps wer made in the Ranks of the Enemy by the cace shot of our Artillery But the Breaking away of a large number of Caseys men in the first attack weakened him and caused conciderable confusion This embolded the Enemy to push harder and faster on our men. Abercrombie our Brigade Commander of Couchs Devision moved us off to the Right in the direction of Fair Oaks Station. the Chassurs belonged to this Brigade and were held in high esteeme by the Old General who said the[y] were his main stay. when we started off I wondered very much where we were going to. it looked as if we were going away from the fight when our men were hard pressed with no prospect of seport from across the River if it was intended as a flank movement I Believed we would require a much larger force. in a short time after we moved off we were Completely shut out from the face of the Conflict by the tall woods and gloomey swamps on each side of the Road.

The roar of Musketry and Cannon at this time was very great the Rebels had taken possesion of some of our Camps and were so fare suckeesfull. Heintzelmans Corps after a march of four or five miles, came into action and fought like veterans and saved the Broken and Disorganised part of Caseys Devision who rallyed into some kind of form in the rear. [...]

Our little force Comprising the Chassurs and Two other Regiments and one Battery of Artillery, after moving to the right and forward, we halted in rear of a great belt of timber and Brushwood isolated from the left wing of our Army who were fighting for there lives round Fair Oaks out numbered and out generald. our Small Force was shifted about from one place to another. now and then a droping shell Bursting in the air or on the ground kept up a little excitement among us and relieved the dullness of our situation. One shell exploaded in the air a short distance over the Centre of our Regiment one of the pieces Striking Private McNallys Rifil and [k]nocking him out of the ranks. he was more frightent then hurt Fourtunatly he was not hit yet his Rifil was Broke in his hands which he held firmly in his fall to the ground. at five O Clock in the Evening there was no signe of the Enemy the battle was still rageing the sound of the fireing was receeding farther away from us. it was evident our men must have Been Beating Back for a Conciderable distance from the position we held in the Morning. about one hundred straglers who wore white stripes of Calico round there hats which was worn by there Regiment or Devision were picked up by some of our men in the thick Brushwood in front of our Regiment. had we remained there a little longer, it might have had very Serious Results fortunately we moved farther to the rear passing trough a thick wood into a large clearing and halted. yet there was no signe of friend or foe. to us Soldiers our Position seemed very strange and unaccountable we were totaly ignorant of the condition of our little army at Fair Oaks and the flooding of the Chickahominy River and the Breaking away of all the Bridges save one which saved the left wing of the Army from entire anialation. about six o clock in the Evening as we were still watching expecting every moment to be Attacked there was a Clatter of toungs and every one looking to the rear in the direction of the Chickahominy several miles away our harts rose we were delighted with joy Reinforcements were comming to us at any other time we would have cheered But we kept quiet, watching them as the[y] came nearer and nearer the bright barrels of there guns gleamed and glinted in the sun, as the[y] emerged out of the Woods and crossing a large opening General Sumner a fine old Soldier about Seventy years of age was in advance and was soone among us he had croosed the Chickahominy with ten or fifteen thousand men when the bridge was sweeped away leaveing a large Portion of his Command who could not get across on the other side. Sumner had fortunately come in the nick of time had he not come it would be hard to tell the consequence of our isolation. The old General had made a fue enquieries, When a Mounted Officer riding swiftly Rode up to us and toled the General that a large force of the Enemy were comming trough the thick Woods in front of us. Imeadiately Sumner formed his line of Battle very quick. Ricketts Battery twelf Pounder Napoleon Guns tooke up position in the centre facing an opening in the woods which had streached Back for a conciderable distance in front of the Battery the Infantry were deployed to the left and right of the Guns. The advance Colums of Sumners men were ready to seport us. The Chassures deployed to the right facing the woods on the line of an old rail fence just as we halted and faced to the front the Enemy opened fire on us Knocking a fue men out of the Ranks. a Corporal very close to me droped to the rear I asked him where he was going to he said he was wounded in the arm that was the last I saw of him as he did not return to the Regiment again. after the first fire we went down on our knees and commenced firing at will which was taken up along the line. Then came one of those Rebel cheers Howling Barking like wolfs or the War whoop of the Indiens. The Confederats made a desperet charge on the Battery. Captain Rickets in the coolest manner reserved the fire of his Guns untill the Enemy was quite close then fired a salvo from his double shotted guns which made the ground shake under them and smashing in the head of the colum strueing the ground with the mangled and bleeding forms of the empetous Enemy who Recoiled and fell Back in disorder the cross fire of our Infantry had a most telling effect on the assaulting party and the direct fire of the Artillery was so murderous it was more than the[y] could stand. The Guns were loaded again with double case Cannister Shot, the[y] did not have long to wait. a heavey Musketry fire was kept up by the Enemy on our line from right to left which kept our attention stedely fixed to the front. The Rebel Yell went out again. on the[y] come to the charge down the Centre of the open towards the guns But our splended Battery with a thundering salvo once more Belshes out fire and smoak its deadly cace shot Bursting and strikeing in the midst of the Enemy the[y] are Driven Back again under the gauling fire of our Infantry the Enemies Bullets fly thick and fast about us. They Ping Sing and Mews past our ears over and By us and so alarmingly close God only knows. well the[y] say the Third time has the charm. on the Enemy comes again for the Third Time. [...] they were again Beating Back and the Ground coverd with there dead. Sumner now seeing his opertunity and the demoralization of the Enemy ordered a Bayonet charge, and drove them Back as fare as Fair Oak Station. Night comming on put an end to the fight and the Battle of the 31st (May 1862) is over.

Not a gun is heard from the most distant part of the Battle field all is silent as the grave, But out of the woods in front comes the cry of help from the wounded and the Dieing. Reliefe parties are sent out and the Docters with lighted Lanterns are going about among the wounded. Water water is the cry which comes from the parched lips of men who cannot help themselfs. The Night was very sad and dreary we were hungery and had no Coffey to cheer and warm us we had no rations and must suffer on God was very good to us that day the losses in our Regiment was very light. the day closed with all the advantages on the Rebel Side. in the Evening our soldiers though Driven Back in most places some held there ground against the Superior numbers and inflicted great loss on the Enemy. we Spent the Night very poorely in a state of uncertinty I sleept very little the ground was damp. I could not lay down. Some times seated on a Rotten stump of a tree or a fence Rail I might take a short nap. what the next day would Bring fort[h] we could not tell. about five o clock in the morning the Battle was renewed again. The Rebels attacked our line in gret force But were met at every Point with firm Resistance. The[y] then put fourte all there strenght but were Beaten Back at the Point of the Bayonet. [...] The firing was very dense and close and worked its selfe up into a continued role, louder and more persistent then the first day. The Confederats were defeated at all points and fled from the Field in great disorder. the[y] were followed up for a short time which added more to there Confuseion and the ignomy of there defeat the pursueing Party were prudently recalled, as we were not in a condition to attack Richmond which would require the combined Strength of the whole Army then split in Two by the fllod in the River. Thus a grand opertunity was unavoidably lost By the forces of nature if Richmond were then Captured it might have ended the War or the cutting off of Virginnia [sic] from the Confederat States [...]

After the Battle the Dead were Burried as speedily as Possible. The moral or spiritual aspect of the work was not concidered for a moment. The Dead lay in heaps in some places and were scathered about where the fighting was done. The Blue and gray no longer enemies, lay near each other. hundreds of Dead were Buried in a very loose and Careless Manner. The Ground was dug up round the Dead Body wherever found and a thin Layer of earth trown over then a Plague of flies came apon us what the[y] call the Blue Bottle sort the[y] did not trouble us much the[y] paid all attention to the Dead Bodys of horses and men which were covered by them it was a most disgusting sight, and the horoble stench emaneted from these little mounds of dirt and flesh. the impureity of the air and the Broiling sun soon added hundreds to the sick list day after day without any abatement while we remained in this unhealthy situation. the Second or third day after the Battle I was taking a look round in the woods looking at the work of the Bureing parties. a number of stretcher carriers were bringing in the dead Bodys from various directions and laying them down on the ground close to a great long pit deep anuf for a cellar there was a large number of Dead Bodys in this great human grave. The[y] were nearly all Confederats, and were placed crossways in the Pit on top of each other in layers like sardians the[y] wore there equipments and were Burried I will say in there war Paint two or three soldiers were in the pit walking about on top of the unfortunate dead and catching hold of another on the Bank by the leg or arm pulls him into the Pit and stretches him out so as not to take up to much room for there is more comming, when the grave was filled and the earth trown over them. [...] War, what a scene for reflection standing on the Brink of that dredfull Pit looking at the faces of the dead and there Blood stained garments. It would be very difficult for me to describe my thoughts on that ocacion which were numerous and varied. I was still in the flesh thank God and the hope which never left me....gave me strenght. after fasting for a Bout two days and a Night a Box of Crackers was served out to each Company in our Regiment which amounted to about four or five a man this was very little But we were very glad to get this much we did not murmur no one was to Blame. The next day we had a full allowence and our Coffey [...]

After Fair Oaks we soon settled down to camp life again the Bridges were Rebuilt our communications were Restord and in Working order, earth works were Built and guns Mounted a forward movement towards Richmond was expected every day, on the arrivil of Reinforcements, which did not come. Now and then a Balloon ascencion took place much valuable information was gained from time to time in this way. The Balloon used to ascend to the hight of a thousand feet the Confederates made several attemp to shoot the Balloon But so fare as I could hear were not suckessfull. our Corps was mooved away from Fair Oaks a long distance to the left of our line. we were very glad to get away from there and its numerous little mounds of earth Called graves. Some of our tents were very near those Pestiferious heaps each Containing a human Body in the worst stage of decomposition. hear and there could be seen a leg or an arm sticking out of the loose Clay which partialaly covered the Remains Yet it is surprising with what indifference we looked upon these sights or how hardened and selfish we had become through the horrers of War in all its inhuman aspects. [...]

On the 25th June the sound of Cannon and Musketry firing was heard on our extream right. we on the left, grew serious while we listened to the Sound of the Conflict. [...] On the 26th My Regiment was ordered to seport a Battery of Artillery placed in a redoubt. all along the line our Army stood under arms. we soldiers thought something of Importance was about to happen the Rebel General Stuaart [sic] with a large force of Cavalry had made a very succesful raid round the rear of our lines, tretning our Communication and doing a great deal of damage and destroying a large amount of stores. about two o clock in the Evening fare away to the right there was heavy fireing. all was congecture on our part. far off in the woods the Enemy were keeping up an apearence as if forming into line and counter marching up and down this was done in order to deceive us while there whole available force was moved to there left. [...] on the evening of the 26th the Rebel Army under the command of General Lee commenced its forward movement against McClellans right wing Which Covered Beaver dam Creek and the Chickahominy River to Gaines Mill, compriseing General Porters and McCalls Devisions. [...] McClellan had commenced his retreat collecting his stores and loading his waggons which amounted to about four thousand five hundred. the night of the 26th my Regiment was under arms the whole night. General Stoneman with a large force of Cavalry was sent to the White House, our Base of Supply to destroy all stores he could not Send away and retire to York Town [sic] if necessary all night the Troops of the left wing stood under Arms no fires were burning except in some places well concealed.

On the morning of 27th the Chassurs were ordered on picket. the Enemies Sharp-Shooters were allways popping at us whenever the[y] got a chance. after the attack on Beaver Dam Creek that night General Porter fell back to Gains Mill taking all his guns with him. it was known By McClellan that Jacksons forces were within suporting distance of General Lee McClellan had giving up all hopes of support and prepared for the worst at Gaines Mill. Having the advantage of of [sic] a good position he determined to await the attack of Lee and Jackson, with thirty thousand men all that could be spared acting on the defensife while he was pre-pareing his retreat to Harrasins Landing [sic] on the James River where he expected to meet supplies and the cooperation of the Gun Boats. Our position on the Chickohominy was a Bad one. [...] About Six o ck in the evening on the 27th June my Regiment was relieved of picket duty the boomming of the guns on our right to which we were listining for several hours still contin-ued. we got Back to our lines at dark. We were then ordered to cross the Railroad in the direction of Gaines Mill. along the way Camps were Breaking up and long trains of waggons wer moveing towards Bottom Bridge and White Oak Swamp. Clouds of dust floated upwards over our heads Regiments and Batterys were moveing at a steady gait sometimes Blocking each others way But Soone stringing out again and moveing along in perfect order. although we had not heard the result of the Battle at Gaines Mill that day it was now plain to see we were in retreat to the James River, droping Back on the right. night comming on the movement of the Troops no longer vesible. we of the left wing who had not taken part in the terrable Battle that day were ansious to know all about it. on we went tramp tramp over the ruff dusty Road while the enormouse train of thousands of waggons was heastning to the rear. it was late that night when we reached our war worn and smoked begrimed veterns at the Chickahominy. after an opstonate (obstinate) and Bloody fight the[y] were crossing over to the Southt side of the river. The Irish Brigade was guarding the Bridge. I had great pleasure in unexspectingly seeing General Meagher hear, whome I had not seen since the year 1848 in Dublin. On the morning of the 28th the troopes Compriseing the right wing had safely passed over to the Southt side the Bridge was destroyed. This movement was a great disappointment to the Enemy. for some time the[y] did not know in what direction McClelland had withdrawen his Troops all the Bridges over the Chickahominy were destroyed which prevented imediate pursuit later in the Day the[y] attemted to Build a Bridge But were prevented by our Artillery which compelled them to Build a Bridge higher up.

The 28th passed quietly our Army was in full retreat with about thirty hours in advance of the Rebels, there was therefore no rest night or day our Troops in advance were pushing on as fast as the[y] Could for the River. Had the Enemy headed us off in that direction the Army was lost. Porters and Keyes Corps were in advance. we marched all night glad to get away from a bad Position for a better one which we were in hopes of making. after a teadious march passing trough White Oak Swamp we halted. The men Broke ranks and saught shelter neath the Bush and trees on each side of the Road from the Burning Sun and clouds of dust circulating about us. we were weary and tired and lay down on the ground. hundreds of our men were soone fast a sleep. Others sat down in a contemplative sort of mood listining to the faint Booming of the Cannon along way in the rear. Some Cavalry men reconitered the woods in front of us. The[y] were discoved By a small force of the Enemy's Cavalry who rode furiously at them Brandishing there Sabres yelping and shouting like Devils. our men retired quickly hotly pursued by the enemy, in the eagerness of there pursuit the[y] unexpectedly came very Close to our lines fue Shots from our ranks sent them whirling back. Some of the horses and Riders tumbled over on the ground. one of our Cavalry men who was wounded and taken prisoner escaped. Two or three officers of the Rebel Cavalry were taken Prisoners and a number of there men killed or wounded. [...]

Late in the evening of the 29th June, Porters and Keyes Corps after a Temporary halt tooke up the march again moving slowly and cautious along the ruff Broken Road all trough the night we toiled along in a sleepy sort of way. The night was fine and camb (calm) not a sound But the Croaking of Bull frogs in swampy places and the dolefull Cry or Song of that very curious Bird the *whip-or-will* which is allways with us in the night time hundreds of pleaseing little lights were flashing about us in the air and flitting trough the ranks those little lightening Bugs, or fire flies illumined our way by dismal swamps and By ways. Scarcely a word is spoke in The Ranks the men stager along the[y] are worn out for the want of rest and sleep and unceaseing watchfullness. a quiet meal is not thought of and our Coffey uncertain. The camb (calm) stillness of the night is now and then Broken by the rattle of the wheels of Artillery and the Crack of the drivers whips passing over a dried up Stoney Creek. Some slight impediment or Block in front causes a temporay halt the men drop down on the side of the road and are soone fast a sleep, But for a very short time. we are then aroused again. I grasp my Musket tight stands up and limp into the ranks again the Command moves forward my limbs are stiff and sore after the very Brief halt. I warm up and is soone right again. Yet no one growls, no one complains. why should we one soldier would say to another aint we very lucky we are not in the rear where all the fighting is done. another says never mind wee'il be into it yet. in every battle since the 25th June only halfe our Army were engaged at one time the losses on the enemys side were much greater than in ours yet in falling Back our dead was left unburrid and hundreds of our wounded men not able to stir from where the[y] lay or unable to keep up with the army, were left Behind in the most deplorable condition Sad and lonely to live or die or be taken prisoner by the Rebels who were more brutal then kind.

The next morning wee arrived at the James River and halted in the Woods til noone. at White Oak Swamp several miles to the rear a terrable Battle was going on. [...] Some hard fighting ensued at close quarters for a short time, when the Enemy brooke and fled to the shelter of the woods. Porter who had now taken up a position on Malvern Hill repulsed an attack of the Enemy at Turkey Bend whose object was to turn our extream left and get in betwen us and the River and thus cut off our retreat to Harrison's Landing our new Base of Supplies about tenn miles lower down the River. while this attack on Porter lasted my Regiment as well as I coud see was a conciderable distance to the right and rear of Porter we were in the low ground laying down in Reserve we could not see what was going on at Turkey Bend. Shot and shell Passed over and about us and some dropping shots came unplesently near us. I was looking at one of our men who had a very narow escape. My Regiment was in Close Colluam (column) of Companys when we lay down a Cannon Ball struck the ground quite close in front of the man I was looking at he was lying forward flat on the ground. the Ball struck the earth a fue feet in front of him It did not Bound But must have passed between the loose soil and his Body he was lifted up for a moment. he was not hurt but well shaken and almost [k]nocked stuped and amased at his escape. [My] Regiment moved off in the direction of Malvern Hill a gently riseing ground with a commanding Prospect looking up the river road and in the direction of Richmond. This was the ground chosen by McClellan with his Army as a whole. it was the Best Position for defence the Army had taken up yet since the commencement of the Seven days fight. our Waggon trains were comming in in splended style hundreds of teamsters were roaring shouting and cracking there whips, But the muels seeamed to know there work. Since they left White Oak Swamp amid the din of Battle and flying Bullets the[y] were now taking shelter Behined our lines near Turkey Bend hundreds of straglers were Comming along dust covered and weary the[y] ought to have been with there Regiments Some of them were looking about as if the[y] were lost. The Provost Marshal was galloping about directing them to there different Commands the Sick and slightly wounded came along in great numbers. fortunately for them the[y] were not Prisoners with the enemy. Regiments of Infantry and Batteries of Artillery were comming on the ground all day there sun Burnt faces grave looking and hardened veterans. as the[y] came along the[y] were asigned to there place in the front line or seporting Batterys of Artillery who were taking up the most favorable positions along our front or to be held in reserve this movement or shifting about Continued all night. our Troops were pouring in from White Oak Swamp and Charles City Cross Roads after there hard fight the day before. [...] The battlefield was pretty well maped out while we lay on our arms all night the next morning we were all ready to resist any attack that might be made upon us.

Battle of Malvern Hill July 1st 1862

On the 29th (June 1862) General Porter who commanded the 5th Corps de Army, was ordered By General McClelin [sic] to proceed in advance to Malvern Hill and take up a position there, in order of Battle, with his Corp and other troops assigned to him. [...] On the morning of the 1st of July about 10 o clock the enemys skirmishers were feeling for us along our whole line. the[y] kept up an irregular fire hear and there, Artillery now and then sending solled shot and shell among us most of the shells Bursted in the air or passing over our heads at times very close to our Bodys whil wee lay flat on the ground wathing for the grand attack which we all expected this lasted till about twelfe O Clock noone there was no return firing on our part we keped under cover as well as the formation of the ground would permit. we were merely acting on the defensive with full Pouches expecting every moment to be hotly engaged. a large body of the enemy attacked the Devisions of Morrell and Couch who were in touch with on[e] another, But were driven back by our Artillery in Confusion with great loss. My Regiment the Chassures of Couchs Devision had changed its position different times during the day. we lost a number of men by shells Bursting in our ranks or in close proximity to us. one shell killed and wounded about twelfe of our men. at one time our Regiment deployed to the Right in the open across a large stubble field extending Back in front of us a long distance we lay down on the ground. at first I could see no signe of the enemy yet the woods beyoned was full of them. a fue words were exchanged now and then among us as we had not the excitement of loading and firing when little is said. [...] Just then a Rebbel Battery opened fire on us direct in front of us at a pretty safe distance. I could see them very plain the[y] were working with a will. the Cannoners had there coats off it was warm work that day the sun was glareing hot the first fue shots passed over us. The[y] improved on this it was evident they were getting the range of us there shot Commenced Plowing up the ground in front of us Then Bounding onwards while we lay still and patient as lambs some of the shot passed very close to us. The loose sand and soil was dashed over us in showers smarting our face and hands and almost smodering us. One man was so completely stuned by these showers he lay motion-les for awhile I thought he was seriously hurt, but there were no marks on him. one of the men shuck him by the arm, he Raised up his head, spitting the sand out of his mouth and picking it out of his ears. he said for a moment he lost his Breath and was so stund that he did not know what to think of himselfe. one of our Sergeants had a leg cut of him he lay on the ground in great agony it was distressing to hear him he beged for someone to shoot him and put him out of pain. about halfe an Hour after the fireing commenced we moved back again to the position we had left. about four O Clock The Enemy attacked us again in the most furious manner. this time our Devision was in the front line hotly engaged My Regiment formed up within easey seport-ing distance of the front line, who wer fireing at will the men were steady and well together our whole Devision was engaged. for awhil the fire of the enemy was extreamly close. our second line lay down yet there was a Constant sweep of Bullets passing over our heads and By our ears, bing, bing, and so deadly near us at times, perhaps the thickness of a shaving, between us and eter-nity. The fireing was keped up for some time the Confederates in no way sparing of there men tried to force there way trough, But our numerious Artillery well posted and well handled Loaded with grape and Cannaster, some times double shoted made such havock among the assaulting Party Brave Men as the[y] were fell Back Broken and in disordered flight to the cover of the woods. wounded men were droping to rear in hundreds such as those who were able to walke. up to about four o clock the enemy had made several attacks or spurts at different Points along our line. the[y] were feeling us in preparation for the grand attack which came later on. My Regiment was moved to the right and front line streching across an open field with a slight incline to the rear in front of us looking towards the enemy the field was Bounded by a road with a low Bank stretching along and a rail fence on top, and a thick wood in the Back ground. Comming up to five o clock there was a a [sic] perfect camb (calm) all was still and quiet til some time after five the enemy opened on General Morrell and Couchs Devision with artillery. Soone afterwards there Infantry moved forward, down along the road in front of my Regiment. The[y] came along unperceived untill the[y] got nearly opposet our front. The[y] halted and faced to the front and gave us a volley in quick time, then dropped down at once behined the fence keeping up a Continual fire on us. The puffs of smoke is all I coud see of them while we were more exposed and in vieu. My Regiment returned the fire Immediately, fireing at will, with no Cessation untill dark Between Seven and eight o clock in the evening I was wounded and left the field.

About halfe past Seven o clock in the evening when the Battle was rageing I received a very serious Gun Shot wound in the left arm Close to the Shoulder Joint completely Severing the Bone and Breaking it into Bits. when I was wounded the sensation was very curious. I felt as if I was struck by a heavey Istrument such as an Ax or a sledge with a lightning like stroke with great force. My Rifel droped out of my hand. My arm hung by my side as if merely held by my coat sleve I was loosing Blood fast. I told the Coloniol who was near me I was wounded. I walked to the rear a short distance and growing very weak from the loss of Blood I sat down Behined a tree for a short time. the Bullets from the enemies front were passing me very lively and over a larg open field which I had to cross in order to get out of range. Tap Tap went the Bullets into the tree where I sat I could hear there compact very well, yet I must cross that field to get out of range if able. I stood up again and made my way towards an old woodden Barren (barn) a Short distance from me. I passed a number of wounded men lying on the ground. A Battery of Artillery was shelling the enemy over our front line, there shells Bursting in the woods beyoned our front. The shades of evening were Comming on I sat down behind the Barren (barn). I was growing weaker all the time. one of the Artillery men collected an arm full of leaves of corn for me to ly on I thanked him and felt very gratefull for his Kindness. I then Crossed the open and came out on a Road where a large Number of wounded soldiers were lying down on the side of the Road and others hobling along to the reare in quest of the Surgeons head quarters. I was now in a very weak Condition my ies (eyes) a bit hasey I was terrable thirsty and would give anything for a drink of water. I walked into a wooded Swamp Close by the Road and was going farther into its gloomey recesses when I realised what I was doing. I walked Back again out on the the [sic] road very much Surprised at myself and my foolish and Dangerous adventure in the Swamp. Water was the cry from many a parched mouth, as I turned down the Road Seeing others going the same way. water more precious then Gold to the worn and wounded Soldier Not able to procure it himself, unless relieved by some kind hand when water is available. Such is an Angeal in disguise a favor not easely forgotten. I had not gone fare down the Road when I sat down unable to stand any longer, when I had the good fortune to meet two soldiers of my regiment Stretcher Bearers the[y] placed me in a reclineing Position on the Road Side and expressed there warmest Sympathy for me. in a Short time the[y] made me a Cup of Coffey which Cheered me and quenched my thirst and like two good Samaratans they stood by me eager to do all the[y] Could for me. One was a Scotchman and the other a German. it was very near dark when the[y] placed me on the stretcher and carried me to the Surgents (surgeon) Camp. The[y] layed me down on the ground the Scotchman put his Army Blanket under me. we then parted for the last time. there were a large number of wounded Soldiers laying about, close to where I lay. Near hand a small farm House was full of our wounded men of all Ranks we outside had the stars for a canophy in our strenght we did not mind that. docters were flitting about with lanterns in there hands looking after the wounded. The Surgeon of my Regiment came to me he said my wound was a very Bad one. he Bandaged my arm and told me he Could do no more for me at present. from every quarter all round about me, the moaning and Bawling of the wounded and dieing was hart rending. about tenn O Clock that night the Surgeon who Bandaged my arm told me the Army was going on to Harrasins [sic] Landing, that the ambulances were full of sick and wounded men and if I could walk to go along with them or be left Behind. I made two or three attemps to stand up But fell down each time trough weakness. I then resigned myself to my fate, But not without hope which I do think never left me when danger was nigh. I lay on my Back all night the rain fell gently for a short time. wheather I sleeped little or much I could not say. the next morning I felt very hungery there was nothing to eat no help of any Kind. By a great effort I got into the House which was full of men laying on the Beds and on the floor. two soldiers were laying on a matres (mattress) and made room for me which I gladly excepted (accepted) this I concidered a great Boone when I Bethought of hundreds perhaps thousands of our wounded men scathered all over the Battle field mingled with the unburied dead. it was Consoleing to think I had at least a roof over my head though I was sorely pinched for room three of us Lying on a small matress. dureing the day we were visited by three or four Confederat officers the[y] told us we were there Prisoners and that we should not attemp to escape. for three or four days we remained hear. during that time I was allways hungery nothing to eat except a few Crackers the men shareing with one another. I could not stand from Weaknes. I used to fall down like a Bag of Bones. we were then taken to Richmond. weak hungery and degected looking, we were put into Waggons without Springs over a very ruff road. I was sitting on some Corn Sacks which the Nigger Teamster very Kindly placed under me, on the hard boards of the Waggon the Niggers were allways Kind to us and looked upon us as their deliverers. before starting a Confederate docter gave me a Powder he said it would num[b] the Pain or Soreness of my arm from the jolting of the waggon over stumps and stones on the Road. when we arrived in Richmond we were distributed among the different wards or lofts of the Libby Prison which was formerly a tobaco ware House. There was a large number of us. We were in a terrable plight all were hungery. I was in a starving Condition. I had nothing to eat for two or three days. There was a Millitery Guard on the Prison. My name Rank and Regiment was taken down and what little effects we had was taken from us. I had a Silver lever watch which I Bought in Donegans in Dame Street Dublin in 1861 which I prised very much. it was carefully rolled up in a tin Box in my pocket. the sercher a soldier looked at the watch then into my face and gave it Back to me again. I was very much surprised at this, as they allways keped anything of value belonging to our Prisoners. I had a fue Newspaper Clipings giving an account of Some of our Battles which he retained. I then passed in and going to the end of the long Room opposet a window, the most airy and lightsome part of the Big Room. fortunately I held on to the Old Blanket whitch my friend the Scotchman gave to me I streched it on the hard dirty floor and lay down with a Billet of stove wood for a pillow and my old Blood stained tunick no longer fit to be worn folded under my head. for the number of days I spent in this wretched place, it would be very hard for me to describe unless I had the abilities of a clever news correspondent taken on the Spot

There was so much misery. we were on starvation allowance. a great many of our Poor fellows in the Libby at that time were severely wounded. we had a great many Deaths during the short time I was there. Many of them I believe would have survived under Better treatment. when a Death took place the Body was removed to the Basement I was told the Cooking was done there. Some time during the night the Bodys were taken away and Buried without Coffins. while Removeing them and placeing them in the carts an intolorable stench pervaded our ward. The helples wounded and dieing men sufferd very much from flys which infested our Prison. The[y] were not the small common fly but Big blue Bottle fellows who could make there mark every time. The[y] swarmed on the face and arms of the helples and dieing, tortureing the life out of them, it was horrable to looke at. one day I was walking round the Big long Room Crowded with prisoners all wounded men some of them Dieing. I came to a Cot near the front door of the Libby a young soldier was lying stretched on the bed with a light dirty covering over him. he was a Bad cace his face and arms were covered with flyes. When he made a slight motion with his arm the horrable insects rose up from him like a Swarm of Bees. The flesh of his arms and face was red and scallded looking the flies were actualy eating him alive. The[y] came back on him again, as the poor fellow was not able to protect himself a Confederat Sentinal was near hand But it did not seem to give him any concern what ever. The Confederat docters had more then anuff to do looking after there own men. Richmond was full of Confederat sick and wounded soldiers. Provisions was scarce and dear and the medicle supplies were Running Short, consequent of the Blockade of the Southern Ports. There seemed to be some Neglect on the part of our Docters some I heared who were taken prisoners, or who had Volunteered to stay with us. I never saw one of them. The horrid spectical of the dieing soldiers was a mellincoly sight for any Christian man to looke at espescialy for a Catholic dieing without the Benefit and Consolation of a Priest or Minister in his last moments. a soldier about two or three yards from where I lay died very hard curseing and swearing almost to his last Breath. After five or six days in Prison I got a very bad attack of Rumatism in the left Knee. I could not stir without Pain. I used some times pour water on my arm which was swollen down to the tip of my fingers and very much discoloured. The Bandage on my arm was very tight and thick with Congealed Blood, my wound was geting dirty wormly for the want of dresing. On the 17th of the month we heard with joy and expectation that a large number of Prisoners would be sent into our lines in a fue days to be paroled untill exchanged. the happyness which we felt in getting Back to our friends knew no Bounds. Oh how I longed and prayed to get out of this Pestilent Prison, and the smell of the living and the dead allways about you. On the 19th July a large number of ambulances assembled in front of the Libby Prison early in the morning, four or five hundred Union Prisoners all wounded men thees were ansious moments for me as I did not kno I was going. all those who were able to walk fell into line. I was put into an ambulance not been able to walk. it was a sort of a funeral like procesion as we passed trough the streets to the Petersburgh Railway Depot, a lot of half neaket (naked) wasted looking men. after a very slow ride we arrived in Petersburgh, on the James River about thirty miles from Richmond we changed cars hear and was put into old freight waggons. after jolting and joging along for some time over a worn out Railroad we arrived near Harrisons Landing. Two large River Steamers flying the Stars and Stripes were laying along side of an old wooden jetty, partly Burnt. The joy we felt at the sight of the flag and the glad and cheerful faces of the Ladies and gentlemen of the Sanitery association who were there to receive us. we were the first prisoners that came from Richmond. no time was lost getting us on Board after been duely turned over By the Confederat officers in charge of us. I went on Board the old Vanderbilt Steamer which used to run Betwen New York and Albany before the war. What a change the kined Ladies asked us what we would have, milk, punch, Coffey or lemonade. we were provided with comfortable, clean Beds in the Salloon and on deck. In a manner it was like falling into angels hands. The next morning going down the River we passed Harrisons Landing the great field of Mars. Thousand of white tents were glistning in the glowing sun while a Border fringe of dark green woods in the Back ground completed the Picture. Soldiers were moving about in all directions. at the River Side a fue vessels were dischargeing goods for the Army then needing Supplies for the next Campaigne. The Confederats were very much disapointed in not been able to smash up McClelens [sic] Army in his change of Base to Harrisons Landing a position which the[y] think is of very great importance to the enemy. [...] passing Harrisons landing I made an effort to take a looke at the great camp. I had been lying on my Bed since I came on Bord. I saw very little of the James River till we came near Fort Monroe. we stoped hear a short time the Captain of the Boat came among us and straiting himselfe up, Now Boys said he where do you want to go, New York or Philidelphia [sic] The Yorkers shouted New York while the Pensilvania Soldiers shouted for Philidelphia [sic]. The Captain concidered the Yorkers were in the Majority and started for New York City, very much to the delight of a large number of soldiers who expected to meet there friends there who were ansiously expecting there arrival when we got there. we landed on the East River side of Bell Vieu [sic] Hospital. we must have presented a very effecting and strange sight to some of the onlookers. I walked ashore with nothing on me But a shirt and drawers Bare headed and forlorn looking we crossed a small square and entered the hospital hear we were met at the foot of the stairs by some of the ladies of the Sannitery association whose kindness

I'll never forget. A number of large Milk Cans were near the stairs and contained milk punch and hot Coffey which the kind and good Ladies in the most charming manner invited us to partake of in a plentious manner. Soon after our arrivil in hospital we were visited by the head Surgents Docter Sairs, Mott and others. docter Sairs examined my arm and taking me unawares trust his fore finger into my wound which he pulled out very quick his finger was pierced by a sharp piece of Bone. The next day he had his arm in a sling I was told afterwards he had a narrow escape from Blood poisening. about half a Dozen pieces of bone were taken out of my arm, from the sise of a grain of shot to about an inch long. I felt a bit more easy after this, and was getting more contented to the ways and usages of the Hospital, when I was taking down with fever. I got into a very low state. a young docter named Shaw whom I gratefuly remember took a great interest in my cace he Broke the fever after three Weekes treatment. I soone recovered and was able to go about the ward. after a short time my health was fairly good. But the nature of my wound was so bad and the uncertanty of the result gave me something to think about. My friend Docter Shaw, would sometimes say to me Seargeant I would like to save that arm for you. I was told by another young docter that attendid me that I would get a New Bone in my arm which he explained to me and discribed some very remarkable instances in that cace, which was new to me and very encourageing. one way or another time passed very pleasently in Hospital there were viseters (visitors) every day The Ladies of the Sanitery association never lost sight of us Bringing us usefull presents, under cloathing some times fowl and other dainties. Prayer Meetings were held frequently and was a source of amusent to a good many of the soldiers The ladies would like to make us all good Boys But did not intrude there Religious Ideas apon us. Two Ladies who came very often to see us were the daughters of the Goverer of the Collumbia Collage [sic] of New York. The[y] invited about twenty of us Soldiers to there Home in the Collage with the Consent of the Head Docter. The[y] had diner prepared for us and Refreshments and plenty of Cigars. We spent a very pleasent evening with the young Ladies. Some of the Boys sung Patriotic Songs. We all tried to make our selfs as interesting as Possible after a real good time we Returned to Hospital more then pleased with our entertainment. Some time in August (1862) to our surprise General McClellan was relieved of Command of the Army of the Potomac. [...] McClellan retired from the army and rejoined his family. at this time there was six months pay due to us soldiers in the Hospital. We were nearly all out of pocket and tired waiting. General McClellan was expected to pay a visit to the Hospital. he came acompanied by his wife and some officers. we were all glad to see our General as we stood by our cots and saluted while he passed along talking to the men indevidualy wen he came to me we talked for quite awhile after answering all his enquiries, well Seargeant said the General if you have any request to ask of me I will see what I can do for you I thanked the General and told him I had only one request to ask. we were all very much in need of our pay then due six months. he told me he would see the Pay master and do all he Could for us. after our viseters (visitors) departed I was surrounded by a douzen of my Comrades giving me all kinds of praise in talking up to the General about there pay and what a good time it was to speake about it. the next day about one O Clock the Pay Master came to the Hospital and Paid us in full which made everything lively and put us all in good humor. Shortly after this McClellan was Called to Washington by the President, who Besought him to take command of the Army again. The Troopes under McDowell, Banks and Pope had Met with Nothing But disaster. [...]

In January 1863, we were sent to Davids Island Hospital on Long Island Sound about twenty one miles from New York City it was a Govenment Hospital recently Built for sick and wounded soldiers it comprised several Buildings all wood. a small River Steamer ran between New York and the Island. In the Summer time it was a very pleasent trip going and comming from New York, allways nise People on Board, some times with musick or singing some of the Patriotic Songs of the day. we were treated very well on the Island and were well cared for in every Respect. about eight months after I was wounded I went under an operation. eight small pieces of Bone was taken out of my arm. after this I got along very well. The discharge from the wound stoped and healed up I exercised my arm very gently at first to prevent stiffness. day after day, I tryed to raise my arm from the shoulder higher and higher without straining myself, till at last my disability seemed fixed and could go no higher. I now looked forward to a possibility of my joining my Regiment again and trust to luck. I was only fit for light duty. Yet I was not unwilling to take up the Musket again. I did not care to go Back into Civil Life again for some time I thought I might tarry a while longer in the Service dispite the severity of the War which was growing more desparate and Bloody, with no prospect of soone ending. I was ambitious to become a Commisioned Officer and to reach the Rank of Captain. This I think would have quite sadisfied me. had I not been wounded at Malvern Hill my chance of promotion as Second Lieutenent was certain. after my arrival in Bell Vieu [sic] Hospital I wrote a letter to the 1st Lieutenant Commanding my Company. I received a very warm and friendly reply. he stated there were several rumors in the Company one was that I was dead another was that I had lost my arm and was a Prisoner in Richmond. There were a fue promotions, but under the Circumstances I could not be promoted as I might not be fit for duty again. I was therefore honourable mentioned in the Report to Washington.

My condition haveing been noted as favorable I was sent to the Convalescent Camp on Bedloes Island New York Harbour where the great Statue of Liberty now stands. Some time in August Eighteen Sixty Three I was sent to Washinton [sic] enroute to join my Regiment at the front. I had charge of seventy one men of various Regiments. after a lot of trouble I got rid of them in Washington which was quite a reliefe to me. I then started on the military railroad to Warrenton, virginnia [sic] after I crossed the Potomack River my eyes was greated once more by that familiar desolation which I experienced before and which met my gaze in all directions. Houses tillage cattle fences all were gone, where there was onst plenty. at Mannassas [sic] the first Battle field of the Rebelion, the ground was disfigured by the remains of Brest works and Rifil pits, where grim death and the smoke of Battle once Clouded the surrounding plain at Mannasses Junction [sic] the ruined Houses Broken down fences and a fue scathered trees the goasts of once happy homes looked lone and Mellincolly. The Burnt remains of a very large number of Railway Cars were scathered up and down the road. it was late when I arrived in the pretty little Town of Warrenton, now faded and falling into decay. farther on I Past General Sedgwicks Head quarters the Commander of the Sixt Corps. hear I met a fue soldiers of my Regiment who were very Kind and asked me to take super with them. I was hungery and gladly excepted the invitation. I told them all I new about New York and such and such persons I met there. I then proceded to hunt up the head quarters of the third devision Sixt Corps to which my Regiment belonged. one of my friends acompanied me and carried my Knapsack, and acted as my guide. in a large Millitery encampment it is difficult to make your way through after been away for some time from your Regiment. if in the night time it is almost impossible without a guide. The Mazes of tents Batteries of Artillery, waggons and all kinds obstruction But my soldier friend saved me a lot of this Trouble. he had a lot of news for me it was then dark My Regiment had moved during the day to another location more disirable leaveing a small detathment in the old Camp ground to guard Some Stores which was left behined. hear again I met some of the old veterns who welcomed me Back and advised me to stop with them for the night. The next morning I reported Back to my Regiment and received a Cordial welcome from some of my old friends. There had been several promotions while I was away which placed me in a Subordinate Position to some of them who had Been my inferior in Rank before I was wounded. one of the New Commisioned I Concidered in a certain Sence an intruder owing to the System of promotion in the Volunteere Regiments. The governer of a State to whitch a Regiment belongs may fill a vacancy in a Regiment without the Recommedation of the Commanding Officer of the Regiment. This is Brought about by Political influence of friends or favor which is in the Power of the Governer But as this Rule is not general onst a Regiment is properly organised, all recommendations for promotion must come trough the Commanding Officer of the Regiment. The Adjutant and the Colonel assured me I would be promoted the next vacansey that would occur. This condoned me for the loss of my opertunity trough no fault of my own But the usage of the service. I once more Resumed my duty as first Sergeant of my Company. everything was going very smood and an unusual quiet Seemed to reigne all a round. our Camps were nisely situated the hostile crack of the Rifil or the distant gun was rarely heard. Camp life was becomming enjoyable but it was too soone yet to expect Repose so early in the fall of the year. our Camps were situated in a Roleing Country in the green valleys and on the hill tops West of Warrenton with the Blue Ridge Mountains stretching fare and wide in the Back ground. in this Briefe and

peaceful intervill many a hart longed for home and were growing tired of this weary war which seemed to have no end. The
Siege of Charleston was the General topick among the men.
The[y] wonder how much more pounding it was going to get to
reduce the Cradle of the Rebellion to Submission Union suckases
(successes) in the North or west was hailed with delight by our
men. [...] about the middle of September we heard Lee was falling Back from our front and had sent a part of his Forces down
Southt to assist the Rebel General Brag [sic] who was operating
against Chatanoga [sic] in Tennessee.

General Mead [sic] our Commander of Irish dessent the
hero of Gettysburgh who had succeded General Hooker after
the Battle of Chancellorsville moved forward with all his forces
in the direction of the Rapidan where General Lee was seposed
to be strongly intrenched. a large force of Cavalry proceeded in
advance of the Army. [...] The Sixt Corps tooke up the Rear following the main Body of our forces it was a very toilsome march
in the hot sun and soone made the men feel the weight of there
Knapsacks. in the evening the heat was very oppressive till
sun down. worn out by fatague and the inervating influence of
Hospital life after marching about twenty miles and getting foot
sore I was Compelled to drop out of the Ranks and rest myself
for a short time I then tooke the Road again and came up to my
Regiment after dark, encamped on Stone House Mountain. to
my surprise I had to go on Picket that night. I never felt a duty
so hard as I did then. My arm was weak and sore from the strain
of the Knapsack. I was in a very poor condition for that kind of
duty But had to go. on the first of October the 3rd Devision of the
6th Corp took up the march for Catlin (Catlett's) Station on the
Orange and Alexandria Rail Road a very important Position on
the line of Railroad from Washington and the princible feeder of
the grand Army of the Potomack [sic], about twenty five miles in
our rear. our devision marched all night not very quick feeling our

way in the woods and Keeping the right Road in the Darkness of night required some caution. daylight came Gloomey and hazy looking the rain was falling lightly and portented plenty of it. we slung our Ponchous or rubber Blankets across our Shoulders and huged the lock of our Rifil under our arm and prepared for the worst as the Rain was then falling heavey and the Road getting soft. in a Short time it was all puddel and water too Bad for anyone but soldiers who must go where the[y] are ordered and Cannot be picking there steps on the line or march. our feet was wet and cold and our lower extremimities bespatered and Coated with mud as we slowly waded along the miry and flooded Road which in some Places stretched out in sheets of water and rushing along like a torrent. on we went trough the yellow flood all day till we arrived at Catlin (Catlett's) Station and Bivouaced on the water soaked plain, the most dismal looking lot of soldier Boys I ever looked at. the Rain ceased a little and by great persafeverance fires were kindled and soon ablaze. There was plenty of timber. we stood Round the Blazeing pile turning round and tosting ourselfs like a spit our cloas (clothes) steaming on our Backs and a Cold Chill running trough us. at last the Clouds began to Break, and the Rain ceased. we put up our shelter tents and in a fue days our Camp arrangements were Complete. thinking we might [remain] hear for the winter we were Calculating on improveing our little Homes and makeing ourselfs as Comfortable as possible when to our great surprise on the second or third night the Generals Call Sounded. the tents were struck there was a hunt for this and a hunt for that in the dark, some curseing and swearing yet the[y] were packing up as fast as possible and falling into Ranks. we were soon on the Road again. where we were going no one Could tell. a fue Drunken Soldiers who were unmanageable were left Behined in there glory the[y] joined us in a fue days. Drungness (drunkenness) in the army was very rare the[y] were let off with a caution. Drink I may say was an un[k]nown quantaty at the front and is not allowed to be sold or smugled into any of our Camps or Sold to our Soldiers. five dollars, one Pound English money has often been paid for a Canteen of the vilest Kind of Whiskey. But so ridged and perfect was the Blockade against this article it was meerly by Chance or favour you could get a mouthful of the vile stuff at any price. At the front it was the rearest (rarest) thing at all to see a drunken Soldier. during the march that night to Kettle Run and Bristow [sic] Station we passed the Camp of the 13th pensylvania Cavalry the[y] had pickets all along the Railway. There seemed to be some excitement among the men it was said there pickets were fired on and the videts driven in Pell Mell and this in the night time makes things very disagreable when Soldiers are deprived of there needful rest perhaps after a long days march. our devision was halted and lay down faceing the Railroad prepared for an attack or surprise by the Enemy. tall darke woods streched out in front of us a meet Cover for the Enemy but the[y] did not come and we were relieved as to any fears we might have of a night attack. [...] our devision rested the remainder of the night in the woods and at daylight Continued our march. we arrived at Kettle Run a deep creek spaned by a small Wooden Bridge which required to be well guarded,and a number of other Bridges along the Railroad requireing large detachments at different points to protect those frail structers from been Burnt down by the Enemies Cavalry who for some time had been hovering about on our front and flank. After a very short time at Kettle Run the army Commenced falling Back again I was very much surprised at these forward and Back movements and Continual marching as we must soone go into winter quarters and rest ourselfs untill Spring. The War had been going on then for about Three years Yet It did not apear we were near the end of this devastating and fearful strugel. our Cavalry under the Command of General Kilpatrick and Some Artillery formed our rear guard The Rebel general Hill with a large force attacked them [...] all day on the 11th and 12th (October, 1863) we heared the Boomeing of Cannon in our rear. [...] The Sixt Corps reached Centreville a very strong position protected by earth works. after the Battle of Bulls Run the Confederates Stationed themselfs hear for some time making the place very formidable Building earth works and entrenshments. our Corps was shifted again and marched to Chantilly about five miles North of Centreville. we then heard the gratifying intelligence that our march was acomplished with very little trouble and our trains were all right. after a fue days the army moved forward again the enemy fell Back as we advanced and finally retired Behined there works on the Rapidan River, which were very strong. Mead [sic] declined to fight them in there strong hold. The season was late and the weather geting cold he fell Back to the Rappahannock. we put up our little Tents but doing nothing of an extra nature the weather was clear and cold our Troops needed rest after there long Campaigne.

One night in my Tent while I lay on my grassey Couch on the ground and feeling very comfortable I was aroused from my Sleep by a drunken Soldier who had procured some Contraband whiskey which he had not tasted for a long time he drunk to[o] much of the fire water. it soone sent him going Sig zag trough the tents and round about shouting like a wild Indien looking for someone he might Scalp. The night was Cold and Windy. I listend for awhile but as the howling Continued I came out of my tent with nothing on but my drawers and over coat and conducted him to the camp Guard and returned to my tent. The next morning I felt very unwell from an attack of Diareie (diarrhoea), from cold I presume Comming out of my tent not properly dressed in the Cold windy air after two days I felt very Bad and was obligded to go on the Sick list. I was sent to the field Hospital. after a fue days my health not improveing, I was obliged to stay in Bed. To our Surprise the army was about to move again. General Hayes of the Confederate

Army had taken up a Position at Rappahannock Station it would apear with the intention of going into winter quarters the[y] set to work Building huts and fortifying there Position. Another force had established themselfs at Kellys Ford, four or five miles from Hayes. The[y] seemed not expecting an attack from our Side and that we were gone into camp for the Winter but in this the[y] were very much mistaken. The sick were ordered to Washington, not less then five hundred nearly all dierria (diarrhoea) caces. we were placed in Ambalances and driven to the Or[a]nge and Alaxandria [sic] Railroad. the Docters were very sharp and vigelent looking after them lest there might be some one shamming among us. a docter came to the ambulance where I was. he asked me do you smoke. I told [him] I did do you Continue to Smoke I said I was unable to do so. That will do said he your sick. at the same time we heard the sound of Musketry and Artillery in the distance on the away to the Station. our men had attacked the Confederate positions and drove them a cross the River taking a large number of prisoners, Bag and Bagage. The Army then went into winter quarters Northt of the Rappidan [sic]. before starting for Washington we were supplyed with hot tea and other warm drinks by the Sanitery People, whom I allways remember for there kindness and goodness to the sick and wounded Soldiers. at the Railroad we were put on Board freight cars with a sprinkling of hay under us. we were in a misarable Condition concidering the nature of our sickness and the foulness of our Situation. Now and then a hat or a cap and its Contents passed over your head and out on the door of the car, then a stifeling smell filled the car for some time, that was almost unbearable. It was well our journey was short. Arriving in Washinton [sic] we were Sent to Lincollin [sic] Hospital a large wooden Building, of a class Built in various parts of the Country for the acomadation of the Sick and wounded Soldiers. the docter told me if I wanted to get well not to drink any water or eat fruit or Cakes. I followed his Instructions and with Gods help made up my mind to get well again. in four or five weeks I was convalasent, while a number of my ward mates died many of them partaking freely of or[a]nges and Pies Brought into the Hospital by there friends. Americans are generaly very fond of fruit sweets and tit Bits which I believe Cost some of them there lives. one day a fue Beds off from where I lay I saw a Soldier sitting on a Chamber, Sucking an Or[a]nge. I was Surprised I could not help smileing at the fellow, it was not nice. That man died. for six weeks I had not tasted one drop of water. my health improved so that I wondered at myself how much I could eat I was then sent to the Convalasent Camp near Alexandria. There was a large number of Soldiers there when fit for duty the[y] were sent out in detachments to join there Regiments. Those not fit were discharged and sent home. There was a large number of Deserters and Prisoners in Washington at the time the[y] had a place for themselfs and were well guarded. Some of those men were Bounty jumpers going from place to place, Inlisting and receiving large Bounties, then Deserting whenever the[y] got a chance the evil became very great til General Mead [sic] put the death sentence in force Millitery exacutions were for a short time very frequent. This had the effect in puting down Bounty jumping. the honest Soldiers at the front had no Sympathy for Such fellows, who took the Goverment and publick money by fraud.

Sandusky, Ohio

January the fift, Eighteen Sixty four I rejoined my Regiment again at Brandy Station, Va (Virginia) after a Cold miserable ride from Washington on the top of a freight Car. the ground was Covered with Snow and a sharp wind Blew right in my face. it was night when I arrived at the encampment of the grand army. The camp fires were Burning Bright and facilitated my movement in Serch of my regiment till I came to a Clump of Pine Trees where the officers Tents of my Regiment were Situated. I reported myself to the Adjutant a friend of mine at one time a Sergeant in my Company he was a little Cockney fellow who was working his way up very safe and nice. after the exchange of a fue words and a drop of old Burbon whiskey I felt a little Bit Cheary after my Cold Bleak journey. about two thirds of the surviveing veterns of Eighteen Sixty one of my Regiment had reinlisted and had gone home on a months furlough. after some reflection I consented to rejoin again. I had no home. I thoutht I woud stay longer in the Army and take the risk our Brigade had orders to move out of camp that night en route to Washington beyond this we did not know our destination. I received my Commision as Second Lieutenent and expected to be Mustered in in a Short time. at Washington we went on Bord a Train of freight cars on the Baltimore and Ohio Railroad the weather was very Cold and our Condition very uncomfordable as soone as we started we heard we were going to Sandusky Ohio. We passed by the Ruins of Harpers ferry. before the War it was the greatest Arsanal in the United States til it was plundered and Burnt by the Confederates. all along the Road of the Baltimore and Ohio Railroad was guarded by detachments of troopes untill we came to Wheeling, Western Virginia. we were treted very kindly by the Citizens, but the disorderly conduct of some of our men prevented many People from Manifesting that Spirit of unionism which was doubtful among them. we stoped in Town for a fue days. all on Bord again we crossed a Beautiful Suspension Bridge which spands the Ohio River and stoped a fue hours in the Station. at Bridgeport a fue Barrells of foul (fowl) were Broken into and there Contents disapeared into some of our Soldiers Haversacks, which were well nigh empty and very unsavery. at lenght we arrived in Sandusky a small City on the shore of Lake Erie. we were worn out for the want of sleep and our Customery Beverage Coffey, and stiff with the Cold for want of execise, after a very tedious journey of about six hundred miles.

at Sandusky we got a very harty Reception from the People young and old flocked round us all ansious to see some of the Soldiers from the Battle fields of Virginnia [sic]. It made my hart glad and took away some of the chill, looking at the cheerful faces of the young girls and matrons with Baskets of cakes and other dainties, handing them to us soldiers as we marched along trough the Town. A ruff looking looking [sic] lot anuff that needed a good washing and Brushing up which would make us more presentable to the Laidies who were allways our friends in this Terrable struggle which we were passing trough. we turned into a large Building where a plentyful and Substancial Breakfast was prepared for us. you may be shure we did justce to ourselfs. as the Board never lightened which was constantly replated By more of the good things which we Call a Square Meal till we finnished our repast, feeling much Better then we felt for the last fue days. Sandusky is a Small City Built on the shore of Lake Erie at its narrowest part called Sandusky Bay. about three miles out from the shore is Johnstons Island garrisoned by a small number of of [sic] U. S. Troopes. about twelfe hundred Confederate officers were held hear as Prisoners of War. for some time there was a rumour a raid was going to be made from Canada, to release the Prisoners. our Brigade was hurried hear North to prevent any hostile attempt on the Island which might take place. The Lake was Covered by a great sheet of ice very thick and looking like a frozen sea. Sledges traveled Back and forward to the Island laden with goods and passengers and was concidered perfectly safe. we crossed over this Ice field allright to the Island and put up our tents. we wished ourselfs Back again in more genial Virginia away from this Cold Border land of the North. one night in the middle of February a Cold North wester came along it Blowed like fury [k]nocking down our tents and scathering every thing portable all over the Island The night was very Cold and a chilling Blast serched us everywhere and pushed us about till daylight came and the weather moderated. a General

Order came from Washington that no more Second Lieutenents would be mustered in any Regiment below the minimum. This order so unuseual and unexpected came on me like a flash and Blasted my hopes from entering the Commisioned Rank for Some time. Yet as 1st Sergeant I had Command of my Company from time to time with more work and greater Responsibility trown apon me and no extra pay. I felt very much anoyed and discontented, But I was Bound and must obey. after a short time on the Island I was promoted to Sergeant Major of the Regiment, and on the Sixt February 1864 I was Discharged by reason of re-Enlistment and went on to New York on a thirty five days furlough. I was acompanied by my friend Woodman the Adjutant who had also re-enlisted. he was a jolly little fellow and was glad to have him with me we Received our Bounty in New York and at the termination of my furlough I Returned to my Regiment in Virginnia [sic], which had been ordered from Johnstons Island to join the first Devision of the Sixt Corps under the Command of General Sedgewick a Brave and Skilful officer who had the good will of his men. They used to call him Daddy Sedgwick.

Grant's Campaign & Sheridan in the Shenandoah Valley

Early in May 1864 the Army of the Potomack [sic] under the Command of Major General Grant Crossed the Rapidan he cut loose from his Base with Supplies for a certain number of Days. on the 5th May our army Confronted Lee in the Wilderness. Thick with woods in all directions which might be Called forests of a primative grote and Screening the Enemy from our vieu until close to them. The exact position of the Enemy was a mistery to us, untill the Battle Commenced. The Sixt Corps under Sedgwick was on the Right of the line, the fift under Warren, in the Centre,

Hancock, with the Second Corps held the left, while Burnside with the Ninth Corps in Reserve in the rear. The Enemy attacked Warren fiercely for about one hour and then fell Back. The[y] then attacked Hancock on our left centre Fighting with Doged persistancy it was a musketry fight as Artillery on either side could not be used affectively owing to the close timber and the Nature of the ground part of the Sixt Corps mooved out from the Right in the woods and advanced towards the enemy a heavey Musketry fire ensued. This movement relieved Hancock for a short time till he was reinforced by a Devision of the Second Corps the firing became more intence and witht that aw inspireing Sound which increased to a Roar among the Timber. the Battle continued with great spirit for some time. In the Evening a short time before dusk on the extream Right where our Brigade was standing leasurely in line my Regiment was on the Right of the Brigade everything seemed very quiet in our front. lower down towards the left there had been some desultering fireing. Now and then, the sharp Sound of a Rifil was heard In our front in the woods. we had no idea of the situation on our left. we had no pickets or skirmish line as fare as I Knew on our front or flank which was very open to an attack in force. I concidered our right flank very weak and liable to be turned I could see no Troops in Reserve where we Stood. a short distance from me to the Right and in the open five or six men were standing round a small fire making Coffey. I could not Resist the temtation of making a Cup for myself. I got water from one of the men and placed my tin cup on the fire when a Bullet Struck the ground close to the fire tearing up the loose soft earth. I moved Back a Short distance ansiously waithing for the water to Boil, then another Bullet struck the ground nearer still and knocking part of our fire about. I looked with the greatest curiosity at the men who notwithstanding, the fire seemed to be a marker for some of the Bullets of the Enemy, who were nowhere to be seen Some of the men cooly put their Coffey in the Boiling water while another would adjust his cup on the fire that was near topling over a Bullet having struck the fringe of the fire disturbing some of the cans it was now my turn I put the Coffey in my Cup. I had merely time to give the water a boil and Layed it down near the fire. the dusk of the Evening was comming on, when a stragling fire opened on our right front which increased in vollum (volume) and worked round on our right rear. It is said no soldiers can stand a fire in there rear. in an Instant the head of the line Broke off. the men runing to the rear. I heared no order of any kind, so sudden and unexpected was the attack I had harly time to looke about us in the rear I could see a swarm of men on the run there was then nothing for it but go, or be shot or taken prisoner by the Enemy. on the run we were subgect to a hevey fire which heastened our steps till we got to a Road Called the plank Road where we halted. I went to the rear in a sort of a jog trot as I wished to save some of my Coffey which I carried with me on the run. This little incident I never forgot yet I have forgotin many things. I may say Coffey was the life and strenght of our human existence we had nothing else to drink except water and so acustomed had we become to it, when we could not get it we were some what low spirited and discontented. we rested on the plank road that night and in the early morning were ready for duty again. Our Brigade General was taken Prisoner. he tried to Rally the men but the[y] paid no attention to him. The Brake as fare a[s] I could hear was Not a serious one. if it occurred early in the day it might have had a Bad result. [...]

In the morning May the 6th the Second Corps attacked the Enemy driving them before them. The engagement became General [...] In the Evening the fight became harder a veray strong attack was made by the Confederates driving Back our line but were met By our Artillerty which drove them Back again This put an end to the fighting for the day with heavey losses on Booth sides Lee fell Back to Spottsylvania Court House. The prospect of a long Campaigne was before us long marches and very little rest night or day. Lying on the ground when chance afforded a short repose and sleeping soundly in the midst of Dainger Perhaps the last sleep who Could tell. [...] if not on the March or changing positions some of the men were as Industrious as moles trowing up the eartht in front of us diging up the ground with our Bayonets knifes or any kind of an instrument we Could get although, it might not be ordered to do so. Instinctively the Soldiers worked til Daligt (daylight) came, as it might afford them some Slight cover in the morning if attacked. In Grants Campaigne from the Wilderness to Petersburgh when the Enemy were compeld to give way the[y] were allways ready to meet us Behined there Breastworks day after day till we Crossed the James River and Commenced the Siege of Petersburg which was the key of Richmond. On the morning of the 12th (May) Hancock commenced Battle again driveing the Enemy before him Captureing three Generals thirty guns and about four thousand Prisoners. Then the Rebels attacked him in great force. The Sixt Corps came to the seport of Hancock and the Battle continued with great fuery untill dusk and commenced again about nine p.m. The fight was Continued trough the night for several hours. at last Lee fell Back again the[y] were pursued along distance by some of our Troops. on some ocasions the loud and continued Role of the Musketry fire was someting awful. It seems to me what narrow escapes hundreds perhaps thousands of men must have unless it was the Mercey of God. Thousands of Bullets high and low and middle Range passing trough the air unseen and with the velosity of Lightning. On the 13th and 14th there was very little fighting. The Roads were Bad. There was a deal of grumbling and murmuring among some of the Troops against what the[y] called Bucking against Breastworks which were of the most formadable Caracter I saw holes in the ground Behined some of those Brestworks Built with logs and covered over on top looking like little casemates which would hold one or two officers under shell fire I concidered them perfectly safe. where I stood looking at these great defences a Terrable Battle was fought the day Before. The looke of everything Round about Bore traces of a dedly struggle the grass the trees and the thinest srub in front of the works were cut down. I noticed one dead Body in Particuler near the Breastworks it was one of our men dureing the whole of my expearience in this War I never saw a Body so completely riddled with Bullets. hundreds of wounded men have been Caught in the Middle of a Deadly fire betwen the lines of there own friends and that of the Enemy. what an awfull situation untill Death relieved them and put them out of Pain. But what about the Poor Soul Such is War. Where is the Glory unless it is the Cause of the Just. On the night of the 15th General Hancock took up a Position on the right he Commanded the Second Corps, whom it may be said done more than its share of the hard fighting in this War. [...] early in the morning the Battle commenced the Corcoran Legion fought in line with the Irish Brigade. It was a hard Battle with heavey losses on Booth sides. On the 19th the Enemy Captured a large number of our waggons but the[y] were retaken again. from Spottsylvania Lee fell Back beyond the North Anna. On the 21st two of our army Corps followed him up Lee turned on them, But with the assistance of the Sixt Corps our troops repulsed the determined assault of the Enemy. On the 26th we crossed the River. afterwards we Crossed the Pamunkey at Totopotomoy Creek there was some fighting at Hanover Court House. The Enemy were found North of the Chickahominy. late in the evening the[y] attacked us but were drivein Back loosing some of there Intrenchments. Next came the Battle of Cold Harbour a very unfortunate one for us. [...] It was some time in the Evening when we came to Cold Harbour my Regiment halted and stacked arms. I counted ninety Rifils in the Stacks for the whole Redgiment. So deplated (depleted) had we came not anuff for a full Company. wee had a short rest siting down on our Knapsacks some injoying themselfs smokeing there Black Pipes, others Brooding over the Miseries of there soldire life and whishing for the end of the War and a change of life. I felt troubled and was thinking of the past and present. In front of us and stretching fare to the Right and left was a hevey Timber Land with an opening hear and there for tillage. all was very quiet. as the Troops came along the[y] turned to the right or left off the Road and were hid away in the Timber. The Enemy opened on us with one or two Batteries of Artillery fireing Shot and Shell there range was good. we lay low waithing for Orders. There fire was becomming more accurate and close to us, there Shells Bursting and scathering there fragments in all directions some times strikeing the earth in front of us and Bounding over us, demolishing a stack of muskets and passing close to our position. Now and then a Blinding dash of sand or gravel was trown up into our faces Biting our flesh and stuning us for a moment this cruial (cruel) and Daingerous suspense did not last long. a Battery of Artillery trotted up to us and soone placed its self in Position, shelling the Woods in front of us. to the Right the sound of Battle was hered. we then moved out in three short lines and advanced into the woods. we Continued onward up and down with a wave like motion expecting every moment to meet with deadly Resistance from the enemy. The Battery in rear sheld the ground in our front as we moved forward now and then one of our shells exploded in the air over us. Some one would say dam them Rottin shells the[y] will do us more harm then good. The noise and din in the woods was very Strange and Weird like. the Battery in our rear ceased fireing. we were then under fire but not of a serious nature. at this Point we were on the extream left whil[e] the hevey part of the fighting was higher up on the Right. I was Struck about the legs with gravel and Bits of stones several times. about six yards to my right I heard a thud like sound. Two men of my Regiment the front and rear rank man were [k]nocked out of the ranks with as much ease as if the[y] were two chickens and dashed against the ground where the[y] lay flat and motionless killed by a Cannon Ball. One was a German and the other an Irishman named Bermingham from Dublin McNamara an Irishman next the German was splashed with Blood and got pale and nevious (nervous) he came down to me I saw the man was weak. I told him to go to the rear and sit down for awhile. I was sorry for Bermingham, he was the victim of a Drunken wife in New York who ruined him and his Business. it was then dusk I expected every moment to see our first line engaged with the enemy. everything seemed very hazey and vapory with a soft mellow glow of the setting sun. yet there was no Signe of the enemy in our front our first line parted in the Middle and the files began to open out and glide off to the Right and left and were soone lost sight of in the Cover of the trees. the second line soone followed, looking round I saw we were alone our little Regiment was standing in a hollow well Covered by the riseing ground in front of us. about twenty of us went up the riseing ground and stood on top of a small knoll. to our amasement a Short distance below us were the Enemies Brestworks. we were Surprised comming almost unexpectedly on top of them in the gloomeing we could see no one it looked to me like a vision or a dream. we could do nothing it would be unwise to procede farther. we turned about to return when a ratling volley was poured into us fortunatly no one was hurt farther to the Right some of our troops had gained a strong Position which the[y] held for two hours despite the attacks of the Enemy til Lee shortened his line and masking his troopes in front of our men drove them Back with very hevey loss night put an end to the conflict, which ended very disastrous for us, but did not stay the forward movement of Grant to the James River. After the Battle of Cold Harbour we had a fue Days rest untill the Pontoone Bridge Across the James River were completed for the passage of the Troops. we then Crossed the River without any interruption [...] On the 22nd of June the Sixt and Second Corps advanced towards the Weldon Railroad, but did not succeed in their obgect. Grant now laid siege to Petersburgh with the James River as his Base. The Enemy's works were very formadable. we commenced to dig and entrench ourselfs round Lees works presenting every feature of enginering skill. about one thousand guns were placed in Position Compriseing field guns Howitsers morters and siege Guns of very large Calabre the Confederate Sharp Shooters were allways peging away where ever an uncautious head apeared over the works. water Carryers often runing great Risks from the dedly aim of the ever watchful Enemy who were allwayes well concealed. one Poor fellow an Irish Man who did not reinlist and who had only one or two Months to serve raised his head above the Parapit and was shot dead trough the neck. On one ocasion I was comming trough the woods in rear when I neared the works about half a Dozen Bullets struck the ground quite close to me. This was not allways the cace, as we had many a Respite from this Murdering Business. Some times the[y] were more spiteful and on the alert. On manny Ocasions dureing the War the Pickets were disposed to keep quiet and friendly towards each other as long as there was no trespass on either side. at the Rappahannock River when on Picket duty the *Johnys* on one side and the *Yankes* on the other. The Irish were more friendly at times with the Confederate pickets then the Americans. Now and then Some little exchanges took place Pieces of wood or a rudely Constructed Boat containing a newspaper was sent a cross in exchang for ainother. Sometimes our men would send over a small quantaty of Coffey in return for tobaca. as Coffey is not an American product the South soone run short of that article There soldiers in lue of Coffey used to roast the Indian Corn and pound it up for use as Coffey.

About the Begining of August the Rebel Generals Early and Breckinridge again invaded Maryland and Pennsylvania first driveing the troops out of the Shenandoah Vally and entering Maryland and Burning Chamsbersburgh [sic]. Raiding and

Carrying away the Crops, the Enemy recrosed the River Rich in Booty and Retired slowly down the Valley. at this time Grant was undermineing a Portion of the Enemies works. The Sixt Corp was Ordered to Washington, which was in a sort of Pannick the Enemy having made an apearence outside the Forts to what extent we did not know. But Grant was not to be drawn away from Petersburg where he had setled down waithing further events by this show of invasion. as long as Lee and the main part of his Army remained in his front Grant would stay where he was. The Sixt Corps Commanded by Major General Wright Broke camp at 12 O Ck in the night and was soone on the march. Some of our Boys wondering where the devil are we goin now. *oh the Lord knows where* was the response, Soldiers are curious there was all sorts of congectures. We turned our Backs on Petersburgh trough the thick woods as if we were stealing away everything was so quiet and orderly. We Passed Grants Head quarters and were soone in rear of our right wing. Now and then the Booming of Guns and the alternate Rattle of Musketry Broke the calm stillness of the night. An ocasionil bom shell darted up through the air with a fiery trail and desending on the Rebel works with a loud explosion. This Continued until we were fare away to the rear, out of sight and hearing and Burried in the dark woods. There long arms stretching out over us as wee marched along the narrow powderly Road Choked with dust, while our little friends the fire fly were constantly flickering about with there little lamps, and the continuous noise and din of insect life and the croking of frogs forming a very unharmonious sound kept our ears awake, with the plaintive Cry of that lone night Bird, our Soldiers called the *Whip or Will*, acompanied us on our nights march till we came to the James River, where we rested ourselves nearly all day untill the transports were ready to take us to Washington. we were now asshured where we were going to. I had a refreshing Bath in the River and a general Brush up and a short knap in the shade which refreshed me very much. In the Evening we were sailing down the River a gentle zeper (zephyr) faned our Sun Burnt faces, leaning on the Rail and looking towards the shore passing Sean after Sean on the River Bank. I bethout to myself how favored America has been by the God of Nature with its Noble Rivers and inland Seas. On the 13th of July we arrived in Washington, and at onst marched out on Seventh Street and on the Road near Fort Stephens. There was some fireing near the Fort betwen some advance Parties of the Rebels and our men Stationed in the defences. Part of our Corps took up a Position in front. I heard there was a Bayonet charge which drove the enemy Back. Night came on and the Big Guns in Fort Stevens ceased fireing. [...] we remained all night in the Forts and entrenchments a strict watch was keped dureing the night. hear and there the Dark Skye was lit up by the Blazeing fire of some home stead as the Enemy fell Back. In the morning we started in pursuit of the Rebels. after a march of about fiveteen miles we halted at the Cross Roads in Maryland. The next day we marched to Poolsville. The enemy made a Slight Stand and then fell Back. on the 16th a Rebel Spy was hung up in presence of a larg[e] number of Troops. On the 17th we started again in pursuit of the raiders. at Whites Ford we halted in a short time our Artillery took up a Position on the hight covering the River after a fue shots the Enemies Skirmishers fell Back again scampering over the hills. We forded the River and pushed on in the direction of LeesBurgh, In the Louden (Loudoun) Valley, and encamped five or six miles from the Town. We rested hear nearly two days, which we needed very much. we were then getting tired marching about without any result. how many times have I heard men whishing that the Enemy would apear in our front and stop our marching on the dusty Pike Road even at the risk of Battl[e]. This timely rest enabled a lot of straglers to catch up and join there Commands. On the 19th we Connected with General Mulligan and Crooks Forces at Snickers Gap, one of the Natureal gateways leading from the Blue Ridge to the Shenandoah Valley, called the Garden of Virginia. about two hundred miles long, very wide in some parts fertile and enclosed on each side by Hills and Mountains well watered and Inhabated by old Time setlers who have an Old fashoned way about them, liveing in comfortable Homesteds and plenty of fruit and other neceseries of life. After passing trough Snickers Gap we heared Cannonading in front of us And a conciderable rattle of Musketry. General Crooks' men were fording the Shenandoah River and were engaged with the Enemy. part of there line gave way and Brooke to the rear and recrosed the River which was shallow at the fords and deep in some places. in there haste I heared some of them were drowned. The Enemy followed them up Briskly But were checked and compeled to fall Back by an Artillery fire from our side of the River. Just then the 1st Devision Sixt Corps came on the ground. Close to the River some of the Enemies Shells Burst near us knocking over some of our men. It was then near dark. The next day we rested and on the twenty first we croosed the River again. The rear guard of the Rebels had left early in the morning, while there main Body with a conciderable amount of Booty were at Winchester farther up the Valley. we were moveing on after them. dark Clouds were gathering over our head when the storm Burst and the Rain came down in Torrents. in a Short time we were wet to the skin and the arder and excitement of the Pursute dwindled down to very little. with a great deal of Care I preserved a picture of my young sister in Dublin which I had recently received from there. This gave me more concern then the drownding Rain storm which we were subgected to for a short time. The rain ceased and the sun shone out Bright and warm again. our water soaked garments commenced to steam and dry up while we continued our march along the mud pudle road towards Winchester. about Noone in the Day we halted and rested all the afternoone in the woods. five or six miles in our front a Smart Cannonade was going on which lasted for some time. we had orders to march in the night for Washington. The pursute was ended and the Raiders were allowed to gang free, after making a very suckessful Tour trough part of Maryland and [k]nocking at the door of Washington and frightning Baltimore, cutting wires and Burning the Governor of Maryland's House. Besides captureing destroying and threatining. But the[y] did not suceede in withdrawing Grant from Petersburgh the key of Richmond. Our Corps arrived near Washington after a march of Seventy Miles. we expected to rest ourselves for Several Days But were disapointed. Confederate Scouting parties were hovering about on the Upper Potomac which caused a state of unrest in Washington and all sorts of rumours were flying about in Camp, when The arrival of the paymaster put us all in good humer (humour). it is a great Day in Army life every one has money old scores are squared and checks are Sent away to Wifes Fathers Mothers and other dependents in all parts of the Country. on the other hand thousands of Dollars is spent in Washington on amusements Drunkness and other exceses. Venders were going about our Camp selling Cakes pies and Cigars while the contreband whiskey smuglers useing all sorts of disguises, done well with those who were in a pleasurable mood. This did not last long we were ordered on the March again going over the same old ground. after marching seventeen miles we halted. The weather was intensely warm. we passed trough Frederick and on to Harpers Ferry and back again to Frederick. we lost a number of men by Sun Stroke and straglers unable to continue on the march left the ranks and sought shelter under the trees and fences or anything that might shade themseves from the Constant heat of the sun till the Cool of the Evening and then start on the Road again. we encamped near the Monocasey [sic] River for about two Days and marched Back again to Harpers Ferry. at last we had a change of Commanders.

Major General Philip Sheridan was sent by Grant from Petersburgh to take command of the Army of the Shenandoah This intrepid Irish American officer lost no time in prepareing his Command for real work insted of marching up and down the valley. at this time a Brooklyn Regiment was consolideted with our Regiment the 65th this Brought us to the required strength I was then mustered in a[s] 2nd Liutenent of Co. H same Regiment and took command of the Company, the Captain been on detached service. for a short time General Sheridan marched and remarched his men while he know doubt was forming his plans, and trying to estamate the strenght and position of the Enemy. [...] after some skermishing and a little affair at Front Royal, when our Cavalry captured 300 Prisoners, Sheridan moved forward from Berryville at dawn on the morning of 19th of September 1864. on the Road to Winchester after Marching for a number of miles we heared the faint Sound of Musketry in front, which became more audable as we advanced. our Cavalry was skirsmishing with the enemy from an early hour in the morning and were much in neede of seport while we pushed on as rapetly as possible. The crack crack of the Seven Shooters of our Cavalry sounded very near and that the[y] were hotly engaged. we expected a Battle this time for Certain. we passed a large wall tent on the side of the road. A fue yards in front of the Tent lay an ugly heap of legs and arms reeking with Blood and mangled flesh inside the tent the Surgents were Busey with the knife while the stretcher Bearers were comming in from the front with wounded men. as we neared the Battle field, relieving our Cavalry who were very hard pressed all the morning. our Troops formed line and commenced fireing our Brigade was in reserve in rear of the left wing. The Enemy atacked our left Centre. at this Point part of our line Brooke to the rear I was very much surprised at this as the Confedarate attack was very weak. our Brigade moved to the Right in duble quick time and filled up the gap and fired a volley in the face of the Rebels who went Back as fast as the[y] came. our line then moved forward while the Enemy continued to fall Back fireing we sometimes moved in the double quick then halting and fireing again. our Artillery were well up to the front. I was very near one of the Batteries and was much pleased at the coolness and promtness of the Cannoners in action. all day long we pushed Back the Enemy who were not strong anuff to offer a serious resistance untill close to Winchester where the Enemy were Posted Behined some worn out earth works. Sheridan halted his Troops and formed line and looking well to his flanks in the arraignement of his troops leaveing nothing to chance. we then advanced our line moved forward and the Cavalry on our left charged the enemy and were soon among them slashing right and left with there sabres. The Enemy Broke to the rear every man for himself princibly making for the Main Street of the Town followed by our Cavalry in hot pursuit, and a Battery of light Artillery, now and then unlimbering and fireing several Shots after the Retreating Enemy who were drivein beyond the Town and dispersed. our losses were light But our Cavalry suffered severly in the morning fighting against od[d]s for several Hours til about noon. one of our Cavalry was Bringing in a prisoner when a Bullet from the Enemy relieved him of his charge who dropet dead at the horses feet. it was then Sun down we all felt relieved and and [sic] in good Spirits. Sheridan had won his first Battle in the Shenandoah where there had been so many defeats and inspired great Confidence in his men who allways Called him little Fill. after the Battle our men staked arms and unslung there Knapsacks expecting to Rest for the night after a long Days work marching and fighting under a Broiling Sun But were doomed to disapointment when the order came to fall in and march again, the Sixt Corps to follow the Caval[r]y in Rear. we passed trough the Town of Winchester unotised (unnoticed) by any of the Inhabatents who did not flee the Town. Now and then a fair hansome face might be sean of the Maryland Type slyly peeping at a corner of a window at our war worn veterns, as we joged along the dusty Road, not knowing how fare we were going or when or where we were going to halt. we had no time for Coffey or a light repast yet our haversacks were not emthy. we were tired out. on the 21st (September) after marching till dark we came very near the Enemies Position at Fisher Hill who were strongly posted on the side of a hill, which Bordered the valley. My Regiment was ordered on picket duty that night. I was in command of the Picket line as fare as my Regiment went. I posted my men very quietly the[y] knew the rest themselves. after a wachful vigilence dureing the night and day light began to appear, I saw a number of little hillocks along the line which the men trew up and Built dureing the night for cover some of them Big anuff for Two men at there Post. about gun Shot Range in front of us we discerned Some of the Enemies Pickets looking to the rear I saw Three long Blue lines aproaching us in perfect order. I at onst took in the Situation and ordered my men to commence fireing which was at onst responded to by the Rebel pickets. I took particular notice to a wild looking Irishman that stood near me whose antecedents and od[d] ways was well none (known) in the Regiment. he was loading and fireing as fast as he coud, his large Blue or grey ies (eyes) looking like fuery his features set with a Slight tip up in his Broad nose which gave him a saucy and defiant aspect. while loading his piece he was reciteing Some prayers in a jumbling sort of way and ansious to have another shot, then Bringing up his gun to the present, he would shout, now Jeff Davis, you Son of a Bitch take that. giveing his head a twist at the same time and his ies (eyes) looking wildly to the front he repeated this severel times til the front line was drawing near we then ceased fireing. The Three lines past trough our picket line and went forward and were Soon engaged with the Enemy, who were caught in the rear By a force which Sheridan sent round there flank during the night. After the lines passed our Regiment pushed on to the front. a Cannon Ball pased me going between a section of fours and clean trough a large tree. fortunetly no one was indured It was a Close Shave. The Enemy finding themselfs attacked in rear, Broke and ran. a large force of Cavalry with the Sixt Corps followed them who in a short time were no where to be seen. we went up the Valley for sixty miles to Stauntin [sic] and rested for a short time and returned Back again to Cedar Creek. on our March Back The Cavalry Burnt all corn and fodder where ever found on right left and centre. at Cedar Creek when we were resting ourselves in faincied security the valley was cleaned out for a Conciderable distance and our Army suffisciently Strong anuff for present Purposes with a wide awake General in Chief we little dreamed the Surprise that was Instore for us. Grant was so well pleased he thought he might order Back again the 6th Corps to Petersburgh. In Compliance with the order we commenced our March for Washington, but someting turned up Sheridan ordered us Back again. on the 19th of October the day of the Battle of Cedar Creek Sheridan was at Winchester about 19 Miles from our encampment General Wright who commanded the 6th Corps was in command in his absence our force Consisted of the 6th Corps Two Devisions of the 19th Corps who came from Louisiana the[y] had very little fighting we of the Army of the Potomack [sic] did not think much about them. we had a fine Cavalry force under Merrit and Custer and about thirty pieces of Artillery. early on the Morning of the 19th we were lyeing Peacefully in our tents. we were aroused from our slumbers By hevey fireing on our left which came nearer while we hurriedly dressed ourselfs and fell into ranks. we moved to the left as quickly as possible and were Soon within Range of the Enemies Bullets which were beginning to take effect on us. we coud not see the Enemy who were covered by the Trees and a dense fog above and below which Shrouded the Landscape in its

Misty form. our men looked serious and thoughtful But yet firm. our left wing was surprised drove Back and Broken up The[y] were no longer usefull and were streaming down the valley and along the Pike Road. with perfect coolness the 6th Corps formed line and Commenced fireing My Regiment was on the left of the line an Irishman in My Company was struck By a piece of a Shell on his Blanket wich was roled up tight on the top of his Knapsack, which save his Life. he was a Bit Shaken But still keped his place in the Ranks. after some time my Company was Thining out fast many of them Lay dead on the ground, and wounded men were going to the rear, making ugly gaps in the line The absence of Sheridan was felt very much as the men had no confidence in the ability of General Wright who was dooing all he could to stem the torrent of the victorious Enemy who were Constantly working round our left. We were loosing hevey and could not stand it any longer halfe of the men in my Company were kild (killed) and wounded, and the Two Devisions of the Ninteentht Corps who were surprised broken up and in retreat.

At this stage of afairs I could See we were Beaten, and the fog not lifting. we must fall Back and get away from the flank fire of the enemy. Our Coloneal gave the order to Bout Face with the intention of moveing a Short distance to the rear when he was shot dead at the same time I was wounded in the left hip just as I faced about. I made my way to the rear in a short time I grew faint after going some distance I was still in range of the enemies fire and not out of Danger. all at onst I saw Sheridan Sweeping round the Corner of a Wood and comming along Pell Mell on his favoret Black Charger the Poor Animal was flecked with foam and as wet as if comming out of a river after his Race from Winchester. the sight of Sheridan comming on the ground Created great enthusiasm in his troopes. I was very glad to see him, and thought to myself the day was not all lost yet, as I knew a Portion of our troops had preserved there organization princibly the Sixt Corps, and our Cavalry and a fue Batteries of Artillery. about this time I met a soldier of my Regiment who was leading a horse belonging to our dead Coloneal. with his Kind assistance I mounted the horse and in a short time came to one of our field Hospitals a great wall tent. when I dismounted, Two or three surgeons were standing outside of the Tent fortunately for me one of them was our Regimentle Surgeon. he handed me a large flask of Brandy and told me to take a good drink of it. I thanked him the small sup of Brandy revived me a little. He then examined my wound and said I was very luckey that my hip Bone was not Smashed. When I unloosed my Sword Belt I felt something cold and hevey drop down betwen my drawers and left leg, it was a connical shaped Bullet flatened on one side near the point The bullet must have struck me from an oblique direction had it struck me squarely on the hip the result would have been more serious for me. the Ball passed round the hip bone and came out near the belt plate. the Brass link where the plate hooked on was stretched out of shape. the tent was full of wounded men lyeing on the ground in two rows witht there feet oposet each other. One poor fellow a German next to me had a very Bad wound he was very weak and moaning all the time. There seemed to be a lull in the fighting as I could hear no fireing. we were Badly Beatin with the loss of nearly all our guns transportation and other property and from three to four thousand kild (killed) and wounded. about 4 o clock fireing commenced again, which continued with more or less Severity which lasted untill near dusk when it ceased, and we received the joyfull new of a Glorious Victory of Little Fill over (General) Early taking Back all our guns, and those of the Enemy forty pieces and all other property which the[y] posest (possessed). Some time in the night after sleeping soundly for three or four hours I awoke. there was nere a stir or a moan from the German. I put my hand on his fored (forehead) the poor fellow was dead. I called some of the assistents and the Body was

Removed. The next day was very quiet. our men were back in there old camps again. The story of the Battle was in every one's mouth I was very ansious to get all the Particulers of this very remarkable fight the day was lost and wone. one little incident pleased me very much. Pat McCormack a young Irishman who had only one years Service was the heroe of the Regiment. in the evening when our men were pressing forward on the enemy the Regimental line became irregular and the files opening out the Officer in Command wished to halt the Regiment and perfect the alignment Pat rushed to the front and shouted come on Boys while we are forming the Johnies will be forming too. The Regiment doubled its pace and with Bold McCormack swept the rebels from there front who brook (broke) up and retreated. There was a Breach of discipline hear, but the victory was so complete and everyone in good humour, Pat escaped censure. The Troopes went Back to there old camp ground again. The valley Campaigne was over. [...] The next day Sheridan issued an order granting a leave of absence for one month to all wounded officers who were slightly wounded and able to avail of the privalage, a source of gratification to a great many. your umble servant was one of those who with the aid of a Crutch started for New York. When I arrived there I was able to do without the stick and with the aid of a stout cane got along very well. dureing the time the Sixt Corps went Back again to Petersburgh. at the end of my leave of absence I reported myself Back at the U.S. Hospital Annapolis Maryland the Cappitol of the State. The Naval Academy is hear where a large number of young men are trained for the Navy. I had a very pleasent time hear and found some very pleasent and jovial fellows among the officers, who when going for a walk, or viseting in the Town allways wished to have me with them. My friend the Major had made a good many friends for himself in the Town, who were nearly all in sympathy with the Southt. My first introduction in the Town was by the Major, to a good old fashioned famaly who occupied a large Red Brick House of the Colonial days. The famaly concisted of Two young Laidies a young man a Brother, and another who was an officer in the Confederat army his portrait in oil hung in one of the spacious Parlors, which the[y] were so kind to show us and other objects of Interest heir looms, everything was good and old fashioned, not often seen in this go a head modern country There Father had been a West Indian planter at one time. when the emancipation of the slaves took place he emigrated to the United States. the Major dubed me Captain in spite of myself when he was introduseing me to the young Laidies I felt very shy of this as the[y] might know by my Shoulder Straps I was only a Second Lieutenant with nere a Bar on my shoulder straps which would require two to make me Captain. These People were very nise friendly and natural in there manner. The[y] entertained us in a moderate and genteel way. in Conversation we avoided Politics and the War as much as possible. One sister was secess (seceeder) and the other union. when we called, not often, we amused ourselves at card playing checkers and musick. The[y] were good Catholics and I think of Irish desent, but regular Southern People. after a short aquaintinship the Brother asked me to join him in opening a Saloone in Town if I coud get my discharge, and that he would Bear all expenses. he did not know I was married, so I declined the offer alledging I could not procure my discharge. I was detained in Anapolis [sic] for about Two months. although it was midwinter my time Past very pleasently, one way or another. I was acting Adjutant with nothing to do but Mount the Hospital guard every morning. At length I was ordered to the front again but like Mickey Free in Charles O'Malley *Its little for Glory I'd care* I had anuff of the long weary War.

The Fall of Petersburgh and Richmond

In the begining of February 1865, I rejoined my Regiment at Petersburgh, Va. On the 3rd of the month I was mustered in as 1st Lieutenant of Company C. we were resting quietly in our Camps save now and then the Booming of a gun in our works reminded us of the Constant watchfulness and alertness along our front. [...] late in the evening of the first of April the officers of our Regiment received an order to turn in all there Bagage and everything that could be dispenced with on the line of march, and to label all our property. we then went to the Surgeons tent and received a roll of cottin Bandage for the next day's work in cace we needed the use of them in Bandaging wounds wheather for ourselves or others. it was an eventful evening Big with hope and contemplation of the work before us. a certain number of axes were distributed to different Regiments to cut away fallin Trees abbatise which might Block our way. when all was done I retired to my tent. I was thinking of tomorrow what a mystery. it was said Grant expected to loose twenty thousand men in the assault, and the most eventful day of the whole War. Big with faitht, there was no certenty on tomorrow. about eight o clock p.m. I stretched myself on my cot in the tent. I tried to get a short knap as there could be no rest dureing the night. I could not sleep. There was an unseual quiet all along our lines. I listened for the Signal gun for the Bombardment of Petersburgh, which was to take place about 10 o ck p.m. and to last for Two hours or more. at last there goes the first gun I jumped to my feet to see the fire works. in a fue minutes near one thousand Guns of various calabre were raining shot and shell bolt and bar on the Confederat works. you would think it hell let loose the din and noise and the hevey vibrations of the larger guns fire jumping from there mouths, and the firey trail of the Bombs after leaving the morters discribeing circles in the air then descending with a loud crash all commingly together was a sight and sound not easily forgottin. The Troops assembled in fighting order and marched out of there works to the different places assigned them. the Sixt Corps, moved out very cautious and moveing Slowly along so as not to alarm the enamies Pickets. we lay on our arms all night trying to see trough the darkness in front listining to the Roar of our Guns. at the dawn of Morning on the Second we started off on the double quick to the front with a very peculiar cry from some of our Regiments which sounded like this hie, hie, hie, hie, hie...As soone as the enamies Pickets saw us the[y] flew to the rear scarcely waithing to fire a Shot. in a very short time we came in vieu (view) of the enamies works which were of a very formadable nature. Some grap[e] shot struck in front of us no harm was done. we could scarcely beliefe our sences or our ies (eyes) no one apeared on the works There was no defence But of a very triveal nature a result so unexpected, we realy did not know ourselves had these works been properly maned the consquence might have been very disastrous for us. we passed trough a small opening in the great stakes stuck upright in the ground close together and pointed sharp on top. hear Lieutenant Grogan of my Regiment handed me a flask of Brandy, and congratulating ourselves on our good fortune we crossed over the embankment and Cut the Southt side railroad the only link which connected Richmond with the Southt. On our Right the 9th Corps, not so fortunate as we were had a very tuff fight. Now and then a cannon ball striking the ground on our right Bounding over or between us Causeing some of us to shift our place and give them Room. The fact of the 6th Corps geting in so easily, Lee must have weakened his Centre in order to resist Sheridan on there Right. [...] The enemies loss was hevey in kild (killed) wounded and Prisoners and a large number of Guns. Sheridans Victory at Five Forks was the key note to the fall of Petersburgh and Richmond. Lee made a firm stand at the Town of Petersburgh attacking the 9th Corps with great vigour. in the last charge he lost one of his famous fighting Generals, A. P. Hill after four years service was Killed. The next day Sunday at 11 A. M. President Davis was Informed while attending Church Service at Richmond of the defeat of Lee and the fall of Petersburgh. during the night Lee collected his Army together about thirty thousand men and retreated Southt West. [...] Our Army followed Lee, Sheridan with the Cavalry and the 5th Corps leading. [...] On the 4th the enemy were at Amelia Court house. on the 5th we came in sight of there Train going uphill and down hollow, oh how we did long to get within Range but they held their pace while we coud gain nothing on them. we toiled along for hours, still there was the Train and there were us, draging ourselves along the dusty road tired out unable to go faster. Close on the Enamies rear a Battery of Artillery shelled the train at a very long range with little effect. a Constant skirmish was kept up on with there rear guard, untill the Enemy reached Sailors [sic] Creek. we passed trough a small place called Farmers Ville. it Contained several houses for dry- ing tobacco the[y] were in flames the heat was intence. the Place was looted. tobaco was very Plentiful most of it of very good quality. it lay about everywhere we were walking on it in the street it was scathered along the Road for several miles. Some of our men trough there Covetousness of the weed encumbered themselfs with the stuff, were droping it on the road as we went along. At Sailors [sic] Creek Sheridan overhalled the enemy a short Brisk engagement took place, Captureing General Ewel [sic] and all that was left of his Corps and four other Generals. I went up to General Ewell, to have a good look at the old Man who was my Commanding Officer five years before at Fort Buchaning [sic] Arizona when I was serving there in the 8th U.S. Infantry. The next day the 7th the Enemy were still in Retreat but were so hotly pursued the[y] had not time to complete the destruction of the Bridge when they were attacked by the Second Corps compelling them to retreat and captureing Eighteen guns from the Enemy. Lee was very much harrashed in his retreat loosing all the time, and his Army growing weaker. On the 9th he found himself surrounded. Sheridans Cavalry was in his front and the Infantry in his rear. he then resolved to cut his way out, By attacking Sheridan. he commanded General Gordon to cut his way trough. Our Cavalry who dismounted and fought on foot retireing Slowly till the Infantry came to there suport. Our Cavalry then mounted and charged the Enemy on the flank. a flag of truce apearing the[y] halted and sat firmly in there saddles some of them leaning over as if to hear and see what was going on. The Infantry brought down the Butt of there Rifils on the ground ansiously waching and waiting for the next order. The whole Army stood still. We heard that Lee was surrounded and coud do nothing But surrender. We were waithing for the news that would at last Bring us Peace when a mounted officer galloped towards us and with uplifted sword announced the unconditional surrender of General Lee. There was loud Cheers our soldiers almost wild with excitement, trowing their caps up in the air and manifesting every symptom of joy and sadisfaction at the termination of the War after four years of the fiercest struggle I may say, known in history. Lee the greatest of all the Confederate Generals and second to none in the Union Army, handed his sword to Grant. he told Lee to keepe his Sword and issued an order that all the Confederate officers keep there swords and horses, likewise all mounted men to retain there Horses, as the[y] might need them for the Springs plowing. Rations was then issued to the starving troops and the Blue and the Gray mingled together talking over there Battles and discourcing with one another in a most friendly manner The Confederate Generall Johnston down Southt had not yet Surrendered. Sheridans Cavalry with the 6th Corps were ordered to Danville North Carolina to assist Sherman if required. when we arrived there after marching about one hundred miles, we came Back again. Johnston surrendered to Sherman. While we were away, the main body of the Army started for Washinton [sic] and on the way passing through Richmond. The[y] were reviewed by the President and his Cabinet. It was a grand spectacle. Our Corps rested a fue days at Burksvill [sic], when the terrable news of the Shooting of President Lincoln by Booth the actor was announced to us. we all felt as if stund for a moment why So good a man as honest Old Abe when Peace was Restored was murdered in Cold Blood by a Southern Symphatiser and a non Combatent. we were amased to think of such wicketness and folly. as for the assassin who if he had ninety nine lives must be giveing up, so much was the wrath of the People, and the Sorrow the[y] felt for such a purposless Crime. Booth if caught should suffer the severest penalty.

From Burksville our Corps marched to Richmond passing trough the City every one eager to get our money. there Bills we called shinplasters were no good the nigers on the sidewalks were ofering Confederate money to us for sale I was offered a Thousand Dollar Bond for ten cents. our Boys were Buying them as souveners of the Rebellion. Part of the City along the River Side was Burnt down and in ruins. we continued our march to Washington and encamped at Halls Hill Virginia a short distance from the City. preparetions were then making for the disbanding of the Volunteer forces a fast as possible. June the first I received a tellagrahm from New York, stateing my Wife was Seriously ill, come as quick as Possible. after Some Trouble I received a leave of absence for tenn days, and at onst set out for New York. when I got there my Wife was dead and burried the day before. when I went Back to Halls Hill I had a great deal to do in winding up the afairs of my Company. I was Discharged on the Eleventh of June 1865 but could not go away. The Regiment was going to New York to be paid off and disbanded. when we arrived there we made our last march up Broad way. we were well received and had a plentiful Breakfast prepared for us by the Citizens. Regiments of United States Volunteers were disbanding all over the Country and were soone absorbed in the Publick life of the country without any seeming effect whatever. trade was good. we were Paid off and everyone went there own way. many of us who formed attachments comradeship for one another felt lonesome Bidding good by with the Kindest expresions of Regard parted perhaps never to meet again…

NEW YORK

On old Manhattan stands
The Empire City of this free Land
Where trade and wealth do multiply
And handsome buildings rearing high,
adorn this great City

Where once the primeval forest stood
Its stillness broken by the Mocking Bird
Whose mimic notes rang through the dell
Where nought but solitude did dwell.

The red man roamed the worlds about
And looked upon the waters
That washed the Beach of the lonely isle
With a sheen of gold on the flowing tide
Stretching out far and wide.

At length one day as history tells
When Hudson sailed away from Holland's shore,
But to explore this strange land far away.
Blessed with success he proudly sailed into the inner Harbour
The red man thought the great spirit had come
with white wings o'er the water.

He viewed the space and looked around.
The beauteous Harbour wide
Burst on the view of the Captain and crew
Of the stout little barque which lazily glides
For the mouth of the river and distant Isle,
A haven of shelter and rest.

From this we trace the Empire's great commercial Capital,
Bold pioneers of distant lands flocked hither with good will.
The hardy Dutch then crossed the sea
and soon themselves located,
They built a Fort, likewise a Town
New Amsterdam they named it.

Thus was New York in early days,
When Holland-Dutch new homes did make
with bricks imported from Amsterdam,
Thus was the Empire City began.
The town grew big, the town grew wide
In a quaint old way on Manhattan Isle.

Next came the English with a treaty granted by the Dutch
Into far away Manhattan and renamed the town New York
It was a great surprise to the sleepy little town
When they saw the English flag run up and
Their loved flag pulled down.

Then the English prospered in the West, their colonies extended,
From North to South they ruled supreme,
A wonderful land of forests and streams,
Of mighty rivers and ocean-like lakes,
Fruitful of soil and wealth.

The Colonials were of a thrifty race,
English, French and Dutch,

And a goodly number of the Irish race
Who held in their heart an undying hate
For the wrongs which their country suffered.

The English passed a stamp Act and tried to make it pay
But the Yankees growled and threatened,
Then the Act was soon repealed.
They taxed tea, paint and paper
Which only made them worse
And like disobedient children kicked up an awful fuss.

An English ship to Boston came loaded full of tea
But a band of Yankee Mohawks flung it in the sea.
First blood was shed at Lexington in a running fight
And the doughty British soldiers got a great surprise.
At Bunker Hill there Warren fell, the patriots
Made a stand. Repulsed, the British charged
Uphill and drove them back again.
On they came the second time, the redcoats up the hill,
Through want of ammunition the patriots lost the day.

A weary War did then ensue and many were the battles
'Til at York Town when victory crowned
The Continental Army, backed by the French
Whose timely aid the bird of freedom nobly saved
And made the British lion yield
That day in old Virginia.

A happy peace is now restored and freedom's
Flag is floating o'er a new-born race.
Long may it be fit emblem of Democracy,
Must guard their rights, the Constitution
maintain, less strife and greed bring ruin on their country.

A. J. Byrne 1830–1911

Military uniforms, left to right: Chasseur, Zoauve, U.S. Regular, Zouave volunteer.

Camp Middleton, New York, 1862.

Mount Vernon, Washington, 1862.

Firing on picket, 1862.

The picket line, 1862.

After the battle, Williambsburg, 6th May, 1862.

Monitor and Merrimac, encounter 1862.

Battle of Fair Oakes, 31st May, 1862.

Federal balloon taking a look at Confederate Camps, June 1862.

Battle of Beaver Creek, 26th June, 1862.

In retreat to Malvern Hill, 30th June, 1862.

The carried me to the surgeon's camp

Part of fortified camp at Harrison's Landing, July, 1862.

Rejoin my regiment at Brandy Station.

The line before the 'break-off' in the rear of the Old Log, 1864.

At Cold Harbour

Battle of Winchester, 1864.

Cedar Creek, October 20th, 1864.

The surrender of Lee, 9th April, 1865.

Chapter Six

The savage loves his native shore,
Though rude the soil or chill the air.
Well may Ireland's sons adore
An Isle which nature formed so fair.

∾

From 'The Irishman'—James Orr

The Fenian Movement

OUT OF TROUBLE IN TO MORE. I was now free But haveing the care of Two young children on me, and no fixed Purpose or a home to Bring them to, I resolved to visit Ireland and See my mother who would take care of them for a time untill further devellopements might take place more favourable to my mind. for about one week I gave myself up to a little pleasure going about sight seeing. But the midsummer heat in New York is to[o] oppressive you become fatagued and soone tires out you must then Betake yourself to a Saloone drink Lager or someting else and rest yourself till Sundown. at this time a very remarkable incident happened to me. I had a Room in the New England Hotell at the corner of Bowery and Bayard St. one night after partaking of too much wine with some friends I returned late to the Hotell and went up to my room. I thought I was all right there are many men, who after partaking of too much dring conciders themselves fit as I did, when under the influence of Drink. My Bed Room window was Closed, a small jet of gass was Burning which gave suffiscient light. a small fan light over the door when open ventilated the apartment. I had no recollection of seeing whether it was open or shut. I Blew out the gass and turned into Bed and was soon fast a sleep. in the morning I awoke with a Sickly feeling and a strong smell of gass in the Room. I at onst realised what I had done I looked up at the fan light it was open I shut of[f] the gas and thanked my God I was saved had the fan light been closed it might have ind[e]ed [been] fatel to me. But God wild (willed) it otherwise. My surprise at what I had done was very great. I felt myself very much humiliated at what might have been my last Mistake.

For some time Past a Portion of the Irish American press had been giveing glowing accounts of the spred of the Fenian organization in Ireland. Money was flowing into the Fenian exchequer. Bonds were printed with the promise to pay when the Irish Republick was established as if it was Certain to happen. a large number I think were Bought by Patriotic Irishmen who longed for the deliverance of there Native Land so dear to them in exile. I was Informed that night Drilling was going on in various parts of Ireland, and that a Semi Millitery organizeation existed which needed officers to lead them when the Riseing took place. I had an intervue with John O Mahoney at Head quarters in New York. I told him I was willing to go to Ireland he spoke to me with confidence. Matters where quickly setled I was not sworn I was pledged. The[y] supplied me with money for expences.

In a fue days I was on the Sea for Quens Town [sic] on Board the National Line Steam Ship Helvetia. On the passage my young Daughter became Sick with fever all my spare time was taken up with hir. I had very little intercourse with the Pasengers. I was not happy but I did not care to show it. The restraint which I felt myself under with my care and the Burden of a Secret Letter which I was to deliver to James Stevens in Dublin head Centre of the Fenian Organzation in Ireland, under the assumed name of Captain Power. in the letter I was Recommended to him as Captain Byrne, all right, and so fortht. after a fine Passage I landed in Queenstown, but coud not proceed to Dublin on account of the week condition of my Daughter. I remained for nine days in Queenstown. I felt a Bit Lonesom But the varied Beauty of the Harbour and an od[d] trip up to Cork on the River Steamers, what Charming Ceanery on the Broad expance of the River Lee, made my time more pleasent. This was my first viset to Cork which gave me great pleasure, but been alone and no one to Talk to except what little intercourse I had witht some of the natives I returned early to Queenstown and muse myself as Best I could, some times under the eye of a detectif well known in Queenstown that time as a Police spie, allways lofeing about the Harbor Side and watching pasengers going and Comming from the Atlantick Steamers. That fellow used to make a target of me with his eyes oh how I heated (hated) and despised him an Irish man with a Celtic name. after nine days spent in this way I started for Dublin. I came by Surprise to my Mother Sister Brother and Relations. The next day Sunday I viseted some of my friends who looked at me with much curiosity fresh looking and unimpared after my long campaigne. That evening I went to visit a friend of mine I felt unwell and returned Home again and went to Bed. I had a severe attack of fever on me which lasted four or five weeks. When I was able to go about I was ansious to deliver my credentials to Stephens which would make me allright. I found this a very difficult matter and was oblidged to proceede with great Caution, as I carried the document about my person when on the hunt for the Captain. after a fue days I was very much perplexed. I did not kno what to do. In my walks trough the City I saw a number of Irish Americans whome I easily recognised, But did not know any of them.

The Irish People The Organ of the Fenian Brotherhood was Published in Parliament Street. O'Donnavan Rossa [sic] was Editor of the Paper. Nealin [sic] the notorious Informer was then an employe of the paper. at last I made up my mind I would go and See Rossa in the office of the Paper, believeing he knew all about the Fenian Organiseation in Dublin, and try and get an interview with him and explain to him my Business and the letter which was several weeks overdue. If I was timed from New York to Dublin and not presenting the Letter on time might cause suspiscion on myself, this annoyed me. The day after I came to this Conclusion the office was Raided By the Police. The Paper was suppressed and O'Donovan Rossa Thomas Clark Lueby [sic] and I think others were arrested. On my way to Parliment Street seeing what was up I came Back again. At last trough a friend who had Known me for a number of years I was introduced to Coloneol Byron late an Officer in the Irish Brigade in America. The next evening I met the Coloneol by apointment we went to the European Hotell Bolton Street, where I met General Halpin one of Stephens Princible agents. He read The Letter and then Burnt it in the fire. It was not long till I was known to all the American Officers in Dublin, who were well known by the Police, and not above suspicion. The Fenian Organization was very extensive it had made its way trough all parts of Ireland. yet I had not much faith in the Movement as I had learned someting about War and the enormus responsibility attached to it. Besides not being Beligerents England could hang and shoot down hir Prisoners in the Most gleeful fashin unless some friendly Power would interfere. We Irish Americans, were amuseing ourselves about Town and waithing for the day without any apearient trouble as if waiting for a foot ball match. a very Poppouler resort of the American officers was Judes Royal Shades in Graftin [sic] Street a Publick House Hotell with a long narrow Consert Hall running back from the saloon and resorted Princibly by young Tory gents Trinity students and Army officers. we were a great eye sore to some of those fellows who conciders themselves the Superiour People. One night a number of our friends were in the Room. I was sitting at one of the little round Tables with Captain

Costello of New York when he called my attention to a scornful looking gent who was walking up and down the Hall, who had sneered at him several times. This roused the hot Blood of the Irish American. Come out to the Bar said he and see how I will fix that fellow. He called for two Drinks when out came the sneerer into the Bar when to my great surprise Costello struck him between the Two eyes and down him on the floor. The Bar maids got frightened and a great uproar ensued. in the confusesion wee shot out on [sic] the door as quickly as possible and jumped on an outside Car which fortunatly was standing Idle at the time the Car Man took in the situation at onst and drove off rappetly at onst down Graften [sic] Street, when wee heard the Cry of Police we were soone out of sight and and [sic] after a Race of about two miles we landed at an obscure Hotell in a Remote Part of the City. I was surprised at our little adventure. We tiped glasses with the Jarvey and gave him an extra shilling for his trouble. wee heard no more of this little incident afterwards, whitch might have caused us some trouble and Bring us more under the eyes of the Police. The Goverment after the suppresion of *the Irish People* then turned there attention to Stephens and locked him up in the City Prison, then concidering there Prisoner Perfectly safe But the Terrable fenians got Stephens out over the wall in rear of the Prison on the Bank of the Cannal. [...] The night that Stephens made his escape I was in company with a lot of our friends in a Room in the City Mansion Hotell Bridge St. The Punch went round and a genial atmosphere pervaded the place all were in good humour. one of our guests, a fine young man a Priest from the country was the life of our party and by his racy humor keeped away any hankering thought or unrest which might trouble me. I suspected someting was going to happen that night. I did not concern myself much about the matter and prefered to wait further developments. I think this was the first time I met Coridan, who some time afterwards became an Informer.

He was no acount to looke at a small Common Place looking individual a great talker, a Bombast. Some time afterwards it was a Surprise to many of our men when Corridan the Informer Confronted them in the Dock. The Close of the great Civil War in America gave a great impetus to emigration in Ireland. I thought it a Bit Curious to see thousands of men trying to get out of the Country as fast as the[y] could while there Brothers were getting ready to strike a Blow for Freedom. From my Point of view, this had a very discourageing effect.

Arrest in Dublin

[…] The habe[a]s Corpis [sic] Bill was rushed trough Parliament, and in a short time the Jails all over the Country were filled with Politicle Prisoners. a large number were suspects taken on suspision. […] in January eighteen Sixty Six I was arrested. I made no atempt to go away seeing the Cause was hopeless. I wished to go Back, Honarable or otherwise, tarry a while if not Molested. after my arrest I was Kept in Green St Station for two days and a night in the Cell, a most knoxious place, part of the time, foul Smelling with Drunken and disorderly Caracters, which I found very hard to Bare with for my first time. Detectives were every where and the willing Instruments of the Castle doing there dirty work man catching. at the end of the two Days I was taken to Mount Joy Prison. Knowing my trunk and contents were examined I was sadisfied no Criminating Papers were found. I did not have any. onst in the narrow limet of my Cell and the Iron Doore Closed behined me, I felt I was then alone a Prisoner in the hands of the English who allways kept a firm grip of their Irish Captives even when innosent. As an untried Prisoner and a Suspect I had the privilage of having my food Sent into me if I chose but there was no telling how long that might be. Soon after I was lodged in prison I was vissited by the Catholick Chaplain. he did not stay long this time. when about to leave he said the English put you in hear let them feed you. I then lived on the prison allowance. The close confinement and the want of exercise and the prison diet soon told on my health.

There was a large number of Irish American officers in the prison. we were let out of our Cells every day for one Hour for exercise if not Raining otherwise we were kept close in our Cells. So we had plenty of time to think of the past while not knowing our fate. Some of us were marked men. fresh information was Comming out every day against some one or other of us, while we were in Blisful igorance as to what the[y] were planing against us. the exercise Ring was a Circular plot of ground Surrounded by a high Railing where we walked round about in single file at four or five paces apart without talking or scarcely looking at one another. any infringement of this rules was confinement in the dark cell on Bread and water or not let out for exercise for a certain number of days. a Millitery Guard was on the Prison Gate. One day while in the Ring General Sir Hugh Rose Commander of the Forces in Ireland acompanied by Some of his Staff and other Big wigs Came to the Prison they seemed to take particular notice of every one of us while we were walking round the Bull ring. [...] Several letters had passed between myself and the American Consul. One of his Letters Stated he was doing all he Could for me, that the authorities were very slow. after about Six months Imprisonment I was released on Condition of going to America. I had a viset from my mother and explained all I could say to hir. I gave hir some money and went Back to my Cell hopeing in God for my deliference and Safe from the Base Informer allways Plenty in our Unfortunate Country. It was a fine morning in July 1866. at Six a.m. I took my departure from Mount Joy after Signing a paper not to Return to Ireland dureing the Suspension of the Hapis Corpis (Habeus Corpus) which I understood was to remain in force for two years. I then got Psesion of my Tunk and my money save a certain amount deducted from it for my passag ticket, and at once proceded outside the gate escorted by a Sergeant and two pvates of the Constabulary. when I got to the Gate the Millitery Guard of Scotch Hilanders [sic] were turned out and formed in front of the Guard House. I thought this rather an amuseing incident. an outside car was standing in the road way. I had Barely times to wave my hand to my Mother and Some friends, when I was off with my Guard trotting down the Road to the Kings Bridge for the early Train for Cork. My health was much weakened and my appatite very poor. Besides troubled with Rumatism which I contracted in the Prison from Cold and want of exercise and fresh air, I was oblidged to use a stick for support, yet I was cheerfull and hopefull and glad to get away from the gloom and restraint of an English Prison. free once more, with a change of air and light exercise would make me allright again when I could work away in the Scramble of Life in whatever Position I may be placed in. I was unavoidable detained in Queenstown for a fue days as the Steamer had not then arrived. I felt mean and uncomfortable as My Body guard accompanied me everywhere I went and sleped in the same room with me in my Lodgins. The[y] were all attention and very carefull of me, I Sepose, lest I might wander off Somewhere out of sight, and were as ansious for the arrival of the steamer as myself. at the end of two days the vessel arrived The Hecla of the Inman Line.

Leaving Ireland Again

I went out on the Tender with my escort and was Soon on Bord when I Bid them a friendly good By. The steam whistle sounded and we started on our voiage. A large number of emigrants were on Board. Soon the distant Hills of dear Old Ireland were fadeing from my vieu (view) and the Hecla not a first rate ship was Cleaveing the Breast of the Atlantick west ward Ho, in her own way which I thought was not the Best. She was slow and uncomfortable, one way or another she Brought us safe over. we had a Slight alarm of fire which was Soone put out. On my arrival in New York and after a fue days Rest I went to see James Stephens who had made good his escape out of Ireland. I met several officers whom I had Seen in Dublin the[y] allowed the cause was hopeless, and the outlook unfavourable I attended a meeting one night at Fenian Head Quarters Stephens was there and a large number of officers who had returned to America on conditions. he made as fare as we thought a very absurde and curious proposition to us after discusing events in Ireland, that if we went Back again, to Ireland, he would go by the way of France and join us there. I thought that was a very wild and strange preposal to make and some of our Best men in British dungeons and in pennel Servitude. this foolish and very strange preposal was not agreed to. I would not like to say incencere (insincere) Proposition failed To receive the Consent of any of the Officers at the Meeting Just returned from Ireland. I had a nuff for a time of our poor distrest Country. The Fenian Movement went down. the People were leaving there Native Land in great numbers with no prospect of an abatement. The Peelers were Suffiscient to Keep Peace in Ireland. It was then time I should looke out for myself with my funds low and my health poor.

Chapter Seven

All now is ancient history, yet visions of the past,
Before me bring some well known faces that I knew,
In the chequered past far and near,
The fond good-bye, the cheerful look,
Now don't forget my boy to write us soon,
And the many kind words and grateful acts,
I must say good-bye
To you at last.

❧

'Musings'—Andrew J. Byrne

Return to Army Life

I HAD NO PLAN and was undecided what to do. I was waiting, But did not worry. It was the fall of the year, then the long Cold Winter was before me. The Goverment were Raising four Regiments of Infantry Called the Vetern Reserve Corps for light Garrison duty, to be Composed of Soldiers of the late War who had been wounded in the Service. I was speaking to several wounded Soldiers who had joined the new Brigade the[y] said the[y] would like to have me with them, and we would have a good time. I concluded I would join this Honarable and Distinguished Corps. it was then mid Winter my health shattered and employment Bad. I joined the Forthy Second Regiment U.S. Infantry in January Sixty Seven at Harts Island, New York. Had I not went to Ireland after the War I would have remained in Civil Life and gone West which would have been more in accord with my mind.

One Evening I was returning to the Island in a Large Open Boat. a snow storm comming on we could not see the Island, and lost our way on the Broad exspanse of Long Island Sound. it was late that night when we found ourselfs near the shore of Long Island. after several attemps to Beach the Boat we Landed. It was Bitter Cold the ground was covered thick with snow, there was no House or light visable in the Darkness. we were half Frozen, when someone said there's a light. We made a straight line for the house a Small dwelling. The people were gone to rest. After a fue nocks on the door, we were let in. There were nine or tenn of us Soldiers and a Captain of our Regiment. The good women of the House started the Fire and made Cakes and Coffey for us. in the main time we thought a little whiskey would be very disirable if it could be got. The Woman's Husband said he could get some. The Captain sent a soldier along with him in a short time they were back with a Jar of Wiskey. We had a Drink all round, and the heat of the stove soone put the shifers out of us. Then we had hot Cakes and Butter and plenty of hot Coffey our cloas thawed out and dried up very soone, and were all in the best of humour. We thanked our Host and Hostess for there kindness and attention to us. The[y] were poor people. we amply compensated them for there Trouble. Daylight comming on we found the Boat all right. We rowed Back to the Island. The[y] thought we were lost.

In the month of May two Company's of our Regiment one of them I was serving in was sent to Plattsburgh Barracks at the Head of Lake Champlain in the Northern part of the State of New York. we had good quarters, our duty was light and the Summer weather made us feel more comfortable after our dreary Winter on the Island. The Barracks is near the Lake and afforded us a good oppertunity for Bathing and washing faned by the Cool Breeses which swept across the water from the green mountain State, Vermont on the opposet shore. We had very little amusement, a Soldiers life is often very dull in this Country. The[y] are never in The Town the[y] are allways away from it, so that the smallest thing in the way of amusement is a treat, but a Ball or more properly speaking a Dance, is the most enjoyable time of all. One of our large Rooms is cleared out and decorated with Cross Swords and Bayonets a fue small flags or pendents with a mixture of green sprigs or Branches and every little device to set off the room and give it a Marshal apearence. The Room is lit up with oil lamps or a candle. After Taps and lights are out then comes along our guests the Girls neatly dressed not costly with some of our Gallants in Blue with white shirt fronts paper collar and cuffs looking smart and neat. There is bound to be a Bell of the Ball if not we will make one by common consent. when Dancing commences, the officers and their wifes Dance the first Set, after a fue quatilons (quadrillons) badly played by our fidler and Banjo Player who are booth Soldiers the Officers retire to there quarters, much pleased at the apearence of the Room and the Company. after the[y] are gone everything goes faster and the merriment begins, which continues til early in the morning the Ball is over and every one is pleased except some poor fellow who has lost his girl, making lots of fun for his commarades who enjoys the joke immencely, besides furnishing a theme for gossop for Some time til it becomes stale and wears out.

At one time I had a very disagreable duty to perform. I was sent in Charge of a Prisoner to Fort Niagra, near Lake Ontario on the Canadian Border, to be tried by a General Court Martial for Drunkness and absent from duty without leave. I had no Guard with me and could not be relifed of my responsibility even for a short time. But as there were many good points in Charley Moss my prisoner, I did not antisapate any trouble with him. I was the only witness in his case compeled to be as a matter of duty, I had a great wish for him. My journey by Rail to Fort Niagra was anything But a pleasent one for me. how I did hate to put the hand Cuffs on Charley, which I was obliged to take off on occasions, while knowing his temperament and not void of princible, I used Kindness with discretion so that I got along very well with my charge. On arriving at Fort Niagra I reported to the Commanding Officer. I had then no longer charge of my prisoner. For some reason which I forget I was detained there for three or four days. I had now an oppertunity of seeing part of this very interesting region at the Fort where the River enters Lake Ontario, and from there up the River to the great Falls, Boiling Surging and tossing about till it enters the River in its mad race trough a great chasm of Rocks which it has cut into perhaps in ages gon by. as this was all French Terotery (territory) at one time the[y] established this Post and Built the Fort long before it came into posesion of the English and then the Americans, whose flag the *Stars and Stripes* in gracefull folds was flying from the tall flag staff overlooking the great Lake and the Cannadian [sic] Shore across the River. After three or four days which I spent very pleasently I was ordered to take the Prisoner to New York, about four hundred miles by rail. I was very much disapointed I expected the Prisoner to be tried at the Fort. when I arrived in New York I reported myself at Governors Island. I was told I would have to wait untill the Board meets for the trial of Prisoners who may be brought before it. the prisoner was put in the Guard House. I had liberty to go back and forward from the Island to the City But as I was not on pleasure bent and very little money I did not care about this. I wished I was back again in Plattsburg. I was out of the Running hear I had quite anuff of New York and some unplesent memories of the City, which was then aglow with the heat of the Sun. Stroleing down Broadway I met an old Millitery friend of mine Captain Truesdell who had served in my Regiment in the late War. I was surprised to see he had lost a leg by an accident since he was Discharged the Service which he left without a scratch. Now as the sailer says there is dainger on land as well as at Sea. we had a very cordial greeting and in cource of our conversation he asked me how I would like a Commision in the Regular Army I told him I would like it very well but I thought there would be a great deal of trouble about it. he told me to never mind that he could work up influence anuff to work that. I thanked him very much for his kindness and the high opinnion he held of me. he promised to write to me and let me know soon how things went on and what influence he could gain in my favor. I was not very much elated of the prospect which he held out to me for certan reasons which he was not aware of. I merely assented to be advised by him as my friend. The Court Martial came off. I was an unwilling witness in the cace yet I did not swerfe in giving my evidence, but nevertheless it was rounded off in such a manner, Charley got a light sentence. otherwise I might have come back without my Prisoner. going Back we went by Rail to White Hall at the foot of Lake Champlain and then by Steamer to Plattsburgh. I was well tired when I got back to the barracks the weather was very warm and the want of change of under cloathing made me feel very uncomfortable. I had several Letters from my friend the Captain in New York. The[y] were very encouraging and looked hopeful. he stated he had in my favor several millitery officers, General Sickles a Brave and Distinguished officer in the late War, Senneter (Senator) Lincoln and some Bussiness men who had been in the Army whom I knew well myself. everything seemed favorable when the whole thing fell trough at onst. The Goverment decided on a reduction of the Reguler Army which had been increased dureing the War. The Vetern Reserve Corps was to go also. [...] There was then a large number of supernumary officers and no vacancy in the older Regiments. I thought no more about my application and let it drop from my mind.

Ordered to Arkansas

In the later part of Spring (1869) By order all men fit for duty in my Regiment were to be transfered to the Sixt Infantry in Arkansas, and those not fit for duty to be discharged. I was 1st Sergeant of my Company and fit for service. about two thirds of the Regiment passed inspection. we took our departure from Plattsburg glad to get away from the Cold Bleak North to the more warm and genial regean (region) of the South West. after a long Jouney by Rail we came out on the Mississippi at or near Saint Louis, and from thence down the River on a Steamer which was more pleasent then the cars, while the change of weather from North to South was very perceptable. it was springtime and the spredding buds and green leaves of the Trees were fast developing under the mild and warm heat of an April Sun. what a delightfull change in a fue days. we turned up the Arkansas River at Napoleon The boat was going to Little Rock. our destination was Fort Gibson farder West. before we came to Little Rock, we lost one of our men over bord no one seemed to know how he got into the water which we all believed to be accidental an alarm was giveing immediately. Man over Bord. There was a rush of men from all parts of the Boat for a looke out on the River. The poor fellow was drifting to the rear on the swelling murky water a Boat was lowered as soone as possible. in the main time one of our Captains jumped into the River, a most Dangrous attemp to save the man. as soone as the Boat touched the water it had to go to the assistance of the Captain who was giving out and in Dainger of drownding. This Brave though it might be said a foolish attemp on the part of the officer, delayed the Boat which headed down the stream again. My eys was intentively fixed on the head of the unfortunate man which apeared over the survice (surface) of the water like a dark round Ball with a slight motion up and down it was a very sad sight. at lenght he went down before the Boat got near him. From

Washington monument (early proposal)

View of Queenstown Harbour (Cobh, County Cork), 1865.

'The English put you in here, let them feed you.'

Fort Niagra, 1868.

A bit of St. Louis, 1869.

Elijah in a sportive mood.

The Grand Union Hotel, Saratoga Springs, New York.

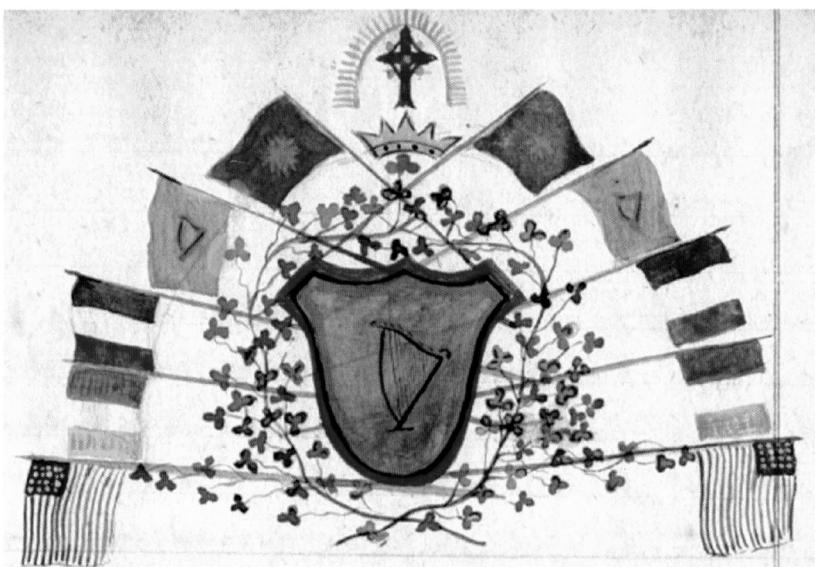

Flag display.

Flag display.

Castle William, Governor's Island, New York Harbour.

Hendricke Hudson in the ship *Half Moon* discovers New York.

Off for the new world.

St. Audeon's Arch, Dublin 1908.

St. Patrick's Cathedral, Dublin, 1841 (taken from an old print).

Harbour scene.

Nora Byrne, deceased 1933.   Andrew Byrne, deceased 1911.

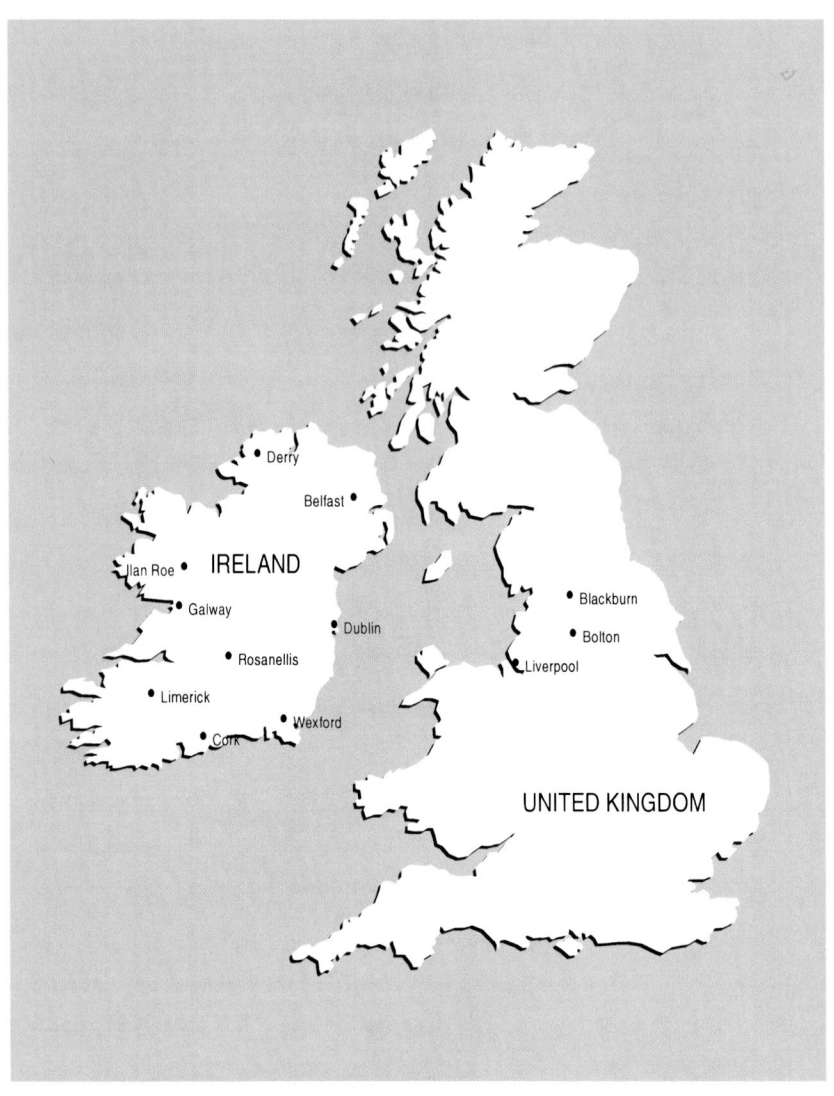

Locations of Andrew Byrne's travels in Ireland and the United Kingdom.

the first I thought the poor fellows chance of been saved very slight owing to the Dangerous nature of the River, and the strong current which bore him away very quick. he wore a pair of hevey top Boots which helped to drown him. on our arrival at Fort Gibson we went into Tents for a fue Days. it was then early in May 1869 the opening up of the Season for all kinds of Labour all over the Country. I was Discharged from the Service consequent on been rendered supernumary first Sergeant by Consolidation of my Regiment with the Sixt Infantry. I was Discharged at my own request, yet the Coloneol of the Sixt done everything he could to induce me to join his Regiment. My health was good and having suffiscient reason for not rejoining again, I parted with my old Friends of the Forty Second who were very sorry for my leaving them, and wishing me suckcess wherever I went. I was soone paid off and lost no time in getting away from Arkansas, as I did not think it a very Desirable place for me to stop.

The Building Trade in America

I tooke passage on a steamer for Saint Louis, prefering the River Route, as I was in no hurry and cheaper than by Rail. I did not expect to be going back on the same route so soone [...] on my arrival at Saint Louis I noticed a vast improvement in the short period of twelf years when I first saw this city in Eighteen fifty Seven on my way to New Mexico, but that is no wonder in free America we get used to such things. going about the City I noticed new buildings hear and there some of them of a very superior class to others that stood near them, at one time concidered the finest Houses in the West. trade was good but I was a bit timid and had almost lost the art of Bricklaying consequint on my long service in the Army. The Building trade had not yet resumed its useual briskness as yet, I found it difficult to drop in, I concluded I would leave hear. I stoped a fue days in Saint

Louis and started by Rail for Chicago. hear I found a friend who had wore the Blue like myself. he was foreman for a Builder. he tooke a very friendly interest in me and put me to work. after a fue days Labour I was obliged to give it up owing to a sore [w]rist on my right hand. I did not choose to stand still or sit down. I went to Milwaukee in Wisconsin then to Recian (Racine) a very Bleak woodden Town near the Shore of Lake Michigan. I did not like the look of the place. I then thought I would go to Michigan on the opposet shore of the great Lake, a fresh water Sea with a Boundless horison. I crossed over on a Lake Steamer the place of landing I forget. then I went North trough a conciderable part of the State stopping a short time at Grand Rappets (Rapids) a small but seemingly prosperous Town. Michigan is a great lumber Country supplying all the princible markets of the West and other places a very large number of men are engaged in this work, chopping down Trees and at the sawmills. immence rafts of timber are floated down the Rivers, to the mills and lumber yards at Saginaw and Green Bay and all over the Country. In some parts the ground is impregnated with salt for miles, which looks as if a white frost had setled down on the Land which has an impovrished apearence. My wrist had now recovered from the strain of a fue days work in Chicago. while I was fullfilling the Proverb of the Roleing Stone, my mind reverted back again to the Big City. I was getting low down in pocket and the Summer far advanced I returned to Chicago again. I procured employment and went to work again. The Building trade was only midling and wages lower then in New York, Saint Louis and other Important Towns. There is a great run on Chicago from various places Chiefly from the East. men out of work, of all classes are attracted hear by the rappet (rapid) progress of the City, which has outstriped Saint Louis, a much older City, in Population and trade. at the end of September after I had worked about Three months, my job was finnished and winter setting in early, out door work, Bricklaying is stoped until the following Spring. this do not apply in all caces. Navigation on the Lake is stoped and the Steamers and Sailing Craft are Ice Bound in the River. I found the Winter and Spring very long and dreary. in the Evenings I felt relieved when all the Borders were in. There was Company then, and a conversation of a mixed nature going on and some card playing or something or other going on that would keep you from thinking and create merriment. Several young Ladies came to the House from time to time to see the Miss Howes Daughters of the Boarding House Mistress. The[y] were nearly all Irish Americans all Business Girls neatly dressed. our Evenings then were much more pleasent then otherwise and relieved the dullness of the sittingroom w[h]ere the Boarders retired to after Tea. But how were we to amuse the Girls wee men were a bit mixed young old and middle aged, there was very little wit and humor among some of us, for the over-worked man and the Battle of life in America is anuff to knock the humor out of most men. Your humbel servent Mr. Byrne was a pasable Singer and would Some Times be called on for a Song. Several little invitatins followed Tommy Dorney who could play the violin farely well and myself were shure to be invited.

At last the Spring came and the joyous sun shone out from time to time growing brighter and more warm every day. for one reason or other trade was Backward this Season about the first of May I started to work again with a long Bill of indebtnes to my Boarding Mistress, which I was very ansious to clear off before I could save a Dollar for myself. I braced myself up and determined I would not let the grass grow under my feet this time and worked away, to the outmost limit of my ability, for such is the Sistim (system) of working hear. in some respects as regards Bricklaying you are worked to the very point of endurence under a glaring hot sun which lasts all Day. after a short time I was out of dept, and commenced to Lay up someting for myself and a Money Order from time to time to my Mother. The Ridget (rigid) economy which I had used for some time was no longer a strain apon me. I was more pleased with myself and enjoyed what ever chance amusement came in my way in a rational and not very expensive manner. I had fue friends and very little company. My time in Chicago might be short or long it depended on Business. I had Two Companions who were of my Trade who were useful to me and good Friends, Elijah Allen and Tom Smith. Both were Irishmen. Smith was a well behaved young man well educated and a good companion. Elijah was a carracter, whom I could not adequetly describe. I was allways glad to meet him. He was genial witty and amusing who could make himself at home anywhere and was regarded by every one that [k]new him as good company. Allin [sic] and Smith were Bricklayers. Elijah played on the Scotch pipes and was the posesor of a very good instrument, which comprised the princible part of his Baggage when moveing about and was allways shure of a welcome among the Irish when he opened out his pipes to play a Scotch or Irish tune, very much to the wonderment of some people who never saw a Scotch pipes before. when the Building I was working on came to a finnish Elijah had myself and Smith booked for another job in Belvadere [sic] a small Town about fivety miles from Chicago. I was promised a good time and a very nice job. I [k]new that very well for the Piper was a host in himself. we went off like Larks in the best of humor. in the evening we were stroleing down the princible street of the little Town, not very flourishing looking but in the midst of a great farming Country, with wide spreding grain fields all round about for miles, and the glistining sheen of some white farm Houses partly shaded by the green Trees which helped to brake the lone sameness of the broad expansif plain. we procured very comfortable Lodgens. Our Land Lady was a widdow and a young girl hir Dauther was sole owners of the place. we were very comfortable both Mother and Dauther making things as agreable as posible. Hir Dauther played on the piano and an od[d] skip up and down and round about the floor and a can of ale on the Table helped to pass off an Evening when at home very pleasently. Elijah was not long hear when he became acquainted with many people in the Town and round about Belvadere [sic] princibly among the Irish, some of them farmers who were old setlers and raised famalies hear. well the result of this was when the[y] found he was a musickil Gentleman was an invite to Dances and parties in the Country a short distance from the Town. Myself and Tom Smith were also invited. One fine summer evening when the gloom that precedes night were closing over us we set out on the soft turf road we did not know the exact road to go to but following our Instructions as near as we could in the Darkness and the Houses fue and far apart. after traveling along the Road for an Hour and no one to direct us we were near turning back again when we saw a faint light across the fields. Now we are alright said Elijah who at onst fixed his pipes and commenced droneing and pipeing a fue discordant notes, struck up *the Cammels are Comming (The Campbells are Comin')* we walked as Bold as any Highlanders going to the Reliefe of Lucknow in a fue moments three or four lanterns were Swaying about in front of us near a grove of Trees. we were met by a merry croud of young girls boys and men and escorted into a comfortable two story frame House where wee were hartly received and made much of. The night went merrily around between Dancing and Singing and some refreshments. The[y] all allowed the[y] never had such a time. The next morning the piper had ent a puff in him. we returned to Town well pleased with our entertainment and the pleasure we gave to our friends in our all night Dance. on the whole our time passed very pleasent hear, But a German wedding which I was invited to was a new thing to me. The Bride groom a German who owned a Laeger Beer Saloon in the Town got married to a good lookeing German Girl of stout proportions. he invited a number of his friends. The company concisted of Germans except myself and my Two friends who were merely looking on. There was plenty of Beer and all talking and laughing together at the one time there was great attention paid to the Bride. The[y] all seemed to make much of hir. The Dancing perhaps I should say waltsing was continued with har[d] ly a stop till a late Hour. The company were nearly all men very fue Woman. This made it very hard for the Bride as all the men young and old wished to Dance with the Bride. I was told a German custum. Poor thing she was nearly kild or worn out from exaustion. The apartment was small and Lager abundent the floor got wet and slippy, five or six couples were on the floor spining round the narrow space. The Poor Bride all smiles and hir partner in the midel, sliped and went down on the wet boards in a minute the[y] were all in a heap on top of each other the Bride under and the[y] all scrambling to get to there feet again Laughfing and roaring with delight […] this nearly put a climax on the Dancing for the Night. vocal musick then commenced the Germans all Singing together or joining in the choros. at daylight the company Broke up and scathered to there homes. a fue days afterwards I went back with my friends to Chicago. it was then in the month of July the harvest was commencing and the Farmers were looking out for men and ofering very favorable terms for Skilled Labourers in the harvest fields or anyone the[y] could get. trade was slack or otherwise the Labour market was overcrouded. Elijah tooke it into his head to go harvesting and prevailed on myself and Smith to go with him telling us we would get three or four Dollors a day and our Board for five or six weekes which would be better then Brick Laying I told him I [k]new nothing about that kind of work, never mind said he it will be only Binding I will show you how to do that in a short time. Takeing a short trip by Rail we were well out in the Country, But as we had no particular place to go to we tooke to the Road. On the way we had the offer of a fue jobs. The Yankey farmers are very dry in there manner and hard task masters. after a talk with one of them who was driveing along the Road in his waggon, we would not go with him. we were looking for work, but more of a choice of master. I did not like the look of that old fellow said Smith. No nor I said myself. Begorra said Elijah, I think it will be purty hard to please you. farder on we met another Farmer who was looking for help and we agreed to go with him, at the rate of three Dollors a Day and Board. the next morning we had an early Breakfast and started for the field of our operations. the farmer was out first, I survead (surveyed) the great field of wheat where a machine was allready at work. there wear three long swarts of the fallin grain stretching out before us. Elijah soone showed me how to tie the Bundles, off we started each man had his swart. I soone found out we could not ketch up with the Machine thinking I might have it a bit easeier, as I was only an ammature. at twelf noon we went to Dinner it was very nice but very light. the Farmer was out first again. we looked at one another and smiled and were soone at work again. we soone got tired of our job, at the end of three days our backs were very sore from the constant stoopeing and our hands red and tender we jacked up the job. We could not be prevailed apon to stop any longer. We were paid off and started on the road again, with the intention of going back again to Chicago. wee were not long on the Road when night came apon us. we could not procure a lodgen anywhere among the farmers. wee wondered at this as we were three Deasent looking men and did not look like robbers or murderers. any kind of shelter would be preferable to us then the Road. we were very tired after our three days work. a large wooden Barren (barn) stood near us in a field we crossed the fence moving cautiously when near the Store House we listened attentively for the foot steps of any person or the Bark of a Dog. all was quiet, a short distance from us was a dwelling House with the glimmer of a light in one of the windows if we were discovered we should have to beat a quick retreat and the ping ping of a fue revolver shots to make us go quicker But we did'int. The barren (barn) door was open and a quantaty of hay was stored in side. we soon made a nest for ourselves, but as the night was cold we slepped very little. early the next morning wee were on the road again. the hunger was begining to pinch us. fortunately we came to the House of an Irishman who gave us a harty welcome his good Woman prepared Breakfast for us. after a plentifull meal and a wash the chill of the night air left us wee started on the Road again. at a way station wee took the cars for Chicago. My friends in the Boarding House were very much amused when I told them of my three Days adventure in the Country.

Returning Home

Comming up to the end of October the snow commenced to fly this is generaly concidered the commencement of winter. then frost which becomes more intence and Biteing winds from the north west some times acompanid by hail or sleet then frost again and no work 'til the following Spring. Then comes a pull out of your saveings, if you have any to carry you over the winter. I recived a Letter from a friend of mine in Plattsburgh in the State of New York who had been working in Saratoga Springs thirty miles North of Albany. My friend recommended me to winter in Plattsburgh on economical grounds. I started on my journey of eight or nine hundred miles with as little trouble as if I was going from Dublin to Cork. Passing trough the great states of Indiana Ohioh and Pennsilvania [sic]. I arrived at my destination in a fue Days. I then settled myself down for the Winter in the dull bleak little town, haveing no where to go and nothing to do and my pocket growing Lighter all the time. about the midle of March I left this dreary place for Saratoga Springs. when I arived there as directed by my friend I was to go to the Town Hall Hotell.

on my arival there I soon found myself at home. although haveing a high sounding name it was a Workmans Boarding House owned by a foxey old Irishman and his wife who picked up a fue crumbs in the late War selling whiskey to the Soldiers. a fue Days after my arrival I went to work the prospect was very good. Saratoga is a nise place to live in so I thought the Town good anuff for me for awhile. the Town containes about eight thousand Inhabitents, slowly increaseing it is a great Summer resort and full of People for two or three months in the year. The principal attraction is a number of mineral springs of different qualities which are acording to the Docters, health giveing and refreshing to Drink. I often thought some of those wells were Doctered for reasons easily understood. There are several large Hotells where the fashionable and Rich People go besides a number of Boarding Houses for those wishing to do Saratoga at a cheeper rate then stoping in the Big Houses among the more wealthy and fashinable Class, who comes from all parts of the States, to chat and talk dance and eat, and sit listening in the Cool Shade of the veranda of the Grand Union Hotell and Congress Hall to the musick of the Band and watching the new arrivals who come in on every train in Large numbers. But when the Indian Summer has come and gone and the birds has flown Saratoga drops back to its normal state of dullness. [...] Shortly after my arrival in Saratoga I became slightly acquainted with a young Irish Woman a native of the County Cork, Ireland. She was a fresh humble looking person becommingly Dressed and an ocasional vissetter at the Boarding House, to see the two Miss Caseys Daughters of the Boss of the Town Hall Hotell. hir Brother and Sister had sailed on a certain date from Queens Town for New York they were comming to Saratoga there name was Connors. In America the[y] became O'Connor. This young Woman whom we called Maggie, was counting the Days and Hours and most ansiously awaithing the Comming of hir Brother and hir Sister Nora. She was growing fidgity and ansious for there arriveal and longed to see them. She bought several coppys of the *N. Y. Herrold* [sic] to looke at the shipping news, the arrivals and tellegrams from Sandy Hook thirty miles seaward from New York. She would come in the evening after hir bussines Hours into the sitting room hir face a little bit flushed and an earnest look in hir eyes and a newspaper in hir hand. hear Mr. Byrne Read this God knows there ought to be some account of the Boat this time. Well the boat did come. She received a letter from hir Sister of there safe arrival in New York, and that they expected to get to Saratoga the following day. little did I think that hir Sister was to become my future Wife. when the[y] came and things had settled down the Connors used to call to the House Nora's vissets becomming more frequent. wee became better acquanted and a mutual attachment sprung up between us and from that to walking together. it was in May Eighteen Seventy one and Saratoga was putting on its Best apearance getting ready for the arrival of the Summer Birds, with Pockets full of money filling the emthy Hotells and Boarding Houses with People and the Shops with Customers. our walks then became more plesant the evenings Beautiful, the sights more animating which put us all in good humour.

Later on in the Summer I met with what might have been a very serious accident while working on a small Church in Schuylerville, about tenn miles from Saratoga. The scaffold broke down, myself and two other bricklayers fell to the ground about sixteen or seventeen feet. Two of the men were very slightly injured I came down on my back on some loose brick on the Church floor. I was picked up by the men and carried to my Boarding House and put to Bed. I received the kindest of treatment. I was very sore all about the Body. the Docter said I had no bones broken but that I was jared and that I would feel sore for two or three weeks. in a short time I resumed work and came back to Saratoga and worked on till November when the snow began to fly the usual harbinger of Winter. in a short time the glass went down very low. I then went into the ark and rested myself for the Winter. early in March Eighteen Seventy two I went to work again my job been a Bad paying one. The Burning down of Chicago was attracting working men from all parts of the Country espescialy Bricklayers who were receiving six and seven Dollors a day, with the prospect of stedy employment for the season. This was very encourgeing I thought this was my opportunty [...] I resolved to go to Chicago with the Intention of comming Back again in the Fall of the year with three or four hundred Dollors better. I then might talk Bussiness to Nora. when I arrived at the ruins of the great City it presented a remarkable scean (scene). the great plane as fare as I could see was covered with heaps of rubbish burnt brick and stone and heavey Iron collums Bent by the action of the fire lay about in the Bussiness quarter of the City. all was Burnt down except a small district which was saved by General Sheridan Blowing down Houses with gun Powder and checking the onward sweep of the devouring flames, and saving a very small portion of the City round Harrison Street on the South Side. with difficulty I made out the Howe family with whom I formarly boarded the[y] were very glad to see me the[y] told me of there expeariance on that terrable night. The[y] were burnt out but were very fortunate in getting apartments in the district which was saved the[y] were overcrouded. a friend of mine tooke me to where he Boarded in a German House. The[y] were good People I had no fault to find. I went to work. wages came down to four Dollors and a half a day yet the[y] were building every where, on an avarage I was told a House a day. Some curiosities of the fire were very much sought after by viseters who came to see the ruins of the City and bring back to there Homes some relick of the greatest fire every known the most destructif and the money loss the greatest on record. passing along the burnt streets which were paved with wood, I noticed a great many large clinkers among the rubbish and crumbling walls, some of them very large lumps, most of them composed of various kinds Glass Iron Brass and various supstances, partially melted into one another many of them retaining there original form in part so as to be recognised for there usefullness at one time such as bolts, bars, locks and keys cups and sausers and many other things used for House hold purposes. all of those clinkers were taken away or sold to visseters or the curious as a relick of the fire and made into Rockerys in various parts of the Country. The Town hall Bell which was destroyed by the fire fell into the Hands of a Speculater, who made a very good thing of it. Small Bells for watch and trinkets were made of the old Bell mettle and sold as a Rilick making a very large profit to the owner. Building was very brisk but the labour market was getting overcrouded.

In June I received a letter from Nora who was then In Albany stateing that work was very good there. I gave up my Chicago speculation and started by Rail for Albany, New York, at five p.m. Sunday. the day after my arrival In Albany I was jobed for work on a new gas works, at the same pay I was getting in Chicago where every one was going to. every thing went on very smood with me till Christmas tide. my job was finished and work closed down. I was then dooing nothing and expected a good job in the Spring. I was married February 2nd 1873 in Saint Josephs Church Albany by Fath. Burk, In a very quiet way. we then went back to Saratoga and started House Keeping. The Building of a Big Hotell early in the Spring made my mind easey and my rest better in my new undertaking. There was nothing new or strange in my everyday life. Most of my time was spent in the house.

Waiting for the sun shine
Wishing for the Spring,
Waiting for the good time
When the Winder ends.

Early in the Spring I went to work again as busey as a nailer and worked steady dureing the Summer and fall til the commencement of Winter and was well disposed to rest myself untill the return of Spring again. thus it is our saveings of the Summer and fall are taken away during Winter and Spring. if there is a Ballance left it will help the next year's savings. It is therefore necessary to use Economy in all its conditions, which must be observed if you want to save money out of a Weekly wage. The long Cold Winters in the Northt and West is a very serious draw back to men of the Building trade especialy Brick Layers. Catherin Byrne the first of this marrage was born January Eighteen Hundred and Seventy four in Saratoga this was a time of a very great depresion of trade all over the Country the[y] call it a Pannick in America. It is not unuseual hear after a long period of Prosperity thousands of People are ruined and loose all the[y] have the wages of the workers come down, work almost ceases. It is hard to get employment at any price. The country becomes infested with tramps and crime increases. a short time before the Pannick I Bought a Building Lot on the border of the Town. after some time the Commisioners had my Lot survead (surveyed), for the purpose of making a new street. I had a Small proffet. I had to put up with that as the Law is different from what it is in Ireland. In the fall of Eighteen Seventy four I had no savings from my Labor. the winter was a heavy one on me. Andrew Byrne Born Febuary [sic] the Sixt Eighteen Seventy five Saratoga New York. When Spring and Summer came trade was very Bad. at this time there was a very strong opposition among the Atlantic linurs running to Europe. The passage was down about one half. I procured a ticket for my Family on the National Line Steamer *Eigipt* (Egypt) to Sail from New York July 3rd eighteen seventy five for Queenstown and Liverpool.

I lost no time getting ready as I was Bound to be in New York one or two days before the day of Sailing. I encumbered myself with a certain amount of Bagage more than I should have taken with me. This caused me a lot of trouble and expense and kept me in a constant state of watchfullness. after parting with my friends in Saratoga who could not understand why I was going Back to Poor old Ireland, I started with my Family by Rail for Albany, and arrived there in good time to catch the night Boat for New York. we arrived in the City the next morning at Six a.m. My wife's Sisters and Brother met us there. I regretted very much our meeting was a very short one, as the Boat was to sail the same day. we left New York on the third of July (1875) and arrived in Liverpooll nine or tenn days afterwards. The voiage was very pleasant, smood sailing and plenty of room to knock about we passed some larg Ice Bergs on the passage. we stoped in Liverpool about a day and a night. in the Evening we saild for Dublin expecting a pleasent run Home, But were disappointed. we were not long out when the weather Changed. It grew dark and Blustering the Rain comming down and the dark Sea Swelling ruff and Choppy. It turned out a very dirty night. In the morning there was no abatement. When we arrived at the North Wall It was still raining and a darke canophy over head. I drove to my mother's residence where I stoped for a fue days till I procured Lodgens and settle down once more in Dublin. trade was fairly good I soon procured employment.

The most interesting and important part of my history was then over, as there is not much to cronicle in the every day life of a working man in Ireland. The circumstances are very depresing and The Curse of Slavery on yet.

MUSINGS

To sit and scribble in my own poor way,
And musing over what I shall say,
In this book of mine from time to time,
When my mind is free and my thoughts unmixed,
And the care of the world feels light.

Then my battles and scars and wandering far,
Come freely to my mind,
But the pros and cons and all the play,
Which some can do with the pen,
Is not in me so I think and think,
And then go on again.

But now my scribbling days are o'er,
I soon shall close my book,
And lay down my pen and say good-bye,
To all good friends I knew..

And the boys with whom I marched and fought,
The boys who wore the Blue,
In old Virginny and Chickahominy swamps,
When the sun poured down on our weary ranks,
And the boom of the cannon was heard in the front,
Then into line and fire at will,
The rest to God or night would come.

All now is ancient history, yet visions of the past,
Before me bring some well known faces that I knew,
In the chequered past far and near,
The fond good-bye, the cheerful look,
Now don't forget my boy to write us soon,
And the many kind words and grateful acts,
I must say good-bye
To you at last.

Andrew J. Byrne (1830–1911)

God Save Ireland

Union for ever

Rally round the flag

Down with faction

God for us all

A. J. O.B
Oct 13. 1909.

Appendices

Section 1

Section 2

SECTION 1

Note on the American Civil War

Over the course of the late 18ᵗʰ and early 19ᵗʰ centuries in America a north south divide had begun to manifest. At the centre of this divide was the issue of slavery. Slavery was dying out in the northern states as they moved towards industrialisation fuelled by emigration. In the North the concept of slavery was also changing and its morality was being questioned. In the South, thanks to the invention of the cotton gin in 1793 and to slave labour, cotton production was expanding at a phenomenal rate. The South was exporting enormous volumes of cotton onto the world market and becoming very wealthy as a result. In 1800 the U.S. exported $5 million of cotton. By 1860 this figure had grown to $191 million of cotton. The success of this industry was based on slavery. Anti-slavery sentiment from the northern states, who were not beneficiaries of the cotton windfall, caused resentment in the South. This divergence on the issue of slavery was compounded by the differences between the two regions. The North was an industrial force that was now looking for the government to provide protection from cheap European imports as well as infrastructure and transport routes to support industry. The South was wholly dependent on the cotton industry, whose success was dependent on slavery. The South opposed protectionism because they traded cotton on the world market and needed cheap European imports. The South was concerned that should the government come under the control of the North, southern interests would not be protected.

The country became polarised and any attempts at compromise ultimately failed. After the election of Abraham Lincoln, a Republican representing the North, as President of the United States, South Carolina voted to secede from the Union and were followed by other cotton states of Mississippi, Alabama, Georgia, Florida, Louisiana and Texas. In February 1861 the Confederate States of America were established with a provisional government and Jefferson Davis was elected president.

The first skirmish of the Civil War took place at Fort Sumter, located near the mouth of Charleston Harbour in South Carolina. The Fort was controlled by the U.S. Army, however it was considered to be a foreign fort in the Confederacy's most important harbour. Confederacy forces bombarded Fort Sumter into submission after Lincoln refused to relinquish it. No lives were lost in the bombardment and the Confederates won the fort.

The regular U.S. Army at this time only numbered 16,000 men, which was just enough to secure the frontiers and the coast. If war was to break out between the North and South it would have to be carried by a volunteer militia. As more states seceded from the Union and joined the Confederacy the Confederate capital moved to Richmond, Virginia. Richmond is located only 100 miles from Washington and the two seats of American government were facing each other across what was to become one of the battle grounds of the American Civil War and the battle ground on which Andrew J. Byrne was to end up fighting, on the Union side.

Lincoln called up a volunteer militia which he intended to use to win back the South. The volunteer militia lacked training and the ability to act as a single regiment. In order to function as a successful military force a regiment must be able to march and fight in formation which called for a variety of highly intricate movements. The voluntary militias were diverse groups who lacked discipline and were led by inexperienced soldiers. The first battles of the civil war took place in June 1861 and were disastrous. Throughout the summer and autumn of 1861 the army underwent extensive training and drilling to prepare for future campaigns. A ring of camps were established around Washington by the Union forces and General McClellan was given command of the Army of the Potomac. McClellan instigated an unending programme of training, drilling and establishing supply and distribution chains. In November 1861 McClellan was made General in Chief of all the armies of the North.

In the late summer of 1861, Andrew J. Byrne, on his arrival in New York, enlisted in the 65th New York Volunteers, 1st U.S. Chasseurs. His division formed part of the Army of the Potomac, initially installed in a string of camps around Washington to defend the Capital. Over the winter of 1861 the army around Washington were drilled in preparation for the summer campaigns of 1862. Byrne's division participated in the unsuccessful Peninsular Campaign which began in March 1862. The Union forces attempted to take Richmond by approaching from the peninsula formed by the York and James Rivers. Byrne's division was involved in the siege of Yorktown and the Battle of Williamsburg. When the Chickahominy River flooded at the end of May, a small portion of the Army of the Potomac, including Byrne's division, were stranded on the South side. This small force were attacked by Confederate forces and the Battle of Fair Oaks ensued. The Confederate forces were defeated when Union army reinforcements arrived. On the 26th June 1862 the Union army began to retreat after battles with Confederate forces at Beaver Dam Creek and Gaines Mill. Byrne's regiment retreated on the 27th June and took up a position at Malvern Hill near the James River. On 1st July 1862 the Battle of Malvern Hill took place. This was the last battle after seven days of fighting and retreat. Byrne was wounded at Malvern Hill and could not continue to retreat with his regiment. He was left behind and captured by the Confederates. Byrne was one of 43 enlisted men of the 65th Regiment who were wounded (but not mortally) in the seven days of fighting. McClellan's peninsular campaign was unsuccessful.

Byrne survived his capture and was returned to the North. He was hospitalised and did not return to his regiment until August

1863. By the time he joined his regiment they were serving in Warrenton, Virginia and were moving on the Confederate General Lee on the Rapidan River. After falling back and advancing several times the army went into winter quarters at Rappanhannock. During the winter Byrne fell ill and was sent to Washington for treatment. He rejoined his regiment in January 1864 at Brandy Station, Virginia. His regiment was then sent to Sandusky, Ohio to guard Confederate prisoners on Johnstons Island on Lake Erie. After several months the regiment was ordered back to Virginia and in May 1864 the Army of the Potomac cross the Rapidan in pursuit of General Lee. After the Battle of Cold Harbour, General Grant, now in command of the Army of the Potomac, laid siege to Lee and the Confederates at Petersburgh.

While Petersburgh was under siege another Confederate force came very close to Washington, marching through the Shenandoah Valley. The 6th Corps, including Byrne's regiment, were ordered to Washington to defend against this incursion. Commanded by General Sheridan the Army of the Shenandoah eventually routed the Confederates after battles at Snicker's Gap, Winchester, Fisher Hill and Cedar Creek. Byrne was wounded for a second time at the Battle of Cedar Creek. After successfully defending Washington against the Confederate forces, his regiment returned to the siege of Petersburgh while Byrne spent two months in Annapolis recuperating. In February 1865 Byrne once again rejoined his regiment at the siege of Petersburgh. On 2nd April Petersburgh fell and General Lee and his Confederate army surrendered on 9th April. The 65th Regiment were mustered out on 17th July 1865. A total of 206 officers and enlisted men of the 65th Regiment died during the Civil War. Of the 206, 89 died of disease.

Nicola Morris,
2008.

Military Career
U.S. Army—Nine years (approx.)—broken service

The author wishes to place on record his thanks to the General Services Administrator, National Archives and Record Service Collections Officer, Washington D.C., 20408, USA for assistance in compiling this record.

Enlisted 1st January, 1850. U.S. Infantry, New Orleans. (Captain/Brevet, Major Pemberton's Inf. Company plus 4th Arty Regt.

∾

16th January, 1852. Two year's service, deserts to New Orleans. February 1853 ship *John Lucy* to Liverpool.

∾

1854, Ireland. Dublin Artillery Militia (Adj. Capt. Charles McCallum). Militia disbands after Crimean War.

∾

1856, enlists Governor's Island, New York Harbour. Pardoned as deserter in 1852 by Lieut. Gen. Scott. Subsequently sent to Fort Staunton to serve for three years (completion of five years which he had originally signed on).

∾

August 1957 Infantry detachment to Fort Staunton New Mexico.

∾

27th May, 1860, discharged, Fort Staunton.

∾

Enlisted August, 1861 44th Coy 65th New York State Volunteers (1st Regt. C Company, US Chasseurs)

Promoted 1st Sgt, September 1861.

Wounded July 1862, Battle of Malvern (Arm injury).

Prisoner Libby Prison, Richmond 1862.

POW exchange to Belleview Hospital, New York, 19th July, 1862.

∽

Rejoined unit (65th New York Volunteers) AUgust 1863. Located west of Warrington.

Dysentery case—sent to Lincoln Hospital, Washington, 3rd November, 1863.

∽

Rejoined unit (65th New York Volunteers) at Brandy Station, 5th January, 1864.

Unit to Johnston's Island, Lake Erie, Sandusky, Ohio.

Promoted Sgt. Major.

Discharged and re-enlisted, 6th February, 1864.

∽

Promoted to 2nd Lieut. 44th Company, New York Volunteers, 1st September, 1864.

Wounded (left hip) at Battle of Cedar Creek, 19th October, 1864.

Sent to US Hospital Annapolis, Maryland. Acting Adj. at hospital.

∽

Rejoined unit at Petersburgh, February 1865.

Promoted/mustered in as 1st Lieut. C Company, 1st Regt. New York Volunteers, wef 27th December, 1864.

∽

1st April, 1865. Bombardment of Petersburgh (unit present).

∽

4th April, 1865. Amelia Courthouse (unit present).

∽

Discharged wef 11th June, 1865, New York.

∽

Re-enlisted wef January 1867, 42nd Regt. US Inf. (for Civil War veterans) Hart's Island, New York.

Spring 1869, transferred to 6th Inf. Regt. Arkansas (1st Sergeant Fort Gibson).

May 1869, discharged at his own request (rendered submnumerary).

Voyages/Ships

2ND NOVEMBER, 1849
Confidence
Dublin–New Orleans
◈

FEBRUARY 1853
John & Lucey
Cargo/cotton ship
New Orleans–Liverpool. A $30 fare with a journey time of 52 days.
◈

APRIL 1853
Old Duchess of Kent
Cattle boat
Liverpool–Dublin
◈

JULY 1856
Columbia
Black Ball Line
To New York via North Channel, a five week journey with English
and German passengers.
◈

1860
Dreadnought
New York–Liverpool. 21 day trip under Captain Samuels
◈

8TH JUNE, 1861
North Brittin
Screw
Moville, Derry–New York

1865
Helvetia
Inman Line
Queenstown–New York

∾

3RD JULY, 1875
Egypt
National Line Steamer
New York–Liverpool and on to Dublin. A ten day journey time.

SECTION 2

I

Father Matthew and the Temperance Movement

Another great man had made his apearence in Publick in Ireland at that time the Reverent Father Mathew the great advocate of total apsence (abstinence). I think it was in 1839 when he came first to Dublin to Preach the Doctrine of Temprance which he had been doing for some time. Before his arrival hear, the good Quakers of Dublin had been advocating the cause, but with little effect. Father Matthews fame went before him. he held open Aire Meetings in various parts of the City. In the Chapel Yard Church Street and the Back of the Custom House his meetings were largely attended. Many came for curiousity but were afterwards prevailed apon to take the pledge. He was a fine Noble looking Priest with a Roman countenance of the Spiritual Order his manner was mild and Pervasive. Teetotalism was spredding all over Ireland Societys were formed and numerous Bands organized. O'Connell was pleading for Repeal and would soone have the Old House open in Collage Green again. Father Matthew was making the People sober, and O'Connell was making them all Repealers. There was a great anual Temperance Procession which paraded the principal streets with flags Banners and Bands playing National airs and Temperance tunes. in the Evenings there were Temperance Balls where the young and sometimes the old Danced to the light fantastic toe and refreshed themselfs with coffey and eg[g] flip made with eg[g]s and hot milk seasoned with ground nutmeg and Cinamin. Temperance songs ware sung in the streets by Ballad Singers. I remember a fue words of one of the songs which was sung in a very spirited manner.

Farewell unto the Land Lord
Farewell to the whiskey keg
Farewell Black ies (eyes)
And Broken nose, blue devills
And dirty rags
This is part of one verse.
Chorus
So I made a vow
And Ile (I'll) keep it now
And never get Drunk again

for several years the Pledge was well observed, though hundreds of the Tetotallers were hard Drinkers at one time. after the Death of Father Mathew numbers of them gradualy resumed there old habbet of Drinking. The Reverend Father Sprat of the Carmelite Church of Whitefriars Street a most respected and good Priest, took up the cause which had made many homes happy. He Devoted all his time and energy to the good work which he continued to the hour of his Death, when he went the way of all men. after this Tetotalism mearly existed in name.

II

Drink

One of the worst evils which we must notice in Dublin is the drinking and drunken habbits of a large sextion of the working Class People of the City. Now I make a distinction between what I call the dringing (drinking) class, and the common drunkard of the lowest type. first take the temperat man who takes a sup with an eye to economy. he will tell you he can't afford it and wonder how some people make it out. he takes an od[d] pint he likes it he is frugal but the habbit never grows on him. he is a rational been (being) a good husband a good Father if there is any good in his Wife, and a man you will not be oblidged to shun in the street and will not be looking up in your face for Porter.

There is another class of Drinkers who can drink a lot but still not come down to the level of the Common Drunkard, yet who spends Two much money in proportion to there wages who never thinks of the Rainy day nor yet not anuff of his famaly who is allways in a Pinched state trying to keep the Best side out. This man is selfish, minds his work, yet slow and slugish, why he Drinks to[o] much which has an inervating Influence over him and are Seldom seen real drunk, simply because it takes to[o] much to set him drunk. he does not give anuff to his famaly and give it cheerfully. he has nothing in his Pocket after Satherday and Sunday. it is either a feast or a famine.

We will now come to the lowest grade of Drunkererd what shall we say about him. it is a painful subgect, a man whome you do not kno wheather to simphatise (sympathise) with or blot out all-together from your conciderations as unworthy, without sence or shame in the treatment of his famaly spiritual and temporal. there are many of this kind in Dublin. Besters when they will dun you in the street and elsewhere. Where is the remedy for this vile sore which festers on the hart of Dublin. a reproach and discourageing to Industry and yet a nationalist he thinks he is and the greatest tax producer in the country, he is a curse and a shame. Moral suasion, the pledge has failed to produce much results, again where is the remidy I have heared a great many suggestions from time to time but the publican's Interest is so well protected by Acts of Parliament we cannot interfare with his rights and his business without an Act of Parliament. there are too many Publick Houses in Dublin and all over Ireland. In the back streets and slums of Dublin, which are a temtation to the weak and degraded class of Persons particularly the women kind with children in there arms, or youngsters following them about who are completely ignorant of the ways of the wretched mother and hir Companions. The Father perhaps is no better. when the child grows up if it dont die th[r]ough want and neglect, if a Boy as the years come on him, he becomes of idle habbits Born and bred in a dirty old tennement not fit for human habatation, in a slum that was onst oppulent and buisey with trade and Industry. There is no work for him. The watchful ie (eye) of the Parent is not over him. Physically he is not up to standard. Consequently is unfit for ruff manual labour but well adapted for factory work. He is nimble and quick to learn but there is no work for all of these class of boys. Therefore many are idle. He then becomes a Corner Boy he grows lazey. If he don't become a criminal he joins the army where almost anything is exceptable he is then lost to vieu for a while at the cor-ner his place is filled by another young unfortunate, so goes the times unless a change for the better takes place.

III

Love of Country. The Old Sod

I have often been asked why i came back from America and stopping at home for good or ill. The best answer i could give to that question was love of Country. I had very little to hope for in comming to Ireland. there was a good deal of Sentiment in it which made me Picture some things more ideal like to my mind and dear old Dublin had not lost all its attraction for me and where I could get as much for a shilling as I could for two or three on the other side a great trade depression was hanging over the Country, which the[y] called a Pannick with wages reduced one halfe and no employment to be got anywhere. I made up my mind to come back to the old Land again, with its Pleasure and its Pain, its hope and fears waiting for the day when the sunshine of Liberty would make this a prosperous and happy country. at this time emigration was in full swing in Ireland. The Panick in America which lasted two or three years did not have any effect on it. The people looked on it in a passive kind of way. now that the Population has run down to the danger point and still the[y] go, it has at last arroused the attention of every true Irishman who loves his Country Better than any other. Something must be done to lessen the evil and to keep the People at home and induce them by various means which are now in opporation. a great many letters from America to Ireland are highly colloured and persuasife, some of them full of lies or misleading, are belived at home to be genuine. The minds of some young People are easely raised by the glowing account which there Brother or friend has sent home to them. the next letter perhaps contains a prepaid passage ticket for Mickey or Pat. This puts the Hall mark on all that has been said in the previous letters the indusements are very strong and temting. off he pops it is not like what it was in the old sailing days it is only a pleasure trip. he is well fed and very little risk. In his thoughts about America he is like looking at a Magick Lantern all is Bright and Cheerful he wont be long there untill he finds out the reality. he is then on his own hook he is far away from home and Mother, who would take a fue shillings from him and keep no account of back payments or arrears. If he is a good young man and is working he may send an od[d] check to the old folks at home, but when the[y] drop off his visions of home grow dim and less frequent to a certain extent he forgets his Motherland and becomes more reconciled in America and is lost to Ireland perhaps forever.

IV

My Baptism of Fire—How a Soldier feels in Battle

I have been asked the question on account of my expearience in War. It is not an easy question to answer. And I will do the best I can and will only speak for my self. My memory is a bit faded and the sceans not so vivid before me after many years. In the Spring of eighteen sixty two General McClelen [sic], in command of the Army of the Potomac commenced his forward movent up the Pininsula in Virginnia [sic] with the obgect of taking Richmond, the capital of the Southern Confederacy. he compeled the enemy to evacuate Yorktown and fought a battle at Williamsburgh. the enemy were falling back on the road to Richmond, where the[y] were collecting a large force for the defence of the City. Keys [sic] Corps of three divisions, Crossed the Chickahominy River which included my devision. General Couch commanding we formed the left wing on the South side of the river, while the great Bulk of our Army remained on the North side. The night before the Battle of Fair Oaks fought on the thirty first May and first June (1862), we had a very heavy storm of rain thunder and lightening. Our shelter tents were blown down. Our condition was misarable untill daylight. The rain ceased and the welcome sun shone out Bright and warm, which put us all in good humour again. Little did we think before night came some thousands of our comrades would be layed low on the Blood Stained Soil of fair Oaks and

Seven Pines. The River over flowed its Banks on the low Bottom Lands. One by one the ruff wooden Bridges was sweeped away thus cutting us off from our right wing on the other side of the River and our Base of Supplies. The enemy aware of all this, and thinking there oppertunity had come, the Confederate General Johnstin [sic] with seventy thousand men while we were not half there number, In order to cut us off from the main Body of our Army before assistance could come to us, about noone they struck our advanced position and were driving them back. We who were in the rear, it came as a surprise to us, til a fue schells droping in front of our camp and exploding, a rush was made for our arms and equipments, And getting into ranks as quickly as possible, my Redgement was sent to the Right. While wee continued to move forward, it seemed to us we were going away from the fight and our men so hard pressed. After marching a short time wee were pretty well screened from the vieu of the enemy and our own men By patches of woodland and forrest belts with openings between. after marching for a short time, wee halted and faced to the front in line. how fare wee came I could not tell. why this movement I could not make out, nor have I ever heard mention of it. The Battle was still raging on our left in the distance. While we listened we knew by the fireing the enemy had gained conciderable ground to there front and had the Best of the fight, and that it would be our turn to be gobbled up as wee could not make much resistance or fall back to the disturbed river which wee could not cross. we moved Back a short distance to the rear, a better position. about halfe past five in the evening a commotion was observed in the Regiment. all eys were turned in the direction of the River. we were not aware that one bridge was saved from destruction but in a shakey condition, but which saved the left wing of McCleland's Army. over this Bridge troops were crossing wee could not see them untill the[y] emerged out of the woods and the glint of the sun on the Bright Barrells of there rifles made our harts lift with rejoicement. The Brave Old General Sumner who led the reinforcements which contained the Irish Brigade was soone among us. he must have learned the situation very quick as he came in the nick of time, not a moment could be lost. a mounted officer dashed in from the front and rode up to the Genneral and with his right arm extended and pointed to the front. Wee knew it all at onst. In an Instant the whole scean changed. Among the detached Body of troops the line of Battle was formed in double quick time. My Regiment deployed to right and faced to the front, Immediately receiveing a volly from the enemy which [k]nocked some of our men out of the ranks. we then commenced fireing at will. All thouthts but that of death and the enemy flew out of my mind with the excitement and so buisey firing. I was not prepared to die, nor had I a presentiment, but hope sweet hope which never left me in moments of Danger boyed me up and was a great comfort to me. yet i could hear the ping ping of the Bullets with a doleful whistle passing my hed and so close to my ear. You could not but wonder that Death was very possible. On the left of my Regiment a fine Battery of twelf Pounder Napoleon guns which the enemy desired very much to capture. Three times the[y] charged the guns which were double shotted with canister and each time sent Back with a thundering salvo which made havoc in there ranks. Genneral Sumner then ordered a Bayonet charge which cleared our front the Enemy falling back some distance. Night comming on the conflict ceased. The next morning the Battle was Continued and the enemy Badly Beaten. My Regiment was not called on wee were hungry and had nothing to eat as wee lost our rations the day before. Our loss in killed and wounded was over five thousand, the enemy over six thousand. How a soldier feels in Battle. I have indevered, by a fue remarks which I have made in Brief.

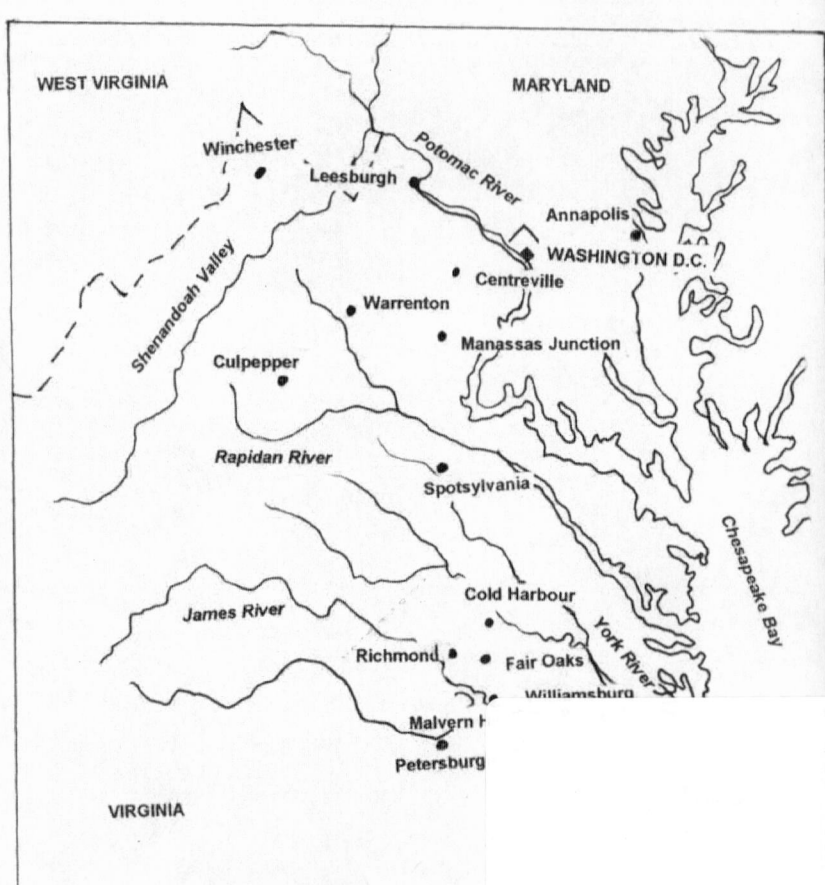

WEST VIRGINIA

MARYLAND

Winchester

Leesburgh

Potomac River

Annapolis

WASHINGTON D.C.

Centreville

Warrenton

Manassas Junction

Culpepper

Shenandoah Valley

Rapidan River

Spotsylvania

Chesapeake Bay

James River

Cold Harbour

Richmond

Fair Oaks

York River

Williamsburg

Malvern H

Petersburg

VIRGINIA

The American Civil War in Virginia

Sites mentioned by Andrew J. Byrne in

accounts of his Regiment during campaigns

in the American Civil War 1861 - 1865